COOPER'S AMERICANS

Kay Seymour House

Ohio State University Press

★ COOPER'S AMERICANS

For Barr and Kirk

ACKNOWLEDGMENTS

MUCH OF MY OWN PLEASURE in working on this book has come from the interest others took in its progress. This study of James Fenimore Cooper's novels was first prompted by Yvor Winters' respect for Cooper, and Professor Winters remained the reader I had in mind as I wrote. My sense of obligation to him—as to such other students of Cooper as James F. Beard, Marius Bewley, Marcel Clavel, James Grossman, Henry Nash Smith, and Robert E. Spiller—is greater than the textual notes can indicate.

Other friends at Stanford University helped immensely, with my greatest debt being to David Levin, who patiently read and reread the manuscript, challenging, questioning, and making suggestions with unwearied attention. Wallace Stegner, as his other former students would know, could always be counted on for generous encouragement and for critical notes that all but repair the flaws they mark. Claude Simpson, Richard

ACKNOWLEDGMENTS

Foster Jones, Irving Howe, and Malcolm Cowley also deserve my thanks for their help at one time or another, and I am indebted to Weldon Kefauver and Thomas Sheahan, of the Ohio State University Press, for their aid in the final stages of editorial preparation.

Finally, I want to thank Alfred A. Knopf, Inc. for permission to quote from Wallace Stevens' "Extracts from Addresses to the Academy of Fine Ideas" and Oxford University Press for permission to reprint Frederick G. Tuckerman's Sonnet XVIII.

KAY SEYMOUR HOUSE

San Francisco
May, 1965

CONTENTS

★ COOPER'S AMERICANS

INTRODUCTION

MILES AND YEARS from Yoknapatawpha, James Fenimore
Cooper created a coherent fictional world containing
hundreds of characters that represented the possibilities
of American life. The heartland of that world was upper
New York State, where Cooper had grown up among
some of the 750,000 acres his father had owned and
where the family history intertwined with American
history itself. Schuyler, Gansevoort, Van Rensselaer,
Washington, Jay, Hamilton, DeWitt Clinton, Gouver-
neur Morris—these men and families the Coopers knew
well, and Morris was, additionally, a link with Germaine
Necker de Staël and the political world of France. To
these household names, Cooper was to add early in his
own career those of Samuel F. B. Morse, Gulian Verplanck, James K. Paulding, Horatio Greenough, and
Lafayette.

Such figures as these, all active outside the world of
belles-lettres, belong to the background Cooper drew

on when he became the first novelist in America to support himself and his family by writing. Conscious of the obligations and opportunities that attend a literary pioneer, Cooper tried a variety of prose styles, invented the sea novel, experimented with the international theme that James was to elaborate, and established conventions of characterization and patterns of myth that prevail in American literature. In the course of writing some thirty-two novels between 1820 and 1850, he discovered much that we recognize as the American novelist's proper material.

Cooper was a man of immense physical and intellectual vitality, and his analytic intelligence and unsentimental sympathy with America's history, peoples, and land well suited him for the task of explaining America to Americans and to Europeans. He considered himself a historian and quoted from Fielding, "I am a true historian, a describer of society as it exists, and of men as they are." Later historians were to affirm his achievement, Parkman confessing that he could not always separate his readings in Cooper from his own experiences, and Bancroft declaring, "Another like Cooper cannot appear, for he was peculiarly suited to his time, which was that of an invading civilization."

Cooper's declared purpose, to which he held with maddening tenacity, was to help Americans achieve their "mental independence." Political and geographical independence America had, but Cooper, born the year the Constitution took effect, was not alone in believing that the country lacked a sense of direction. The bravely launched state seemed awash; while an uncouth and mutinous congressional crew challenged the authority of the captain, some of the passengers looked nostalgically

4

astern, others demanded to be taken instantly to ports they had only dreamed of, or busied themselves endlessly in the rigging, or stood benumbed, so grateful for a deck beneath their feet they cared little where it bore them. Cooper believed that America should, must, take its bearings from the Constitution and chart a political and cultural course. It was a question of navigation, of following a course chosen rather than one chanced upon, and he warned in one sea novel after another that what seemed the easiest procedure—running before the gale— was by all odds the most dangerous.

What direction would America take? What values would it honor? What quality of life would it make possible? What culture would it produce? Did its disparate peoples predict the harmonious co-existence of all countries and all men? These questions had been, and would continue to be, largely contained in a discussion of the American character. Seven years before Cooper's birth, Crèvecoeur had asked, "What is an American?"; when Whitman's essay asked the same question, Cooper had been dead for two decades.

Interested above all else in America's "mental independence," desiring to be America's "true historian," Cooper funneled his life's activities into the study of American character that is the essence of his novels. He went back into the past to uncover and describe the peoples and cultures that represented the "given" of American life. He turned himself into an expert on the Constitution and tried to relate democratic concepts to daily life. Without losing sight of "men as they are," he displaced fictional characters in time and space in order to relate past, present, and possible Americans to one another.

II

While his concern for character is typical of his time, Cooper's discoveries are not, for he found dour facts and stubborn dilemmas that are missing from the hopeful prophecies exuded by such writers as Crèvecoeur, Emerson, or Whitman. Crèvecoeur had sketched, dimly but enthusiastically, a messianic American who would be a "new man, who acts upon new principles"; an American was one who "leaving behind him all his ancient prejudices and manners, receives new ones from the new modes of life he has embraced, the new government he obeys, and the new rank he holds."

The confidence of Crèvecoeur had yet to be justified when Cooper began to write. Modes of life were multiple and sometimes conflicting; government was remote and its powers tentative; rank there was none. (As late as 1836, Cooper followed Benjamin Franklin and Charles Brockden Brown, and anticipated Hawthorne, in denying distinctions of rank in America: "There is no costume for the judge, no baton for the general, no diadem for the chief magistrate.") Crèvecoeur, eager to strip the new man of European encrustation, had nevertheless revealed his own European origin in expecting government to shape and clothe the citizen. To Cooper, it seemed that Crèvecoeur's method threatened to leave the American naked and shivering in a cultural wasteland. Cooper would have sympathized with F. R. Leavis' statement that it is possible to "call the state of those who have lost their distinctive heritage and acquired nothing comparable in its place, distinctively American; but the tendency to treat this state as a positive American tradition . . . is depressing."

6

As Cooper saw it, only the eventual establishment of a high culture could justify the loss of folk culture.

The main reason D. H. Lawrence's essay on Cooper has been helpful is Lawrence's ability to sense that the process of character formation was complicated. Old forms had to be sloughed even while a new man was forming himself underneath. Through most of the nineteenth century, American writers gave priority to the formation of the new man. Only after establishing his own integrity could he choose modes of living, balance all three corners of his triangular government, and decide whom, if anyone, to honor. Thoreau spoke for the age: "I think that we should be men first, and subjects afterwards."

Meanwhile, American life was buffeted by such rapid and apparently discontinuous changes that Cooper warned, "To see America with the eyes of truth, it is necessary to look often." His historical novels did just that, revisiting scenes and linking characters until American history becomes a human continuum. The reader can follow subtle changes in families (in the Littlepage trilogy, for instance) as characters are molded by the events of their own history. Yet this ability of people to change in response to historical fact was, Cooper thought, particularly worrisome in the formative years of a nation. The urgency he felt was expressed in his preface to *The Spy* (1821) when he wrote: "The nation is passing from the gristle into the bone." Cooper's Chinese understanding of pressure and shape suggested to him that Americans could no longer ignore the silent forces at work in American life.

Such a political leader as Daniel Webster had a similar sense of danger; in listing the nation's needs, in 1831, he placed "national character" first. If America's concern with character seems obsessive to us now, we should remember that America was made still more sensitive by the number of European visitors (like Alexis de Tocqueville) who kept coming over to see what the new man would look like. Such spectators were annoying, yet one could understand their interest, for nearly everyone seems to have agreed with Walt Whitman's opinion that "the only large and satisfactory justification of it [democracy] resides in the future, mainly through the copious production of perfect characters among the people. . . . "

Less sanguine than Whitman, Cooper never hoped for perfect characters out of the "godlike-devil man"; yet he believed that America offered man the greatest opportunity since classical times to pursue his total perfection. Americans believed that Europeans had no comparable chance; and Cooper's good friend, W. C. Bryant, explained at length how in Europe a "rigid intellectual and melancholy destiny" went to "contract and stint the intellectual faculties, to prevent the development of character." That Bryant really had in mind the freedom to form one's own character is made clear by his further statement that America boasts "infinite variety of forms of character" in immigrants whose "characters and manners were formed by institutions and modes of society in the nations beyond the Atlantic."

Unlike Crèvecoeur, Bryant and Cooper both assumed that religion, race, and imported values still shaped most Americans. They did not insist, as Crèvecoeur had done, that the American automatically reject his old "prejudices and manners," for they saw clearly that cultural chaos bewildered the average man. Like the Hawthorne who edged into the front row of spectators at "Earth's Holocaust," Cooper had misgivings about setting afire all the customs and values of the past. To adopt, as Americans seemed tempted to do, the method of the Phoenix without first making sure of the Phoenix struck Cooper as vandalism.

The problem was one of choice; wise choice depended on education and eclecticism, and Cooper set about trying to show Americans what values and models were available to them. He first identified and then fought forces that constricted, bleakened, or impoverished. Like Bryant, he distrusted parties and factions, and his ability to detect counterfeit labels was sharpened when, in France, he saw Lafayette duped, trussed, and used as a shield by aristocrats masquerading as liberals. (In Cooper's lexicon, an aristocrat is any person who obtains special powers and privileges; the term has nothing to do with social classes, and the "aristocrat" often demanded, in the name of the multitude, those powers he appropriated to his own exclusive use.) Cooper defined his terms and analyzed his characters thoroughly, and James Beard has rightly insisted that his thought is consistent. Much of the factitious writing about Cooper's political beliefs rests on what he considered the erroneous assumption that consistent thought coincides with the professions of a particular political party. Character, which had to come first, was not built on an unexamined faith in any faction, and individual integrity was the best defense against all tyranny. John Jay Chapman had to ignore Cooper in order to boast of Emerson, "By showing the identity in essence of all tyranny, and by bringing back the attention of political thinkers to its starting point, the value of human character, he has advanced the political thought of the world by one step."

III

Cooper's novels are like so many notes dictated, as Robert Spiller has said, from his "whole reading of life." It was for this amplitude and complexity that later novelists were to respect him, Conrad praising the way in which Cooper's setting "interpenetrates with life," and Melville insisting that his very faults were the faults of his genius. All Cooper's novels are flawed; but where he succeeds, he does so less through conscious artistry than through intelligence and temperament. To be alive, for Cooper, was to be aware of and responsive to fine distinctions among men and scenes. Sometimes, reading his journals, one feels that Cooper had an exaggerated sensitivity to cultural differences. Traveling with him through Europe, one crosses a border and finds that post-horses, drivers, and innkeepers are all delightfully different from those on the other side.

Cooper's ability to synthesize character, setting, and theme, in other words, rests on his ability to analyze. At the core of his fictional world, we find over four hundred clearly recognizable American characters; they are subdivided into two general types. Most of these characters derive their essential identity from some cultural group; certain of their prejudices and manners are intact. These characters are drawn in accord with one of Cooper's few literary theories. He wrote, in the preface to *The Pioneers*, that characterization "had better be done by delineations of principles and of characters in their classes." By "classes" he meant not the social stratification that belonged to Europe, but natural genres growing from racial, cultural, or religious differences. Such characters think and act in accord with their communal affiliation; and while they may be themselves unaware of their own group's history, they bear its identifying marks. Richard Chase, mentioning Cooper's interest in "propriety," insufficiently stresses the sense of belonging, the *proprior*, Cooper recognized in the word.

A scene from *Wyandotté* can stand as a paradigm for Cooper's larger world. As Major Bob Willoughby tells the members of an isolated frontier community that the colonists and Great Britain are at war, Cooper describes the hearers' reactions. The New England group, descendants of the Puritans, listen attentively, exchange "meaning glances," and retire to choose the profitable allegiance. The single Irishman present grasps his shillelagh and looks for a head to hit. A Scotchman begins what will be a day-long process of scratching his head and pondering. The Dutch gape in bewilderment and nightfall finds them toiling toward an understanding of what has happened. Grinning with excitement, the Negroes return to the kitchen to multiply the casualties and magnify the damages with each retelling of Willoughby's description of the initial battle of the Revolutionary War. Only the Tuscarora Indian is unmoved, his indifference indicating both his impassive nature and his secret knowledge of the Battle of Lexington.

This group of characters, reacting in various ways to one bit of news, is typical of Cooper's fictional world. One stockade shelters and the wilderness surrounds them all, but they are anything but united. Occasionally a character may show signs of departing from what would be the normal behavior for his group; he may reach out to the Bible or search history for a standard.

But the quotation he retrieves or the model he finds to emulate is always one that can be fitted with his original ethic. Actually, therefore, these characters are closed to experience. No matter what happens to them, they cannot essentially be changed. No desire ever beckons to them from beyond the periphery of their defining community.

When such characters are only sketched, they are, of course, stereotypes. When they are fleshed out with detailed histories and actions that differ, even slightly, from those of their group, they become recognizable as individuals. The Yankee Jason Newcome, the squatter Ishmael Bush, the Indian Chingachgook, the Dutchman Guert Ten Eyck, and scores of seamen—all are identifiable. Yet they can all be understood most quickly through knowledge of the "class" (as Cooper would call it) they belong to. If challenged, Cooper would have defended his method as realism; this was the way most men were in America. As a fictional method, moreover, the use of stereotypes let Cooper move class representatives around as counters in the action. The technique is most familiar to us from drama, and it may not be irrelevant that Cooper's lifelong avocations were playing chess and reading Shakespeare.

Cooper's debt to Scott is as superficial as it is obvious; his reputation as "the American Scott" has unfortunately obscured more significant affinities with classical authors, with Shakespeare, and with eighteenth-century dramatists and novelists. While he was not himself successful as a dramatist, many of his novels were staged and his familiarity with dramatic techniques explains, if it does not excuse, much of his discursiveness. Interested in character formation and cultural pressures, Cooper attempted to convert the adventure romance into a novel of ideas. In so doing, he dared the discursiveness of Virgil's *Eclogues*, of Sidney's *Arcadia*, of much of Shakespeare, or, to mention a later writer whose interests were similar, of George Bernard Shaw.

The kind of material that Shaw put in his prefaces and plays Cooper incorporated in the novel by twisting two plots—one of action, the other of ideas—into a narrative line. To remember the action plot of such familiar works as *The Spy*, *The Pioneers*, or *The Prairie* is to recognize how the action (conventional, at best; at worst, ridiculous) can be justified only by the thematic plot it activates. Cooper's remark that a novelist needed "inventiveness" suggests how casual was his interest in the construction of the conventional plot; his real interest lay in the ideas that formed the thematic construction of the novel. The action plot, often based on the heroine's perils, is parasitic, a device to keep the reader interested and the characters in motion.

That the characters move is essential; for if most of them are representative figures, they must interact in order to reveal the moral and historical conflicts that involve them. By identifying issues with various characters, Cooper could revive ancient values, assess new ones, and reckon instantly the cost of any choice. Where, furthermore, the life had gone from a tradition (as it had for Cooper's latter-day Puritan, the Yankee), the vacuity and inconsistency of the tradition's carriers are the measure of its loss. Cooper's romances were never intended to conjure a remote but perfect world that never was. Rather, he wished to relate past to present and present to future, to show causation and continuity in American experience. Relevances are exposed and traced through the aversions and loyalties of those darlings of the nineteenth century—representative men.

To identify the uniquely American opportunity, however, Cooper created a second and very different type of character. This second group is numerically smaller than the first, but its members are greater in stature and in interest. These are the characters who are still unformed, open to experience, and capable of surprise.

All of these open characters are men. Each of them leaves his defining community and risks the experiences offered by the sea or the wilderness where, in Cooper's fictional world as in America itself, a man could escape his native culture. The world such men inhabit is less tidy than that of the first group, for it is cluttered with doubts and dilemmas. As fictional characters—mobile, plastic, and in many ways ambiguous—these are the most "modern."

IV

This study follows the divisions suggested by the material itself. First, I consider those characters that are defined by their community. Since these natural communities are to be found in all Cooper's novels and roughly coexist in time, the order in which they are introduced is somewhat arbitrary. I discuss the women first for a number of reasons, none of which has anything at all to do with chivalry. Cooper's world is definitely a man's world and, except for their importance to the action or romance plot, women are almost completely outside it; they are generally his poorest characters, and they are also the most burdened by the conventions of Cooper's time.

The other two disenfranchised groups come next. With the Indians and Negroes, Cooper confronts the two races whose cultures are the most foreign to his predominantly English world; for these, Cooper worked out certain fictional techniques that became, particularly for the Indians, themselves conventions in American literature. The fourth group is the Dutch, closely related to the Negro in Cooper's fiction and yet, like the Indian, a vanishing part of American life. Next appear the two groups that contain most powerfully what Lionel Trilling calls the "yes" and "no" of the culture; these are the gentry and the Yankees. Finally, with seamen, we have Cooper's lone attempt to describe an artificially engendered community of appreciable size and duration.

The second and third sections of the study roughly follow the chronology of the novels as Cooper liberated, one at a time, five characters from their original communities and tested them in the American scene. These few characters—Harvey Birch, Miles Wallingford, Conanchet, Onoah, and Natty Bumppo—show Cooper at his most ample, analytic, and visionary. These characters ask what harmony is possible between what individual and what environment. As they meet representatives of the groups described first, we find that the static communities represent the "given" of the American experiment, and the solitary figures, its hypotheses. It is largely through the former that Cooper explores America's connections with aboriginal and European cultures, and through the latter its separation from them.

In his essay, "The Ruins of Time," Yvor Winters has described Cooper's works as a "mass of fragments, no doubt; but the fragments are those of a civilization." Such a description is exact, for Cooper never believed that the lumber of the new world was new in kind; the newness was all in the American's freedom to choose and shape a culture from shards of old civilizations. Only by knowing himself and history, by choosing wisely and eclectically from the essences, not the artifacts, of great cultures, could the American shape a character that would fulfil the promise of the government and the land.

I

"WOMAN IS WOMAN"*

The writer of these pages is a man—one who has seen much of the other sex, and he is happy to have an opportunity of paying tribute to female purity and female truth. That there are hearts so disinterested as to lose the considerations of self, in advancing the happiness of those they love; that there are minds so pure as to recoil with disgust from the admission of deception, indelicacy, or management, he knows; for he has seen it from long and close examination. . . . He believes that innocency, singleness of heart, ardency of feeling, and unalloyed, shrinking delicacy, sometimes exist in the female bosom, to an extent that but few men are happy enough to discover, and that most men believe incompatible with the frailties of human nature.

—Cooper†

DECLARING his faith in "female purity and female truth" in his first novel, James Fenimore Cooper only accepted the literary and social conventions of his age.[1] The

---

* Dr. Obed Bat, Naturalist, in *The Prairie* (119).

† *Precaution* (101).

[1] The type of woman Cooper describes here was simultaneously appearing in Washington Irving's *The Sketch Book of Geoffrey Crayon, Gent.* (published in seven parts during 1819 and 1820). Irving's "The Wife" describes the qualities of Cooper's best heroines while "The Broken Heart" could be used to defend the worst. Also like Cooper's are the heroines who emerge from Herbert Ross Brown's study, *The Sentimental Novel in America: 1789–1860* (New York, 1959).

Some of Cooper's female characters are discussed in later chapters; the most notable of these are Lucy Hardinge, Narra-mattah, and all the women of the Leatherstocking tales except Elizabeth Temple. Nothing said of them, however, contradicts the pattern of characterization established here.

passage describes the romantic heroines of all his later novels. This it is to be a proper woman, and to be a woman is enough. Men are always something else in addition—Irishmen, seamen, borderers, or Indian chiefs—but the fact of femininity transcends and makes almost irrelevant race, environment, or religion. The woman who departs radically from the woman described here can only be comic or grotesque; she ceases to be a woman. If she has, for whatever reason, betrayed what he considers her true nature, Cooper usually sees to it that she suffers for her abnormality. Thus his attitude, which often seems that of a gentleman, is actually, as Richard Chase says, "determined by age-old folk superstition."[2]

Cooper's first two novels, *Precaution* (1820) and *The Spy* (1821), establish the extremes of behavior allowed his "females." The virgin and the virago were the "either" and "or" of characterization; and two of his last four novels, *Jack Tier* (1848) and *The Ways of the Hour* (1850), show how he not only retained but almost parodied the original restrictions. These two types can be found in any setting in Cooper, but a third group of women emerges only in tales about the frontier, wilderness, or sea. Such characters as Elizabeth Temple and Anneke Mordaunt remind one of Cooper's wife, Susan, as his letters and journals depict her. Capable (even in business affairs), willing to adapt their behavior to the actual situation, yet never backward about expressing their own wishes, these characters do not deserve the opprobrium associated with "Cooper's females." To do them justice, however, we must first define what they are not; consequently, we begin by discussing the

---

[2] *The American Novel and Its Tradition* (New York, 1957), p. 64.

two extremes (the douce heroine and the virago) that set the limits of behavior for Cooper's females.

Precaution, the novel of manners that was his first book,[3] convinced everyone (including Cooper) that he could not succeed with Miss Austen's material. Considering novels primarily as "formidable weapons in the cause of morality" (*Precaution,* p. 159), Cooper took an abstract noun, related it to the "lottery" of marriage, and produced a tale full of characters who held "diversified views of the evils to be averted" (122). He stocked the marriage mart with figures already familiar in literature: a trio of sisters, a foolish mother, a pious aunt, and a mysterious foreign woman. The eldest sister is safely married to a minister, but the second, Jane, has been brought up by the mother and is consequently proud, worships rank and heraldry, reads poetry, and "lacks a well-governed mind." Worst of all,

> To that principle which was to teach her submission in opposition to her wishes, to that principle that could alone afford security against the treachery of her own passions, she was an utter stranger. (82)

Jane is morally weak, but Emily (her younger sister) is physically the more delicate. The pious aunt, Mrs. Wilson, recognizes this fact and predicts that Emily

---

[3] Cooper's career is supposed to have started when he threw down a new English novel he was reading and exclaimed, "I could write you a better book than that myself!" When his wife encouraged him, he wrote (and then destroyed) a long moral tale; *Precaution,* a second attempt, imitates Miss Austen's novels, particularly *Persuasion* and *Pride and Prejudice.* See Marcel Clavel, "Fenimore Cooper: Sa vie et son oeuvre" (dissertation, Aix-en Provence, 1938), pp. 253–64; George E. Hastings, "How Cooper Became a Novelist," *American Literature,* XII (1940), 20–51; and Susan Fenimore Cooper, *Pages and Pictures from the Writings of James Fenimore Cooper* (New York, 1861), pp. 13–22.

"has so much singleness of heart, such real strength of native feeling, that, should an improper man gain possession of her affections, the struggle between her duty and her love would be weighty indeed; and should it proceed so far as to make it her duty to love an unworthy object, I am sure she would sink under it. Emily would die in the same circumstances under which Jane would only awake from a dream and be wretched." (47)

Cooper's wise aunts and governesses are never wrong. Jane marries the wrong man and is wretched; Emily is temporarily attracted to an unworthy suitor, but gets only as far as the weighty struggle. Cooper explains:

The truth was, that in Emily Moseley the obligations of duty were so imperative, her sense of her dependence on Providence so humbling, and yet so confiding, that, as soon as she was taught to believe her lover unworthy of her esteem, that moment an insuperable barrier separated them. (249)

Emily eventually marries a proper Christian (who has all the money and titles Jane sought) and is handsomely rewarded in this life for remembering that "her existence here was preparatory to an immensely more important state hereafter" (249).

Precaution is a woman's book in every sense; men are the "Unknown." Many are attractive, but as they are tested and as their true characters and histories are revealed, only one is worthy of the heroine. The women are largely what they seem; the male characters must be unmasked. The only mysterious woman in the book is an unhappy foreigner who is, it seems, still doing penance for her grandmother's mistakes. Mrs. Wilson points out that her plight is

". . . the sad consequences of one false step in generations gone by. Had your grandmother listened to the
voice of prudence and duty, she never would have deserted her parents for a comparative stranger, and entailed
upon her descendants a train of evils which yet exist in
your person." (234)

In Cooper's world, the double standard endlessly applies.

Cooper never again attempted to build a whole novel
by imbedding heroines of gossamer temperaments in
passages of elephantine moralizing. Unable to construct
a world of such delicate proportions that it could be
shaken by a nuance, Cooper henceforth moved the
occupants of the drawing room out-of-doors. The types
of women established here, however, and the scrambled
psychology given them, recur in most of his novels. The
heroine's principles check her inclinations, and all that
remains is for the hero to survive whatever combats
engage him, rid himself of misunderstandings about his
character, and stand revealed as worthy of the heroine.
She can then capitulate, suffused with blushes. The
author says she is dependent on Providence, but the
action says that the Protestant confusion of works and
faith affects courtship so that the hero has to earn her.
Marriage is a matter of wages.

As Cooper's interest turned from the love story itself,
the process became almost automatic and rather circular.
The heroine's inflexible demands determine what the
plot reveals, and the plot in turn must select the man
worthy of the heroine. One is tempted to think of this
man as the "heroine's hero," for he is never, after
Precaution, of more than occasional interest in the

novel.[4] The heroine's hero is a character built to a formula, and that is determined by what the heroine demands in a man. All these heroes could be shuffled and dealt back into the novels at random without causing any serious difficulty. The hero and the heroine are, in short, each other's reward for their common fidelity to truth, virtue, principles, and (in some novels) religious faith. As Herman Melville said in his review of *The Sea Lions*, " . . . The moist, rosy hand of our Mary is the reward of his orthodoxy. Somewhat in the pleasant spirit of the Mahometan, this; who rewards all the believers with a houri."[5]

Cooper himself seems to have had little interest in the affairs of such lovers; most of his careless mistakes, such as letting the heroine's hair change color in mid-volume, occur in connection with them. Yet, at the time, a novel, by definition, was a love story, and the chief purchasers of fiction were sentimentally educated

---

[4] Henry Nash Smith refers to such characters as young, handsome, and genteel "doubles" of Leatherstocking (*The Virgin Land* [New York, 1957], p. 76). Actually, they are all (as is Leatherstocking himself) indebted to stock heroes of romantic fiction and drama. The prototype in Cooper is Peyton Dunwoodie of *The Spy*. A Virginia cavalry officer with a gentleman's skills and code, Peyton correctly indicates the hero's affinity with the cavalier of Southern plantation myths. After Peyton, these heroes are: Oliver Effingham of *The Pioneers*, Griffith of *The Pilot*, Duncan Heyward of *The Last of the Mohicans*, Paul Hover and Duncan Uncas Middleton of *The Prairie*, Wilder of *Red Rover*, Ludlow of *The Water-Witch*, Don Camillo Monforte of *The Bravo*, Berchthold of *The Heidenmauer*, Sigismund of *The Headsman*, Paul Powis of *Homeward Bound* and *Home As Found*, Luis de Bobadilla of *Mercedes of Castille*, Wycherley Wychecombe of *The Two Admirals*, Bob Willoughby of *Wyandotté*, Harry Mulford of *Jack Tier*, and Ben Boden of *The Oak Openings*. Roswell Gardiner, one of the two central characters in *The Sea Lions*, is vitiated by the same tradition.

[5] *Literary World*, IV (1849), 370.

women.[6] He kept the love story (which had certain structural advantages also), but occasionally his impatience with the demands of the casual reader broke out in a preface:

> *The Pilot* could scarcely be a favorite with females. The story has little interest for them, nor was it much heeded by the author of the book. . . . His aim was to illustrate vessels and the ocean rather than to draw any pictures of sentiment and love. (vii)

> . . . The reader will do us the justice to regard *The Two Admirals* as a sea story and not as a love story [although a sub-plot contains a love story]. Our admirals are our heroes; as there are two of them, those who are particularly fastidious on such subjects are quite welcome to term one the heroine, if they see fit. (Preface of 1842, deleted later)

With his second novel, however, Cooper subordinated the love story and established the pattern his books usually followed. He wrote of *The Spy*, "Ashamed to have fallen into the track of imitation [in writing *Pre-*

---

[6] William Charvat is the undisputed authority here (see Bibliography). In his introduction to the Riverside edition (1958) of *The Last of the Mohicans,* he says, "The love affair of Duncan and Alice in the *Mohicans* is insipid precisely because it was for Cooper a mere pandering to public appetite" (viii). The *North American Review*'s article on Cooper's *Lionel Lincoln* (1826) states that Cooper is trying a new method in not offering a "regular, impeccable, and all-accomplished hero or heroine. But these inimitable patterns of square-toed perfection are now regarded as very uninteresting fellows . . . " (XXII, 400). Readers apparently did not agree; *Lionel Lincoln* sold badly, and Cooper continued to use the conventional figures throughout his career. He not only was, incidentally, trying to support his own family, but had assumed responsibility for the debts and families of his five brothers—all of whom died between 1813 and 1819. See James Grossman, *James Fenimore Cooper* (New York, 1949), p. 17.

caution], I endeavored to repair the wrong done to my own views, by producing a work that should be purely American, and of which love of country should be the theme."[7] *The Spy* consequently entangles the love story in questions of loyalty and submerges it beneath battlefield and adventure scenes. Cooper retains the pair of heroines, the wise female advisor, and the mysterious dark lady, but their experiences form no more than a narrative line to which he can attach a series of discrete adventures. Harvey Birch is the largest character in the book and connects most importantly with its theme; whereas Harvey sacrifices everything to his patriotism, a conflict of loyalties only embarrasses temporarily the heroine's Royalist brother (Henry Wharton) and her lover (Peyton Dunwoodie).

The Wharton girls' mother is conveniently dead by the time the novel begins. America seems to have been affected early by the glorification of motherhood; and since Cooper was unwilling to make mother a comic character, he made her a rare one. An appalling number of heroines (all but two) are motherless, while many are orphans. The alternative, to provide a wise mother, did not suit Cooper's purpose. If rebellion against mother is unthinkable, principles are irrelevant to the heroine who possesses an admirable mother. Nor did Cooper follow the sentimental novelists in getting rid of mother in order to portray the daughter as a persecuted innocent. Instead, he roughed in the situation of a Jamesian novel: the heroine has beauty, money, freedom from maternal domination, and as much mobility as the historical facts allow. The important difference is that Cooper's heroines never have to make choices without having been exposed

---

[7] *A Letter to His Countrymen* (New York, 1834), p. 98.

to guidance from some person whose correct advice they may reject if they wish. A proper heroine accepts this tutelage gratefully, marries successfully, and is obviously destined to become herself a wise advisor; a foolish virgin follows her own inclinations, which lead to death or madness or a symbolic death as a virago. The Wharton sisters are typical.

Sarah, the elder, has learned in the city to admire the British and ignores much of the advice offered by her aunt, Miss Peyton (of the Virginia Peytons). Consequently vulnerable, Sarah falls in love with an Englishman, Colonel Wellmere, and learns only at the altar that he has left a wife in England. Like Scott's bride in the same situation, she goes mad. Frances Wharton, by contrast, elects to do just as her aunt directs and eventually marries Peyton Dunwoodie, her hero. Partly to check the course of true love, partly to reinforce his theme, Cooper makes Peyton responsible for capturing and turning over for trial as a spy Frances' brother, Henry. Cooper also provides a rival, the beautiful Isabella Singleton, who openly admires Peyton until she is accidentally shot by a band of human predators known as the Skinners. As Richard Chase says, Cooper fired the shot, and he keeps Isabella alive long enough for her to explain to Frances (and the reader) the reason for her own death.

"I was born under a burning sun, and my feelings seem to have imbibed its warmth; I have existed for passion only. . . . That mild, plain-hearted, observing aunt, has given you the victory. Oh! how much she loses, who loses a female guardian to her youth. I have exhibited those feelings which you have been taught to repress. After this, can I wish to live?" (296, 297)

25

The strongest connection that can be made between Isabella's passions and the rifle shot is that both she and the Skinners are ungoverned. She is effectively removed, however, and Frances has what Isabella terms "the victory."

As the word "victory" suggests, other wars besides the Revolution are being fought. Anyone who acknowledges the element of warfare in sex (as Isabella does) must be done away with so that the passive can triumph. In the whole sentimental tradition, according to H. R. Brown's study, marriage was governed by "only one law, the survival of the unfittest."[8] If the sentimental novel in America unstrung Diana's bow, it compensated by simply giving women without a struggle the man they wanted and all the morality there was. Cooper's heroines are consequently like and yet unlike Richardson's. Morality, in Richardson, is chastity and a cause for battle; morality in Cooper's novels is asexual and uncontested. Cooper could have used Pamela in a novel only by elevating her social status, lowering her pen, and sending Mr. B. on about his proper business. Whereas Richardson's obsession with sex makes Pamela's predicament interesting (whether we believe her or agree with Fielding does not matter), Cooper allowed no prurient suggestion. Only a few villainous Indians (such as Mahtoree and Magua in the Leatherstocking tales) betray even a faint physical desire for the heroines. It is strange, however, that even in the absence of Richard-

---

[8] *The Sentimental Novel in America,* p. 292. Brown says that Miss Sedgwick, whose novels Cooper reviewed early in his career, described what she called "lean-to" heroines as a compound of "amiability, docility, and imbecility." Irving's *Sketchbook* contains the clinging-vine analogy; more interesting, after Hawthorne's Hilda and James's Milly Theale, is Irving's comparison of such a heroine to a wounded dove.

son's sadistic and sexual males, Cooper's heroines retain the complementary masochism and asexuality of Richardson's females.[9] They were fortunate in retaining the masochism, for, as we shall find presently, they were sometimes called upon to suffer beautifully and endlessly.

If all went well, however, they were the victims only of that kind of double-talk that "relieves" an officer of his command. Cooper joined other novelists in assuring women that powerlessness was power: "If women thoroughly understood how much of their real power and influence with men arises from their seeming dependence," he wrote in *The Sea Lions,* "there would be very little tolerance in their own circles for those among them who are for proclaiming their independence and their right to equality in all things" (223).[10] By accepting the conventions, Cooper committed himself to the portrayal of what V. S. Pritchett calls "that powerful cult of the will, duty, and conscience by which Puritanism turned life and its human relations into an incessant war."[11]

Pritchett's statement clearly applies to the marriage-or-death struggles of Richardson's heroines, but it is no less pertinent to Cooper's. The difference is that Richardson described the struggle, whereas Cooper only recorded the victory of his inflexible heroines. If Cooper's most vaporous females had any physical presence, they

---

[9] See Ian Watt's *The Rise of the Novel* (London, 1957), p. 232, *passim*. Watt's discussion of the lily symbolism in *Clarissa* reminds us that D. H. Lawrence used the same symbol in describing Cooper's heroines.

[10] William R. Taylor quotes one expert of the times who assured women that the quiescent woman "wields a power, compared to which the lever of Archimedes was nothing more than a flexible blade of grass."—*Cavalier and Yankee* (New York, 1961), p. 162.

[11] *The Living Novel* (London, 1954), p. 10.

27

would be frightening, so perfectly assured is their control; the strength of their will is undeniable. When one of Cooper's most angelic heroines (Grace Wallingford of *Afloat and Ashore*) finds that she cannot have the man she loves, she leaves him all her fortune and wills her own death. She dies in spite of everything her family, friends, and physicians can do, and disregarding the serious problems her willfulness creates for her brother. With her character Cooper completed the prediction we heard earlier from Mrs. Wilson; a proper heroine who cannot have life on her own terms "sinks under" and dies.

Such displays of will underscore the inflexibility of these heroines. Questions of greater or lesser good never occur to them; they deal only with absolutes. Consequently, the heroine's truth-telling occasionally jeopardizes the life of someone she loves. Just as Jeanie Deans' testimony almost costs her sister's life, Frances Wharton's almost hangs her brother. Frances, however, lacks Jeanie's clear connection with history. Firmly rooted in uncompromising Scotch Calvinism, Jeanie has damnation behind her conscience. Cooper not only fails to identify the dregs of religion contained in the formula for the sentimental heroine but undercuts his heroine by treating damnation comically in *The Spy*. Frances is left, consequently, with no more than a virtuous dedication to abstract truth.

As the foregoing suggests, Cooper's douce heroines lack complexity. Sarah Wharton, Frances Wharton, and Isabella Singleton, if combined in one character, would have been interesting. Sarah, understandably bored in the Wharton household, exhibits an attractive girl's desire for becoming clothes and a social world to ornament. Frances has all the virtues any woman could need, while Isabella has emotions—a body. (One suspects that the bullet that kills her would have gone harmlessly through Frances.) By assigning various types of behavior to separate characters, Cooper could dispatch troublesome female tendencies. Yet this practice leaves him, far too often, with a heroine who is both insubstantial and unchangeable. She stands rigidly, essentially untouched by the experiences the tale offers, and it is quite obviously the business of the plot to cast a suitable husband at her feet.

When he appropriated the douce heroine to his own fiction, Cooper also took over the prose in which she was usually described. His description of the Wharton sisters is a fair sample of this:

> The sisters, for such the resemblance between the younger females denoted them to be, were in all the pride of youth, and the roses so eminently the property of the Westchester fair, glowed on their cheeks, and lighted their deep blue eyes with that lustre which gives so much pleasure to the beholder, and which indicates so much internal innocence and peace. (6)

Here, linked by the "feminine *so*," are asserted a beholder's reactions and the sisters' internal states; there are only two images, the roses and blue eyes, and these considered seriously are absurd. The roses on the girls' cheeks we can accept as reluctantly as the next cliché, but not roses that somehow light blue eyes with a "lustre" that in turn pleases the onlooker and reveals the state of their souls.

In *Jack Tier*, Cooper wrote that the two most beautiful things he knew of were high-bred and graceful women and ships. His remark justifies a comparison, and we find that his prose is usually more just to the ship than to the woman. Given the chance, he can describe a ship in terms suggestive of her mission, her crew, and her fate—and still make her visible as few heroines are.

> A three-masted lugger, that spread a wide breadth of canvas, with a low, dark, hull relieved by a single and almost imperceptible line of red beneath her channels, and a waist so deep that nothing was visible above it but the hat of some mariner taller than common, was considered a suspicious vessel. . . .
> The lugger was actually of about one hundred and eighty tons admeasurement, but her dark paint and low hull gave her an appearance of being much smaller than she really was; still, the spread of her canvas, as she came down before the wind, wing-and-wing as seamen term it, or with a sail fanning like the heavy pinions of a sea-fowl, on each side, betrayed her pursuits. . . . (*Wing-and-Wing*, p. 3.)

Ships are described with particularity; heroines, in sentimental terms or not at all. Yet Cooper only suggests, as he does here, the power of ships, while he asserts the powers of his heroines: "Love is a holy feeling with the virtuous of the female sex, and it hallows all that come within its influence" (*The Spy*, p. 247). So much more visible, vital, and credible are Cooper's ships than his heroines that we can understand those seamen whose affections remain with their ship.

Indefensible as Cooper's frail heroines are, they solve some of his structural and thematic problems. The love story often acts as a narrative line, as it does in *The Spy*. In addition, the resolution achieved when the heroine's hero proves worthy of her is often the one happy event in the ending of the book. Cooper's hurried disposal of other principals is often unconvincing or confusing, and his bustling conclusions sometimes obliterate rather than resolve major themes and problems. In *The Spy*, for instance, the events necessary to the marriage of Frances and Peyton are settled, but Harvey Birch is rushed into old age and death; the predators still roam the valleys of the Hudson; Washington's behavior is as enigmatic as ever; and the question of proper loyalties has been aired but scarcely codified. This is not an adverse criticism; one of Cooper's great strengths is his ability to recognize the complexity of moral questions. Nevertheless, the marriage of a romantic heroine is often the sole affirmative action he can find to set against the losses the novel describes and the future it foreshadows.

The converse of the douce heroine we have been discussing is, of course, the virago. Cooper was unusually skillful at portraying characters at various stages of their lives, and there are clear connections between the types of viragoes he attacks or ridicules and some of the younger women he criticizes. Girls who are outspoken and make a pretense to learning will become dogmatizing fools like Mrs. de Lacey (*Red Rover*) or Mrs. Budd (*Jack Tier*). Passionate girls like Isabella Singleton can become evil and managing women (like Lady Hamilton in *Wing-and-Wing*) or cunning hags (like Abigail Pray in *Lionel Lincoln*). Proud girls may find their fate forecast in the story of Mrs. Lechmere (*Lionel Lincoln*), who is critically injured when she trips on her train and falls downstairs. (Cooper's incidents are often dramatizations of folk sayings.) His New England towns are full of satirically drawn women (usually

widows) who pry into other households while neglecting
their own. They seem the settlement's counterpart of
Indian hags. Like the old Indian women, they no longer
have a function in society, and they retaliate by tormenting others.

The true viragoes in Cooper are all mature women;
again, they fit a conventional pattern. Their characteristic actions in American romances are, according to
Carl Van Doren, to "anticipate their suitors, nag their
husbands, and beat or savagely protect their young."[12]
Cooper did so well with the genre, however, that Maria
Edgeworth herself praised his Betty Flanagan, the Irish
camp-follower who appears in *The Spy* and reappears
as Betty Hollister in *The Pioneers*. Neither she nor
Katy Haynes, the other virago in *The Spy*, attempts to
conceal an unrelenting interest in marriage and money.
Neither knows her proper station or recognizes her
limitations. These women will argue warfare with com-
manding officers or medicine with surgeons; they pursue
men who are obviously superior to them, but the men
are single and solvent and that is all that matters. Like
Scott, Cooper sketched lower-class women with ease,
assurance, and sympathy. He showed the least mercy
to the *nouvelles riches* and to women who abuse the
power that wealth and privilege give them.

Toward the end of his career, however, he broadened
and deepened his attacks on viragoes. The most vicious
characterization, that of the titular "hero" of *Jack Tier*,
may have some connection with a much-publicized convention of women who met in Seneca Falls, New York,
to open a concerted drive against the "tyranny of man."
Jack Tier was written in 1848, the year of the conven-

---

[12] *The American Novel* (New York, 1940), p. 46.

tion, and contains two viragoes. One, a foolish widow, is murdered; the second, "Jack," turns out to be Molly Swash, a woman who has been deserted by her husband. Dressed as a man, she follows him to sea for a number of years, but the experience and hardships have unsexed her until she remains a grotesque even when restored to her proper name and clothing at the end of the book. Although she has been treated badly by her husband, Cooper wastes no sympathy on her. With this freak, the virago (in the archaic sense) who is more man than woman, Cooper reached what would seem the furthest possible extension of the character.

What, in Cooper's world, should Molly have done rather than follow her husband? How should a woman respond to the "tyranny of man"? Cooper's answer is conventional and unequivocal: Suffer. In contemporary novels, Griselda and Penelope were being extolled as models of wifely conduct, and "to know how to suffer was the first duty of virtuous wifehood."[13] Novelists pointed out how historically, biblically, and physiologically *right* it was that women suffer—and praised them for doing it so beautifully. In *The Two Admirals* and *The Heidenmauer* Cooper had written admiringly of two European women who were patiently waiting for death to release them from unhappy marriages.

Among the American women, however, only one gentlewoman is portrayed as a sufferer. This is Ruth Heathcote of *The Wept of Wish-Ton-Wish*. As a young

---

[13] Brown, *The Sentimental Novel*, p. 109. For the references to Penelope and Griselda see also pages 108 and 290. Brown describes one novel (E. D. E. N. Southworth's *The Deserted Wife*) in which the heroine learns just after the marriage ceremony that she has married a lunatic whose former wife drowned herself to escape him. The heroine refuses to have the marriage annulled, saying piously, "The Lord has given me something to do for His sake and endowed me with strength to do it" (298).

wife and mother in the early part of the book, Ruth is
unexceptional; sweet and pious, she is not particularly
intelligent and is incompetent in emergencies. Her
daughter is captured by Indians, however, and Cooper's
psychology rings true as he shows how uncertainty
about the child's fate exacts the heaviest possible toll.
As the years pass, Ruth decays under the strain.

> That softness and sweetness of air which had first touched
> the heart of Content [her husband] were still to be seen,
> though they existed amid the traces of a constant and
> corroding grief. The freshness of youth had departed, and
> in its place was visible the more lasting, and, in her case,
> the more affecting beauty of expression. . . . The ma-
> tronly form, the feminine beaming of the countenance,
> and the melodious voice, yet remained; but the first had
> been shaken till it stood on the very verge of premature
> decay; the second had a mingling of anxious care in its
> most sympathetic movements, and the last was seldom
> without that fearful thrill which so deeply affects the sense
> by conveying to the understanding a meaning so foreign
> from the words. . . . Like the mastertouches of art, her
> grief, as it was beyond the sympathies, so it lay beyond
> the ken of those whom excellence may fail to excite, or
> in whom absence can deaden affections. (228)

This is the mature romantic heroine in apotheosis. The
voices (to which Cooper was extremely sensitive) alone
allow an instant comparison; Ruth's has a "fearful thrill"
while Molly Swash's is simply "cracked."

Cooper's admiration for patient suffering even softens
his characterization of two women who belong not, as
Ruth Heathcote does, to the heroines but among the
viragoes. These two, both squatters' wives, have been
worn down in lives so harsh that the maternal instinct
seems the only one left them. Of the two, Prudence

Thousandacres of *The Chainbearer* and Esther Bush of *The Prairie,* Esther is the better character. Well enough educated to read from the Bible, Esther has in desperation taken as her second husband the uncouth Ishmael Bush. Adjusting to his life, she becomes almost as fiercely militant as Rob Roy's Helen, but the plot forces from her a much wider range of responses than Helen displays. On her finally come to rest the mythic primal crimes of her brother and husband, and her suffering asks a sympathy from Cooper that counters his distaste for her type. She consequently emerges as one of his most memorable female characters.

The relative success of Esther Bush suggests no more than we already know: interesting characters contain some dissonance. Since women had fundamentally only one choice in Cooper's world (to be or not to be a "female"), we find the most interesting women in tales that force ambivalence on them. *The Ways of the Hour* (1850), his last book, fails because it attacks too many things at once, but Cooper's confusion of purpose and the fact that Mary Monson is his only female protagonist make her worth considering.[14] Mary is much like Eve Effingham, who herself is thematically central to *Homeward Bound* and *Home as Found* (1838). Where Eve is, however, but a part of a coterie of social critics, Mary is alone and the defendant in a murder trial. Since Cooper wanted to show how provincial attitudes and the jury system could convict the innocent, Mary is pictured as a beautiful and innocent young woman who has

---

[14] This novel may be the first American detective novel; Anna Katherine Green's *The Leavenworth Case* (1878) is usually considered the first. Experimenting in fiction to the last, Cooper placed the climax of the action in the courtroom and made two professional men major characters. Neither is satirized, and Dr. McBrain does the basic detective work that supports the mystery's solution.

been educated abroad; the trial is held in a small town, and the inhabitants swarm through the action and harass the defendant like so many feists. Mary's accomplishments (such as playing the harp and speaking French) are here almost enough to hang her. By keeping the point of view outside Mary, Cooper adds to her mystery and makes his social criticism more telling and amusing than in the Effingham novels. Eve Effingham's perfection had been her one unforgivable fault as a character; yet this same perfection led Cooper to use her as spokeswoman for his views; and since he never solved the problem of giving a virtuous woman the last word without having her say it, Eve becomes unfemininely dogmatic.

Perhaps because of the difficulty he had had in keeping Eve from appearing a virago, Cooper saw that Mary could be made a champion of women's rights. Although no one knows it at the time of the trial, Mary has been hiding in the small town to escape her husband, a fortune-hunting European nobleman who is unpleasant but not so sinister as those who plague Hawthorne's heroines later. Since she has to function both as an injured innocent and as a wealthy woman who acts independently and supports feminism, Cooper makes her subject to a cyclical insanity which is reflected in her "illuminated countenance" (38).

As the trial begins and Cooper becomes increasingly interested in his attack on feminism, he starts to build a case against Mary. (Cooper routinely sent off manuscripts to the publisher as he wrote; consequently, his changes of purpose are often clear.) First, Mary's attorney begins to suspect that she is guilty, not of murder, but of "management." Then, almost halfway

through the novel, a douce heroine is brought to the
foreground so that she can be contrasted with Mary. This
girl, Anna, replaces in the action an attractive and outspoken character (the lawyer's niece) Cooper had carefully established in the opening scenes. The reason for
the substitution is obvious; the niece, who plunges into
an argument about constitutional law, is too much like
Mary. Anna, by contrast, is a perfect foil. She assures
her fiancé that if she had money (she has none), she
would "pour all into his lap, and then come and ask of
him as much as was necessary" (181); the lovers agree
that women should content themselves with "accomplishments, and small talk, and making preserves, and danc-
ing, and even poetry and religion"; they scorn women
who think they are intelligent and who desert their
husbands. The reader soon finds that Mary is wealthy
(but has refused to turn over her money to her fortune-
hunting husband), that she has little interest in religion
and less in preserves, that she is hiding from her husband, and that she is taking an active interest in her own
trial. Mary's interest is explained as "love of domination"
by Anna, who goes on to suggest that the defendant
may have a criminal record. Cooper insists that Anna's
motives are "benevolent and truly feminine," but to
a modern reader her actions appear to be those of a
scheming hypocrite.

Meanwhile, Mary's "shrewd and useful suggestions"
and her talent for "reasoning with singular acuteness"
have shaken her attorney's faith in her. Only once does
she act properly; at that time "a flood of tears, for the
first time since her imprisonment, so far as anyone
knew, burst from this extraordinary being; and, for a
few minutes, she became a woman in the fullest mean-

ing of the term" (292). As soon as she dries her eyes and recovers her composure, however, everyone (including the author) leagues against her. Cooper reports:

> The observer had an opportunity of tracing, in a face otherwise so lovely, the lines that indicate self-will, and a spirit not easily controlled. Alas! that women should ever so mistake their natural means to influence and guide as to have recourse to the exercise of agents that they rarely wield with effect; and ever with a sacrifice of womanly character and womanly grace. (363)

Although the novel ends in a snarl, Mary is clearly mad. Her idea has been that since she is innocent she should be acquitted, in a just legal system, because of insufficient evidence and without telling all she knows. She has just been sentenced to hang when one of the "murdered" reappears; she then takes over her own defense and singlehandedly solves the mystery by correlating what she knows with McBrain's detective work. Her action is obviously improper, according to Cooper; yet it seems harsh of him to suggest that she hang rather than act.

The novel leaves Mary reading the New Testament to learn "humility" and taking instruction from little Anna in how to be a proper woman. The big difference between Mary and Anna is that Anna has been taught her "duty" and "her character has been formed in what I shall term harmony with her sex . . . " (442). The novel ends by attacking divorce and women's property rights; quite obviously current feminist activity and legislation made Cooper champion, in his last book, the same douce heroine he appropriated from the sentimental novels for his first. Throughout most of his writing, the "natural harmony" of a woman's sex is a monotone.[15]

All of Cooper's novels taken together state that a female character could enrich her life without becoming unfeminine by leaving the domestic routine of towns and going where there was action. Paradoxically, it was only when a well-educated heroine invaded what was most eminently a man's world (ships, battlefields, forests, frontier settlements) that she acquired physical presence and complexity of character. The liberating influence of setting was not automatic (as the horrible example of Alice Munro proved), but a few heroines managed to seem credible—even likable—when they shared what were essentially men's experiences. If such a heroine were a racial mixture, Anglo-Saxon and something else, she had even more latitude, unless the foreign blood was Negro or Indian. Either of these was fatal.

Cooper's best heroines, in short, respond to and are really created from the action of adventure tales. They inhabit settings in which they can be useful; and since they are well-intentioned and capable, Cooper only infrequently worries about their deportment. Thus when Ursula Malbone, heroine of *The Chainbearer*, darts from a crowd of onlookers to place a prop under a church's roof structure, the action is described by one

---

[15] Certain biographical facts are pertinent to this last novel. His long and wearisome libel suits obviously influenced his opinions about judges and juries (see Ethel R. Outland's *The "Effingham" Libels on Cooper* [Madison, 1929]) and *The Letters and Journals of James Fenimore Cooper*, ed. James Franklin Beard (Cambridge, Mass., 1960 and 1964), III, IV. Cooper also had reason to be sensitive about women's property; Mrs. Cooper's family (the de Lanceys) set up her property in trust "for her sole and separate use independent of her husband." *The Letters and Journals of James Fenimore Cooper*, I, 86-89, 343.

of the men the roof threatens to crush. Once he is safe, this narrator comments briefly that the act required quick-thinking rather than strength and that a girl could consequently save them. Except for remarks such as this, or an occasional reminder that their voices are melodious and their hands soft in spite of frontier conditions, the authorial voice rarely speaks of femininity. The heroines themselves never give it a thought; yet they never faint, rarely blush, and speak their minds freely. Maud Meredith of *Wyandotté,* in fact, commits two sins against propriety and goes unpunished: she cleverly lets her affection for Bob Willoughby be known, and she is guilty of levity.

The extent to which such heroines undercut the frail female Cooper more often supported is nowhere clearer than in *The Pioneers,* his third novel. Elizabeth Temple, its black-haired, jet-eyed heroine, is paired with Louisa Grant, a minister's daughter and a perfect example of the pious virgin type. Elizabeth is described as she is first seen by the jealous New England housekeeper, Remarkable Pettibone. At the sight of Elizabeth's "dark, proud" eyes, Remarkable is "a little appalled"; she feels that "her own power had ended" and rightly suspects that her new mistress has a quick temper (57). Impatient and impulsive, Elizabeth chafes at some of the restraints imposed by frontier living; she has to check her horse because of the conditions of the trail, and she complains that the lack of society makes her " 'a nun, here, without the vow of celibacy' " (288). Yet, in a crisis she is controlled. When she and Louisa encounter a panther in the mountains, Louisa's "form yielded like melting snow," but Elizabeth sets her dog on the panther and stays by her friend until Natty Bumppo rescues them. Moreover, while Louisa refuses to go near the spot again, Elizabeth goes alone up the mountain to take Natty the gunpowder he wants. Her self-command is so great that the panther incident only troubles her dreams, in which her "active fancy" conjures up scenes wherein she is again threatened by the beast.[16] Some of Cooper's heroines draw strength from their religious beliefs, but Elizabeth Temple is not notably religious, and admits to her father that she tried to think of "better things" while in danger, but failed (336).

Since Elizabeth has rapport with more of the major characters than anyone else, she is soon caught in a conflict of loyalties. Her father criticizes her for letting her heart interfere with her head, but actually he sees the world more superficially than she does. The judge categorizes people with relation to the community; Natty is a "friendless" old hunter, and Hiram Doolittle, a scoundrel, once given a badge becomes "deputy." To Elizabeth, Hiram Doolittle with a badge is still a scoundrel, and Natty Bumppo has rights and a dignity that have nothing to do with his civic status. Elizabeth, sympathetic to the position of Natty, Chingachgook, and (for much of the novel) Oliver Effingham, seems not at all abashed at the suggestion that she looks as though she might have some Indian blood.

---

[16] Like Richardson before him, Cooper often used dreams and animal imagery effectively. Cooper was convinced that a character could not be held morally responsible for the content of dreams and used them to suggest those fears and fantasies that the proper hero or heroine would not consciously entertain. Elizabeth responds to the beauty of the wilderness, yet feels it as a threat; furthermore, she is at this time attracted by Oliver Effingham, but has refused his offer of escort minutes earlier because of his "equivocal" state (his identity is uncertain and he is said to have Indian blood). Panthers are Cooper's favorite animals to express savagism. See also the discussion of Natty Bumppo's dream in Chapter XI.

"It would be a great relief to my mind to think so, for I own that I grieve when I see Old Mohegan walking about these lands, like the ghost of one of their ancient possessors, and feel how small is my right to possess them." (287)

Actually, of course, she seeks a relief from guilt; she does not "possess" the land, never will, and would probably not give it to Mohegan if she did. We are reminded that the actual and fictional restraints placed on women helped Cooper have things both ways. Emotionally, Elizabeth realizes the wrongs done those to whom the unspoiled forest is a necessary condition for life; she volunteers for the invader's guilt and even toys with the image of herself as a product of miscegenation. Yet her reason tells her that her father is right; laws are necessary and farms cannot be turned again into forests. And making her reason somewhat redundant is the supreme fact that as a woman she is relatively powerless; by comparison with her father's actions, which are shaping society, even her most daring acts are gestures.

In the narrative, however, she appears to be independent and more than a little rebellious. What she can do, she does. Sent to reconcile Natty to jail, she helps him break out and then, in a marvelous moment of daring, lends the fugitives the judge's own boat so they can escape. This done, she displays some of that "management" Cooper denied most heroines in getting gunpowder from the store without the owner's knowing it.

All the better heroines have this same tendency to self-reliance. All are receptive, as Elizabeth is, to a broad range of opinions and customs. Anneke Mordaunt, the heroine of *Satanstoe*, and Dus Malbone of *The Chainbearer* have the same empathy Elizabeth shows.

Dus, in fact, speaks both Onondago and English and is described as being "half wild." They achieve this latitude by refusing to submit, as the douce heroines and Negroes do, to other people; like the Indians, these heroines give in absolutely only before what they construe as Fate. Elizabeth quarrels with her father and surrenders, finally, not to her father, but to the fact of her sex. Cooper emphasizes the parallel with Indians by placing Elizabeth and Mohegan together on Mount Vision and surrounding them by a forest fire. Mohegan knows that it is time for him to die and refuses to help himself; so long as she sees no chance of being rescued, Elizabeth's resignation matches his. Once Natty arrives, however, she takes hope and helps effect her own escape. The ability to recognize the inevitable and then to submit to it with composure sustains Cooper's most memorable heroines.

The resemblance between frontier women and Indians is repeated with Cora Munro in *The Last of the Mohicans.* One of the most interesting things about Cora is her indecision, through much of the action, as to whether her Negro blood is or is not a form of Fate. She hopes that Duncan Heyward is free of prejudice (15, 55). Duncan is, however, "conscious of such a feeling, and that as deeply rooted as if it had been ingrafted in his nature" (188). Once Cora learns this, and that he is to marry Alice, she recognizes the inevitable and draws for Tamenund a parallel between her state and that of his people: " 'Like thee and thine, venerable chief . . . the curse of my ancestors has fallen heavily on their child' " (368). By contrast with this, little Alice's fainting spells seem evasive rather than submissive.

Perhaps because it is important to them to distinguish

between the actual and the apparent, these women are slow to accept popular notions. As a group, they are less prejudiced than men, and they tend to trust their own instinct. Fortunately for them, in Cooper's world a good woman's instincts are never wrong. As a result, Anneke, Dus, Cecil Dynevor (of *Lionel Lincoln*), and Maud Meredith (of *Wyandotté*) can, like Elizabeth Temple, safely journey through the wilderness with what appear to be highly unsuitable companions. This ability is most amusingly considered in *The Water-Witch,* whose heroine, Alida de Barbérie is half-French and has a marvelous lack of concern for appearances of any sort. She is simply "missing" throughout much of the novel—cruising about Long Island on a smuggler's ship. No one, not even the reader, knows what she is doing, what she thinks, or even where she is much of the time. Since the other characters (all men) are rather urgently trying to find out one or all these things, Alida is a focus of interest, and the speculations of the men about her behavior endow her with a complexity that is never denied by her own statements or action.

The Water-Witch is really an international novel, and Alida is something like Daisy Miller. When she runs away to board the mysterious ship, her two suitors and her uncle (representatives of a corrupt world) suspect the worst. Her uncle, who is himself playing Pandarus to the Patroon of Kinderhook's slogging Troilus, sees Alida only as a marketable commodity. He laments,

"When a female reputation gets a bad name in the market, 'tis harder to dispose of than falling stock; and your young lords of manors and commanders of cruisers [the other suitor is the British Captain Ludlow] have stomachs like usurers; no percentage will satisfy them; it must be all or nothing." (173)

Like Edith Wharton's Lily Bart, Alida exists in the twin contexts of sex and cash. The uncle, the Patroon, and Captain Ludlow pursue the smuggler's ship, trying to recover Alida and redetermine her fair market value. Captain Ludlow suggests to the uncle:

"I know not how highly you may prize your niece, Mr. Van Beverout; but were I the uncle of such a woman, the idea that she had become the infatuated victim of the arts of yon reckless villain, would madden me!" (259)

The uncle tries to mollify Ludlow by suggesting that the girl has a "French fancy," is only rummaging through the smuggler's silks and laces, and will return "more beautiful than ever for a little finery." But Ludlow groans, "'Oh, Alida, Alida! this is not the election that we had reason to expect from thy cultivated mind and proud sentiments'" (259). All this speculation is enhanced by casual comments about women and ships throughout the novel. A sailor called Trysail tells of a young wench he knew who "'luffed athwart all her old companions, when the young lord of the manor fell into her wake.'" She did well until a "'squall'" overtook her; then others "'snugger in their morals hove-to'" under the protection of religion, while she "'drifted to leeward of all honest society'" (216). Trysail's story is hardly the commentary to reassure Captain Ludlow.

Through some fantastic contortions of plot, even for him, Cooper restores Alida, safe and presumably sound, and reveals that the bearded man she went to sea with is really the Alderman's daughter in disguise. Cooper refuses to say whether the daughter is legitimate or not, and he never explains Alida's motives for boarding the ship. In this novel, as in such European novels as *The Bravo*, the author seems little concerned about appearances. Alida has apparently followed her instincts about whom to trust, and we can only assume they did not betray her. When Cooper liberates a heroine and lets her rebel successfully against authority, as he does here and in *The Bravo*, the society which she escapes (and whose bad opinion she dares) is always corrupt.

Cooper's douce heroines quickly bore the modern reader; at the other extreme, the viragoes are sometimes genuinely comic, at other times tedious. His female characters have, as we have said, very little latitude; they are either feminine or they are not. Yet, beginning with Elizabeth Temple in his third book, Cooper did portray a few women who are not too unlike the heroines of popular modern fiction. He did this in spite of opposition, for one review of *The Pioneers* is typical when it complains that surely Elizabeth and Louisa walked by the lake in the moonlight and discussed young Edwards but that Cooper neglects to describe such scenes; the anonymous critic also feels cheated at not finding any of the "thousand little acts of tenderness" that "must have escaped" the hero.[17] When we add criticism such as this to Cooper's own attitudes, it is rather more surprising than not that even a very small group of females can teeter at the verge of masculinity and help themselves to some of the self-reliance, emotion, and adventurous spirit that romances allowed men but denied women.

---

[17] *Port Folio*, XV (March, 1823), 236.

II

DEFINING THE ABORIGINE

JUST AS Cooper's readers can predict a woman character's behavior once they know whether she affirms or denies her sex, they can also relate his Indians to a schema. Indians are more complex than women, however; the bestial savage shades into demonism at one limit, while, at the other, stands a chief so old and sage that he seems almost pure spirit. Whereas women, even Indian women, are always what they seem and can be instantly placed within a woman's limited realm, Indian characteristics form a spectrum that involves the reader in distinctions between appearance and reality.

When Cooper began to write about Indians, two contradictory notions about them prevailed. They were beasts (usually maudlin or bloodthirsty) or they were romanticized as "noble savages." Roy Harvey Pearce argues convincingly that in American fiction it was Cooper who first portrayed the Indian as complex and who synthesized these antithetical views. After Cooper, he says, writers of fiction always

tried to argue feelings of guilt and hatred, of pity and censure, out of existence by showing how Indian nobility was one with Indian ignobility. We can observe how Cooper set the pattern for writers who would treat of the

Indian, and how after him imaginative realization of the idea of savagism became a prime means to the understanding of American progress in its glories, tragedies, and risks.[1]

While Pearce is apparently correct about the idea of savagism in and after Cooper's novels, the old dichotomy is latent and sometimes visible in them. As a consequence, the Indian attracts perceptual doubts. In folklore and fiction, the Indian is variously described as diabolic, noble, proud, drunken, cunning, treacherous, honorable, and frightening. Even students of Indian life found him strange, and the few men who pretended to know him did not agree.

Cooper uses this uncertainty to advantage. It is the Indian's strangeness and the white man's fear of that strangeness that trick Duncan Heyward when he creeps toward an Indian village and mistakes, in his fright and ignorance, a pond of beavers for lurking savages (*Last of the Mohicans*, 262). Even when the senses are acute and the Indian familiar, comprehension is not immediate, as Cooper suggests in a scene from *The Pathfinder*. Mabel Dunham, hiding alone in a loft, hears a noise below.

. . . Never had there been a time in her brief career, when Mabel heard more acutely, saw more clearly, or felt more vividly. As yet, nothing was visible at the trap; but her eyes [*sic*, but Cooper surely means ears], rendered exquisitely sensitive by intense feeling, distinctly acquainted her that some one was within a few inches of the opening of the floor; next followed the evidence of her eyes, which beheld the dark hair of an Indian rising so slowly through the passage, that the movements of the head might be likened to that of the minute-hand of a

[1] Roy Harvey Pearce, *The Savages of America: A Study of the Indian and the Idea of Civilization* (Baltimore, 1953), p. 197.

48

clock; then came the dark skin and wild features, until
the whole of the swarthy face had risen above the floor.
The human countenance seldom appears to advantage
when partially concealed, and Mabel imagined many
additional horrors as she first saw the black, roving eyes,
and the expression of wildness, as the savage countenance
was revealed, as it might be, inch by inch; but when the
entire head was risen above the floor, a second and better look assured our heroine that she saw the gentle,
anxious, and even handsome face, of June. (365)

Since June is a woman, she can be trusted to act as she
appears to Mabel once the heroine's fright subsides; had
the Indian been a man, however, Mabel would have
confronted a dusky riddle that only subsequent action
could solve.

Of the Indians who exist in casual conjunction with
white men, the Tuscarora who gives his name to
Wyandotté (1843) embodies most clearly the weaknesses and strengths Cooper believed inherent in Indian
temperament. Wyandotté , a development of the earlier
character of Le Renard Subtil in *The Last of the
Mohicans* (1826), is really two Indians; his duality,
recognized by him and by others, is dramatized and
commented on by Cooper. Wyandotté was once a chief
since he was one of the tribe's bravest warriors and
"what was scarcely less honorable, among the wisest
around the council-fire" (36). In Cooper's understanding of Indian hierarchy, certain Indians become tribal
leaders either through physical superiority or by showing
unusual wisdom. It is a rare Indian who has both abilities, and Cooper's somewhat careless explanation that
Wyandotté "had made himself an outcast from his
tribe, more by an excess of ungovernable passions, than

from any act of base meanness" (36) seems designed less to explain the chief as a character than to leave him the widest possible latitude for action.

Wyandotté first appears in the novel as Saucy Nick, "a sort of half-outcast from his own people . . . a singular mixture of good and bad qualities, blended with great native shrewdness" (6). The reactions of the white settlers to this "half-outcast . . . mixture" are appropriately varied. Captain Willoughby, head of the frontier settlement at Hutted Knoll, feels securely that "this Tuscarora has a salutary dread of me" (117) and scornfully tosses him an occasional dollar for drink; he fails to notice that the Indian never picks up the money. Mrs. Willoughby trusts Nick with a confidence that is partly justified (she has saved him from smallpox and he is grateful) and partly sentimental; she pleads that Nick has "some good qualities" and complains that the retired Captain is too prone to "apply martial law to the weaknesses of your fellow-creatures" (118).

Like the Willoughbys, other characters in the novel judge Nick without understanding him, and some suggest that he is ubiquitous—even demonic. Even the insensitive Captain realizes, "'A drop of water might as readily be banished from that stream as an Indian from any part of the forest he may choose to visit" (117). Physically, Nick has the "dark, basilisk-like eyes" Cooper attributes to many Indians. The initial fears of a superstitious Irishman further invest Nick with demonic suggestion. On first meeting Nick, Mike is convinced that he is a devil; "'he says himself that he's Ould Nick, and I'm sure I never fancied the cr'ature but it was in just some such for-r-m'" (40).

Cooper explains Mike's reaction by describing Nick's paint, which is "confused" as a result of a "night or

two of orgies." Nick's face is an emblem of his life.
One-half red and one-half black, his paint is symbolically accurate, for the Tuscaroras (a branch of the
lower Iroquoian families) used red as a symbol of success and black as a symbol of evil, death, or mourning.[2]
The red indicates the Chief Wyandotté half of the
Indian, the black represents the Nick half; but at the
beginning of the action they are "confused" as is Nick–
Wyandotté. The confusion of paint, like that of identity,
is related to "orgies." Here, as elsewhere, Cooper uses
symbols more carefully than critics generally have been
willing to admit.

While his paint indicates his psychological state and
his personal history, Nick's name and the fear he arouses
in the little settlement remind us that Indians were long
suspected of being leagued with the devil. The affinity,
in the New England mind, of devil and Indian is, of
course, familiar to readers of colonial literature, New
England histories, and Hawthorne; the same thought
seems to have prevailed in the southern colonies, where
it endured past the middle of the nineteenth century.[3]
Henry R. Schoolcraft's *Personal Memoirs* (for March
13, 1835) record a letter from the editor of the *Theological Review*, who writes: "I was particularly gratified
with the coincidence of your judgment with the opinion
I have entertained for some years, *respecting the reality
of Satanic influence at the present time.*" Schoolcraft
confirms that he has concluded, from questioning one

[2] A. Grove Day, *The Sky Clears* (New York, 1951), pp. 154, 124.
According to H. L. Mencken's *The American Language*, Cooper
invented such expressions as "pale-face," "war-paint," "to go upon
the war-path," and "Happy hunting-grounds" (*Supplement I* [New
York, 1945], p. 180, *passim*).

[3] For Indian diabolism in American histories of the nineteenth
century, see David Levin, *History as Romantic Art* (Stanford, 1959),
pp. 135–37; Roy Harvey Pearce records the southern opinions in the
first chapter of his *The Savages of America.*

Ottawa prophet in particular, that "the Satanic influence, although invisible, was veritably present, adapting itself to the devices of the Indian priesthood, for the purpose of deceiving the tribe." [4] Cooper, by contrast, cautiously suggests that demonic interference belongs to the American past, as he does in the opening pages of *The Wept of Wish-Ton-Wish*.

> There is some ground for believing that the great parent of evil early looked with malignant eye on the example of peacefulness, and unbending morality, that the colonists of New England were setting to the rest of Christendom. (4)

Such characters as Michael O'Hearn, David Gamut, and Duncan Heyward may suggest that the Indians are diabolic, and Cooper himself may allude to them as devils, but he obviously does not believe and never exploits the contemporary fear that the Indian was an agent of Satan. Like Turgenev or Parkman, he is aware of supernatural suggestions that he deliberately suppresses in order to keep the narrative clear and unhampered.

The natural qualities of the Indian, in fact, interested Cooper more than supernatural affinities. Both halves of Nick–Wyandotté are "true to his nature . . . which taught him never to forget a favor, or forgive an injury" (448). How staple was this simple psychology is shown by Noah Webster's 1828 *Dictionary*.

> The *savages* of America, when uncorrupted by the vices of civilized men, are remarkable for their hospitality to strangers, and for their truth, fidelity and gratitude to

---

[4] Henry R. Schoolcraft, *Personal Memoirs* (Philadelphia 1851), p. 510. This statement is not typical of Schoolcraft's attitude toward Indians; his wife was half Ojibway.

their friends, but implacably cruel and revengeful toward their enemies. . . .

How much Webster owed Cooper himself for this definition, and to what extent both men were indebted to general opinion, cannot be known. The important thing is that Indian psychology hinged the pre-Christian drives of loyalty and revenge. Cooper and Webster alike accepted and imposed a conception of the Indian as one whose very nature resisted the forgiveness preached by Christians. Nick expresses this as, " 'Blood in Injin body; thick blood—nebber forget good—nebber forget bad' " (380). Repeated and reinforced by action in novel after novel, this motivation determines the behavior of every Cooper Indian except his last, Onoah of *The Oak Openings* (1848). The specific injury Nick needs to revenge is a public flogging he received thirty years earlier at the orders of Captain Willoughby.[5] Willoughby never questions the military axiom that " 'the most flogging regiments were the best fighting regiments.' " Cooper concedes that the rule might hold for "the lower English character." He warns, however, that it was "a fatal error" to make about an Indian. When the Revolutionary War begins, Willoughby's foreman (a Connecticut Yankee) incites the people of the settlement to revolt in an attempt to wrest Willoughby's lands from him. Nick is the only person Willoughby can send through the forest for help, and in order to "insure" his loyalty, the captain reminds Nick of the flogging. Unfortunately, Nick has just started to see

---

[5] The public humiliation of a flogging also explains the vindictiveness of Le Renard Subtil (Magua) in *The Last of the Mohicans* (which antedates *Webster's* dictionary by two years), and the hatred of Chief Musquerusque for Jaap, the Negro in *Santanstoe*. In their metaphorical language, these Indians complain that their backs are still sore.

himself again as Wyandotté, the responsible and respectable chief. Reminded of the disgracing blows, he sternly reproves the captain: "' . . . he flog warrior's back; make blood come. Dat bad enough; worse to put finger on old sore, and make 'e pain, and 'e shame come back ag'in'" (300).

The situation, in which an admitted inferior patiently comments on the injustice of an ostensible superior, is that of Jim's admonition to Huck Finn: "'Trash is what people is dat puts dirt on de head er dey fren's en makes 'em ashamed.'" But whereas Huck acknowledges shame and feels it himself, the military manual and Willoughby's own insensitivity keep him from seeing Nick as a man, let alone one whose temperament reacts violently to honor and shame. Nick yields as "the wavering purpose of thirty years was suddenly and fiercely revived" and by killing Willoughby regains the chiefhood Willoughby had denied him. "He believed that, in curing the sores on his own back in this particular manner, he had done what became a Tuscarora warrior and a chief" (433).

Just as, according to the rough chronology of the novel, the flogging had called into being Wyandotté's second self (Nick), the murder of Willoughby exorcises it.[6] Speaking of the flogging later, Wyandotté says, "'Dat happen to Nick—Sassy Nick—poor, drunken Nick; to Wyandotté, nebber!'" Having regained his integrity,

---

[6] Cooper's portrayal here of a double personality antedates by forty-three years Stevenson's Jekyll and Hyde, but follows the 1805 publication (in German) of Diderot's Rameau's Nephew, with which there is an interesting correspondence. Willoughby, we remember, occasionally tossed coins at Nick; Diderot's initial description reads: "Today his linen is filthy, his clothes torn to rags, he is virtually barefoot, and he hangs his head furtively; one is tempted to hail him and toss him a coin. Tomorrow he is powdered, curled, well dressed; he holds his head high, shows himself off—you would almost take him as a man of quality."

Wyandotté explains the difference between what have been his two selves: "'Nick always dry; Wyandotté know no thirst. Nick beggar; ask for rum—pray for rum—t'ink of rum—talk of rum—laugh for rum—cry for rum. Wyandotté don't know rum when he see him. Wyandotté beg not'in; no, not his scalp'" (304). When young Major Willoughby addresses Wyandotté by this proper name, the Indian answers "with emphasis, assuming a dignity of manner the major had never before witnessed. 'Wyandotté come—Nick gone away altogether. Nebber see Sassy Nick, ag'in! . . . '" (421). Nick—Wyandotté is an extreme example of Indian duality, but a clear one nonetheless; Cooper's more usual method was to contrast the stolid and vacant expression of the Indian in repose with his magnificent vitality in action. At the end of the book, Wyandotté is pictured as a Christian convert, but he still believes in revenge and, like Chingachgook and many others, he dies still an Indian—his character only clouded by Christianity.

Capable of nobility or degradation, guided only by a few simple precepts having to do with loyalty and revenge, and able to react so belatedly to an old injustice that the action seems unmotivated, Wyandotté–Nick defines the Cooper Indian. His extraordinarily acute perception of human emotions (only he recognizes the heroine's love for the hero) is typical, as are his scorn for gossip and curiosity, his automatic yielding before the beauty or kindness of a white woman, and his "desperation of one who ran amuck, and with the delight of a demon" in battle. By showing some of Wyandotté's traits, asserting others, and suppressing all information about his whereabouts for long periods in the narrative, Cooper presents the Indian as a complex character who has an existence in a second world—one unknown if not actually unknowable to the white settler. Furthermore, the Indian's ubiquity, as he emerges from the forest or is silently engulfed by it, establishes him as both a part of the wilderness and an agent for it. This particular function of Indian characters was carried on through nineteenth-century fiction and became a convention of its histories.[7] Parkman, for instance, in comparing the Indian with even the most adept woodsman, insists that the basic distinction is the Indian's relation to nature.

> . . . There are niceties of the woodsman's craft in which the white man must yield the palm to his savage rival. Seldom can he boast, in equal measure, that subtlety of sense, more akin to the instinct of brutes than to human reason, which reads the signs of the forest as the scholar reads the printed page, to which the whistle of a bird can speak clearly as the tongue of man, and the rustle of a leaf give knowledge of life or death. With us the name of the savage is a byword of reproach. The Indian would look with equal scorn on those who, buried in useless lore, are blind and deaf to the great world of nature.[8]

Even Natty Bumppo, expert woodsman that he is and much as he has learned from them, acknowledges their superiority as beings instinct with nature.

Against the full range of Nick–Wyandotté's villainy and nobility we can chart "Cooper's Indians." When people use this term, they think of the Indian brave in the prime of life who is a norm for Indians as a group.

---

[7] See David Levin, *History as Romantic Art*, pp. 132–35.

[8] Francis Parkman, *The Conspiracy of Pontiac* (Boston, 1899), I, 166.

Young Susquesus *(Satanstoe)*, Uncas *(The Last of the Mohicans)*, Chingachgook *(Deerslayer)*, Pigeonswing *(The Oak Openings)*, Hard-Heart *(The Prairie)*, and Rivenoak *(Deerslayer)* are all of a type and approximate most closely the common conception of the noble savage. From this group, the Indians shade toward demonism in one direction and toward the abstract idea of a wise chief in the other. The warriors of this group, often likened to Apollo, are sometimes posed in flickering firelight while Cooper admires their physique, dignity, grace, piercing eyes, and noble mien. Cooper's frequent classical allusions when writing of Indians are more than physically pertinent; his Indians are ethical descendants of those pre-Christians for whom revenge was a part of honor and honor was all.

Magnificent in motion and statuesque in repose, these braves are physically superb; and when Cooper can get two of them together in single combat, as he does in *The Prairie*, he invests the action with appropriate conventions from epic battles. As the Pawnee and Sioux warriors line the banks of a river to watch, the two enemy chiefs, Mahtoree and Hard-Heart, meet on a sandbar in its middle.

The Pawnee awaited the time of his enemy with calmness and dignity. The Teton made a short turn or two, to curb the impatience of his steed, and to recover his seat after the effort of crossing, and then he rode into the centre of the place, and invited the other, by a courteous gesture, to approach. Hard-Heart drew nigh until he found himself at a distance equally suited to advance or to retreat, and, in his turn, he came to a stand, keeping his glowing eye riveted on that of his enemy. A long and grave pause succeeded this movement, during which these two distinguished braves, who were now for the first time confronted with arms in their hands, sat regarding each other like warriors who knew how to value the merits of a gallant foe, however hated. (395)

The discussion that follows is part fliting and part an appeal by Mahtoree for union against the invading white men. Hard-Heart refuses and eventually triumphs in the combat. Never does Cooper surround a white-Indian battle with the classical conventions and high seriousness that mark the struggle of these latter-day Spartans.[9]

If both chiefs are heroic, what makes Mahtoree a villain? Indian villains in Cooper are defined in their relation to white society. Some, like Mahtoree and Philip, wish to exterminate the white man; others, less noble, are bent on personal (not racial) revenge and succumb to the white man's vices. Either way, they belong to the Senecan tradition of the villain protagonist. Mahtoree is a fair example of two things that mark the villain: his passions overwhelm his self-command occasionally, and he abuses his oratorical power. Since he is a chief, these are serious charges. Cooper's tribes are like little Renaissance worlds; the actions of a chief redound upon each member. Thus when Mahtoree yields "to his nearly ungovernable delight" at the sight of Ishmael Bush's horses, "it was at the precise moment" that the man set to watch Mahtoree's prisoners "chose to indulge in the malignant pleasure of tormenting those it was his duty to protect" (58). The collapse of tribal order even spreads to the horses.

---

[9] The battle between Deerslayer and the Indian at the edge of Lake Glimmerglass has an entirely different tone and purpose, though it, too, is serious. The proper context of this combat is Natty's initiation as an Indian killer. The combat of Harry March (a superb physical specimen of the white race) and the Indians at Hutter's "Castle" in the same book borders on farce. Harry belongs not to the epic tradition, but to that of the tall tale; he is of the half-horse, half-alligator combination that produced Mike Fink.

The impulse was communicated to the Teton horses, who were long accustomed to sympathize in the untutored passions of their owners. . . . The wild animals snorted with joy and terror, and tearing the earth with their heels, they dashed away into the broad prairies, in a dozen different directions. (59)

When Mahtoree does command himself, he does so not for the good of the tribe but to achieve his own personal desires. Like most of the villains, he is characterized as a persuasive orator who appeals to the passions rather than to the wisdom of his hearers. Cooper followed closely the metaphors and rhetorical patterns recorded by students of Indian customs,[10] but he overlaid these, in portraying villainous Indians, with his own particular fear of demagogues. As a result, Mahtoree, Weucha *(The Prairie)*, Magua *(The Last of the Mohicans)*, and other villains share the ability of the Weasel *(The Oak Openings)* to "flatter the mass that he might lead it," to stir the passions of his audience, and to suppress "whatever was frank, manly, and noble" (323). Such oratory usually provokes and unleashes a public fury that the speaker himself can no longer control. As these scenes accumulate and as red demagogues give way to white in the Littlepage and Effingham novels, the anachronistic political nature of this particular villainy becomes apparent. The shades of Desmoulins and Patrick Henry have crept unseen into Cooper's Indian camps.[11]

Indian villainy, then, can be seen as a failure of

---

[10] See John T. Frederick, "Cooper's Eloquent Indians," *PMLA*, LXXI (1956), 1004–17.

[11] Cooper had few illusions about the nature of man; he feared, in a democracy, the kind of oratory that leaves the audience "bereft of their senses" as Henry's was said to have done. (See William R. Taylor's discussion of Patrick Henry as he emerges from the 1817 biography by William Wirt, *Cavalier and Yankee*, pp. 67–94.)

command. The drunken Indian, the lustful, vengeful, or ambitious Indian has lost self-control; and the higher his position in the tribe, the more censure his irresponsibility deserves. The Indian scoundrel relates to white society in this way: the encroaching whites exert a pressure on the Indian that opens the flaws in his nature. Cooper's Indian villains are young and reveal the race's psychology. An Indian's failings are preeminently sensual; even money (which turns Cooper's white men into scoundrels) has value only for the debauchery it can buy. The novels imply that had the white man never come, even the villains could have controlled themselves. When the Europeans gave them rum, armed them, and set them against each other in what was essentially a European war for possession of the continent, the natural balance of the Indian world was destroyed. In this struggle, all that is pacific and rational, whether in a tribe or an individual, is threatened by what is warlike and brutal.

When Cooper was writing, few of his readers had actually seen an Indian; those who had, had seen, usually, the degraded remnants of a few Eastern tribes. In the 1830's, however, the government's removal policy reawakened interest in the Indian as the victim of civilization. Roy Harvey Pearce summarizes the situation:

The Cherokees were the most "civilized" of Indians, patently an agrarian people, settled, on their way to learning and literacy, hard-working, and brave. Georgians demanded their lands, insisting that they be moved west where they would be safe and where they could be edu-

cated safely into civilization, apart from the paradoxically evil influences of high civilization itself. Many
Americans who in general favored the Removal policy
did not favor it for the Cherokees, and even those who
saw Removal as a necessity, denounced the government's
actions. Yet the government went ahead, President Jackson [whom Pearce calls a "practicing Indian-hater"] in
1832 refused to carry out a Supreme Court order which
would have safeguarded Cherokee lands, and Americans
suddenly saw in the plight of the Cherokees the plight
of all Indians. . . . Still, no one thought to denounce
American civilization. The point was that the Cherokees
represented the certain hope that savages might become
civilized. And even this certainty would not hold.

Americans thus were of two minds about the Indian
whom they were destroying. They pitied his state but
saw it as inevitable; they hoped to bring him to civilization but saw that civilization would kill him. (*The
Savages of America*, p. 64)

Since it is far easier to lament a race than preserve it,
Americans accepted Indian extinction as inevitable and
indulged themselves in sentimental nostalgia for a lost
cause that was assuredly lost but that had never truly
been a cause. As we shall see in the third part of this
study, Cooper groped for an answer throughout his
career, but he also accepted the notion of the "vanishing
American"; it hangs like a nimbus over most of his
warriors and is personified in the chiefs who are his
most admirable Indians. In the preface to *The Wept
of Wish-Ton-Wish*, Cooper says that the chiefs Miantonimoh, Metacom, and Conanchet " . . . proved themselves worthy of better fates, dying in a cause and in a
manner that, had it been their fortune to have lived
in a more advanced state of society, would have enrolled
their names among the worthies of the age" (vii).

Cooper distills his nostalgia for the vanishing American in the closing pages of *The Last of the Mohicans*, concentrating it in the persons of young Uncas, the last of his race, and old Tamenund, whose day has, as he says, already "been too long." As a chief, Uncas is more important symbolically than actually; he proves in battle his leadership ability, but he no longer has a people to lead, and his own death is heavily foreshadowed early in the novel as Chingachgook pronounces the *ubi sunt* theme:

"Where are the blosssoms of those summers!—fallen, one by one; so all of my family departed, each in his turn, to the land of spirits. I am on the hill-top, and must go down to the valley; and when Uncas follows in my footsteps, there will no longer be any of the blood of the Sagamores, for my boy is the last of the Mohicans." (29)

Captured by the Hurons, Uncas looks on a tormentor with "an expression that was superior to contempt" (289) and behaves as though he were "an exquisite and faultless representation of the warlike deity of his tribe" (299). As he grows from a warrior to an abstraction of a warrior, Uncas' symbolic value as the last of his race increases simultaneously, and Cooper begins to prepare for the extinction of the Indian *qua* Uncas. A hag thrusts a torch in his face and "his eye, so far from deigning to meet her inquisitive look, dwelt steadily on the distance, as though it penetrated the obstacles which impeded the view, and looked into futurity" (292).

Cooper rescues Uncas from the Hurons less for the chase and battle in which Uncas dies (though there is that, too) than for the tableau that is to give Uncas' death additional importance. He is brought before Tamenund, a human anachronism who is so little man and so nearly manes that he is said to have "the rare gift of holding secret communion with the Great Spirit" (353). At the revelation of the bright blue tortoise tattooed on Uncas's breast,[12] the old man's mind telescopes time.

"Is Tamenund a boy?" at length the bewildered prophet exclaimed. "Have I dreamt of so many snows— that my people were scattered like floating sands—of Yengeese, more plenty than the leaves on the trees! The arrow of Tamenund would not frighten the fawn; his arm is withered like the branch of a dead oak; the snail would be swifter in the race; yet is Uncas before him as they went to battle against the pale-faces! Uncas, the panther of his tribe, the eldest son of the Lenape, the wisest Sagamore of the Mohicans! Tell me, ye Delawares, has Tamenund been a sleeper for a hundred winters?" (374)

---

[12] As this study proceeds, it will become increasingly apparent that Cooper's encompassing vision is based on ancient Greece. Not only does he compare Indians with Spartans and Apollo and compose battle scenes as though Indians were epic heroes, but he uses their symbols. The tortoise was the Greek symbol for woman; the Delawares or Lenni Lenapes (of which the Mohicans are a branch) were known to the Six Nations as *gantowisas* or "women." In Iroquois, *gantowisas* was a compliment rather than a reproach; Iroquois society was matriarchal and women had joint ownership of land and (if of a certain lineage) could appoint or recall chiefs. The white man, however, imposed his own pejorative sense of the word and the question of Delaware–Iroquois relations was soon involved in a fascinating semantic and historical confusion. Cooper got his ideas about the Delawares and Iroquois (the Mingos of his novels) from John Heckewelder's *Account of the History, Manners, and Customs of the Indian Nations, Who Once Inhabited Pennsylvania and the Neighbouring States* (Philadelphia, 1819). See Paul A. Wallace, "Cooper's Indians," in *New York History* (Cooperstown, 1954), XXXV, 423–46.

In comparing the Indian with classical heroes, Cooper was in accord with convention. So widespread was this particular cliché that Benjamin West, seeing the Apollo Belvedere for the first time, is supposed to have said, "My God, a Mohawk." (See Roy Harvey Pearce, *The Savages of America*, p. 110, *passim*.)

Here, in language that should interest Freudians, the impotent old chief endows Uncas with all the history of his race and its hope of perpetuation. The name Uncas belongs not only to the present Uncas, son of Chingachgook, but to the Uncas Tamenund had known in youth; it is a generic name for chiefs of the tribe. When Uncas answers, therefore, he responds as deputy for a century of Delawares.

> "When the Manitou is ready, and shall say, 'Come,' we will follow the river to the sea, and take our own again. Such, Delawares, is the belief of the children of the Turtle. Our eyes are on the rising, and not towards the setting sun. We know whence he comes, but we know not whither he goes. It is enough." (375)

The hope is abortive, of course, and Uncas is killed; yet Tamenund pathetically expresses the wish, at Uncas' burial, that the reign of the white man may be temporary. Admitting that the "'pale-faces are masters of the earth,'" he adds, "' . . . the time of the red-man has not yet come again'" (423). He has not given up all hope for the race, but he complains that his own day "'has been too long'" since "'before the night has come, have I lived to see the last warrior of the wise race of the Mohicans'" (423).

Tamenund is a magnificent figure. He, like such other superannuated chiefs as La Balafré in *The Prairie*, speaks oracularly from a position between this world and the next. They are sepulchers for the cumulative wisdom of their tribes. As characters, they have something of the quality of wish-fulfilment; they are the elder statesmen Cooper failed to find in the national capital—those whose dignity demands, fully as much as their wisdom deserves, the absolute deference of their people. In *The Oak Openings*, the last novel he wrote about Indians, Cooper finally assembles a large number of these chiefs in a scene that seems more dreamlike than real.

> The Indians already present were not seated. They stood in groups, conversing, or stalked across the arena, resembling so many dark and stately spectres. No sound was heard among them, a circumstance that added largely to the wild and supernatural aspect of the scene. If any spoke, it was in a tone so low and gentle as to carry the sound no farther than to the ears that were listening; two never spoke at the same time and in the same group, while the moccasin permitted no foot-fall to be audible. Nothing could have been more unearthly than the picture presented in that little, wood-circled arena of velvet-like grass and rural beauty. (242)

As Cooper surrenders to the unearthly quality that invests his greatest chiefs, it is as though the shades of the ancients had convened in Arcadia.

While most of the chiefs are seen only briefly, two of them, Chingachgook (of the Leatherstocking series) and Susquesus (of the Littlepage trilogy), are characterized over a period of years. Both are without tribes, but their fortunes run counter to each other. The story of Chingachgook is essentially a jeremiad; he moves from the status of an uncivilized warrior to a drunken, semi-civilized, imperfectly Christian, and thoroughly tamed savage. As a foil to, and friend of, Natty Bumppo, Chingachgook has a function and consequent importance (see Chapter XI), but as an Indian chief he is narrow.

Susquesus is more interesting as an Indian. Cooper meant him to be a model warrior, and the characterization succeeds until, because of his thesis, he attempts to turn Susquesus into a social symbol. Susquesus, first seen as "Trackless" in *Satanstoe,* belongs to the group of warriors who approximate the noble savage.

> Trackless was a singularly handsome Indian, the unpleasant peculiarities of his people being but faintly portrayed in his face and form; while their nobler and finer qualities came out in strong relief. His nose was almost aquiline; his eye, dark as night, was restless and piercing; his limbs Apollo-like, and his front and bearing had all the fearless dignity of a warrior, blended with the grace of nature. (331)

Although he is a faultless guide, the explorers have some initial doubts about his reliability. They have been warned that Trackless lives apart from his tribe and that "such Indians are always to be suspected" (339). Furthermore, the convivial members of the party distrust him because he refuses to drink. " 'T'e man t'at refuses his glass, in good company,' " says one Dutchman, " 'has commonly something wrong in his morals' " (340). In the ensuing adventures of the party, Trackless proves himself, and Cooper sets him in contrast with Jaap, Cornelius Littlepage's Negro man. At the battle of Ticonderoga, the Indian refuses to take part; yet he appears, after the rout of the British-American forces, and asks quietly, " 'You want go? Got 'nough, eh?' " (371). He then leads his group to safety. Jaap, on the contrary, fights alongside the white men, but by flogging a captured chief he incurs an enmity that later proves disastrous to the group.

In *The Chainbearer*, the second novel of the trilogy, Susquesus' role is less crucial, as the conflict is between those who are trying to measure the land for settlement and the squatters who are trying to appropriate it. Both parties accept the Indian's word as valid, and he acts as a medium, moving at large through the forest. Only at the end of the book, after the squatter has murdered the chainbearer, does Susquesus assume any real importance. He is then suspected, by the narrator, of having avenged the chainbearer by firing the bullet that kills the squatter. There is no real proof of his action, however, and the account is considered morally square.

In the last book of the trilogy, *The Redskins*, Susquesus assumes an importance that overwhelms the novel. Both Susquesus and Jaap are over a century old as the novel opens, and both are living in quiet retirement on the Littlepage estate. Their venerability makes them possible elder statesmen; as Susquesus says, " 'Youth is full of hope; but age is full of eyes; it sees things as they are' " (480). Their symbolic function is made clear to Hugh Mordaunt, the new heir, when his uncle says early in the novel,

"Hugh, I never see these men without a feeling of awe, as of affection. They were the friends, and one was the slave of my grandfather; and as long as I can remember, have they been aged men! They seem to be set up here as monuments of the past, to connect the generations that are gone with those that are to come." (124)

Like Faulkner's Sam Fathers, Susquesus and Jaap are links with the past; they are also racial prototypes. The

uncle comments that they are both "'true to the feelings
and habits of their races, even after passing so long a
time together in this hut'" (125). Jaap pokes around
in the garden that surrounds half the house, "'still a
slave to his work, in fancy, at least,'" while Susquesus
lounges in the forest that surrounds his half of the
property. Jaap feels himself superior but shows himself
as inferior to Susquesus, and the racial comparison is
kept up throughout the action.

Cooper was even more interested, however, in a
second kind of comparison: that between the real
Indian, as represented by Susquesus, and the white
"Injin" who painted his face and dressed in calico to
raid the country and burn barns during the anti-rent
wars in New York State. Cooper is here counterposing
two ends of an historical process. Susquesus is enough
like Tamenund to represent him adequately, and the
"Injins" are of that barnburning and leveling faction
that gained control of Tammany Hall in the 1840's. In
taking "Tammany" as the name of an organization
which Tweed was to take over in 1867, the "white
usurpers of his ancient territory" have corrupted not
only Tamenund's name but also his principles. The
history of Tammany Hall would be fresh in the reader's
mind as he read, in 1846, the following words:

There is "Indian" and "Injin." The Injin is a white man,
who, bent on an unworthy and illegal purpose, is obliged
to hide his face, and to perform his task in disguise. The
Indian is a redman, who is neither afraid nor ashamed
to show his countenance, equally to friend or enemy. The
first is the agent of designing demagogues, the hireling of
a discontented and grasping spirit, who mocks at truth
and right by calling himself one who labors to carry out

"the spirit of those institutions" which he dishonors and is afraid to trust; while the other serves himself only, and is afraid of nothing. One is skulking from, and shirking the duties of civilization, while the other, though a savage, is, at least, true to his own professions. (286)

Once this background is established, a delegation of western Indians arrives; they seek Susquesus who, as it turns out, was once a great chief. He left his people long ago, but is famous for his virtue. Their spokesman says "that is a thing a redskin never forgets" (293). "Virtue" is later defined by the context as keeping one's word and having an overwhelming sense of individual responsibility. The real Indians, finding they admire the same principles held by the Littlepage gentry, take up the Littlepage battle against the "Injins"; and the interstices between quarrels and skirmishes are filled with the aggrandizement of Susquesus (often at the expense of Jaap).

In the first two novels of the trilogy, Susquesus has had surface, but now Cooper starts to fill in depth. We learn that Susquesus has yet another name: The Upright of the Onondagoes. His reason for leaving his tribe was his love for a young girl who had already given her word to another brave. Having sacrificed his happiness for his integrity, he is still honored by the tribe. When Susquesus left the tribe, he asserted the timeless validity of the forest as an intellectual retreat by telling his people that he must go into the woods, but that he would return when his mind was at peace. As the interpreter retells the story,

"Brethren, the stillness in that tribe . . . was like that which comes in the darkness. Men saw him go, but none dare [*sic*] follow. He left no trail, and he was called the Trackless. His mind was never at peace, for he never came back. Summer and winter came and went often before the Onondagoes heard of him among the pale-faces. . . . The chief was gone, but the law remained. Go you, men of the pale-faces, who hide your shame in calico bags, and do the same." (488)

While all this is obviously intended to point the difference between the Indian chief, who values his word and a settled government above his personal felicity, and the "Injin," who tries to break his legal agreements, the novel does give Cooper the opportunity to display a number of set-pieces in which an elderly Indian chief addresses an encircling audience in a context of setting suns, doing what is right, and pleasing the Great Spirit. Susquesus explains to his admirers that " 'the wicked spirit that drove out the redman is now about to drive off the pale-face chiefs [the gentry]. It is the same devil, and it is no other' " (483). He points out that the real, though displaced, Indians are their own masters as the bragging and greed-ridden "Injins" are not. The white man tries to take whatever he wants from his neighbors; the Indian, desiring a wigwam, builds his own. The white man boasts of his liberty, but it is the Indian who lives a free man.

"My children, the redman is his own master. He goes and comes as he pleases. If the young men strike the warpath, he can strike it too. He can go on the warpath, or the hunt, or he can stay in his wigwam. All he has to do is to keep his promise, not steal, and not to go into another redman's wigwam unasked. He is his own master. He does not say so; he *is* so." (494)

At the end of the book, Susquesus elects to stay with his friends, the Littlepages, rather than make the long journey west. Yet he recognizes his symbolic importance. "'I did not think ever to be a father; but see how different it has turned out! I am now the father of all redmen'" (480). Sublimated, through probity, to symbolic stature, Susquesus is still living at the end of the novel—long after the Injins are defunct.

In Cooper's world, as in Faulkner's, the Indian survives as a symbol or spirit while the Negro (whom both writers juxtapose with the Indian) endures physically. Treating the Indian as noble and the Negro as comic, Cooper was apparently unaware of the implications of the Littlepage trilogy for the two races. The action states, nonetheless, that the Negro accepted, without question and as his due, a protection for his people that the Indian could not bring himself to ask.

III

SLAVERY, SECURITY, AND DOUBT

BADLY as America has done by the Negro in life, it is
the only nation to treat him seriously and as one of its
major figures in literature.[1] Cooper was the first American author to characterize repeatedly, and with some
complexity and depth, the American Negro. Jaap, the
Negro we have just seen contrasted with Susquesus, is
the most maligned Negro in Cooper's novels, and it is
necessary to establish briefly the background for such
characterization before returning to Jaap and the other
Negro characters.

Cooper's ideas on equality in general and slavery in
particular are hard to distinguish from those stated by
Aristotle and accepted (though for different reasons)
by St. Thomas Aquinas. The "equality" the Greeks
sought, according to G. Lowes Dickinson,

> was proportional not arithmetical—the attribution to each
> of his peculiar right, not of equal rights to all. Some were
> born to rule, others to serve; some to be ends, others to
> be means; and the problem to be solved was not how to

---

[1] John Herbert Nelson, in *The Negro Character in American
Literature* (Lawrence, Kansas, 1926), writes, "With the Indian and
the frontiersman, he [the Negro] shares the honor of being the most
original and distinctive contributions which America has yet made
to the world's small company of great literary types" (15). Cooper
was, of course, the first author to establish the ruling conventions of
all three types.

obliterate these varieties of tone, but how to compose them into an ordered harmony.[2]

In his essay, "On American Equality," in *The American Democrat* (1838), Cooper wrote:

The celebrated proposition contained in the declaration of independence is not to be understood literally. All men are not "created equal," in a physical, or even in a moral sense, unless we limit the signification to one of political rights. This much is true, since human institutions are a human invention, with which nature has had no connection. (47)

The distinction between natural and human orders is carefully made.

The best basis for comparison of ideas on slavery comes from Euripides, who wrote that "one thing only disgraces a slave, and that is the name. In all other respects a slave, if he be good, is no worse than a freeman."[3] This is almost literally transferred to Cooper's *The Spy*, although color is substituted for condition since Caesar is not a slave. Thus Caesar says, "'A black man so good as white, Miss Sally, so long as he behave heself.'" Sarah Wharton assures him, "'And frequently he is much better'" (32). Like Aristotle, Cooper believed that there were certain men whose abilities at the moment made it "as much to their interest to be ruled

[2] *The Greek View of Life* (Ann Arbor, 1960), p. 81. The problem here stated, of composing an "ordered harmony," was Cooper's chief concern and that of his age. When Daniel Webster addressed the senate on January 26, 1830, he exclaimed, "Would to God that harmony might again return!" According to William R. Taylor, schoolboys memorized the line for almost a century, Webster built his career on it, and "this word and this speech penetrated very deeply into the American's consciousness of himself."—*Cavalier and Yankee*, p. 114.

[3] *Ion.* 854, as quoted by Dickinson, *The Greek View of Life*, p. 81. The quotation from Aristotle that follows is also from Dickinson's translation, p. 79.

as it is to their masters' interest to rule them." Such an edict clearly applies to childlike Negroes. Speaking of Caesar, Cooper laments that such family servants are

> giving place in every direction to that vagrant class which has sprung up within the last thirty years, and whose members roam through the country unfettered by principles, and uninfluenced by attachments. For it is one of the curses of slavery, that its victims become incompetent to the attributes of a freeman. (36)

While his potential abilities were unknown and only his ignorance a certainty, to free the slave by fiat would be to abandon him. "Freedom" would deprive the slave of any tolerable future in America so long as his complete acceptance by immigrants from Europe proved impossible.[4]

---

[4] Alexis de Tocqueville's *Democracy in America* (translated into English in 1835) and Cooper's *The American Democrat* (1838) agree on this problem. Tocqueville wrote: "The Indians will perish in the same isolated condition in which they have lived; but the destiny of the Negroes is in some measure interwoven with that of the Europeans. These two races are attached to each other without intermingling; and they are alike unable entirely to separate or to combine. . . . Thus the negro transmits [through "the physical and permanent fact of colour"] the eternal mark of his ignominy to all his descendants; and although the law may abolish slavery, God alone can obliterate the traces of its existence. . . . You may set the negro free, but you cannot make him otherwise than an alien to the European. . . . Whosoever has inhabited the United States must have perceived, that in those parts of the Union in which the negroes are no longer slaves, they have in nowise drawn nearer to the whites. On the contrary, the prejudice of the race appears to be stronger in the States which have abolished slavery, than in those where it still exists; and nowhere is it so intolerant as in those States where servitude has never been known."—*Democracy in America* (New York, 1899), I, 380, 382, 383.

So Cooper, after stating that the consequences of slavery were the sins of limiting the slave's moral existence and keeping him in ignorance, continued: "American slavery is distinguished from that of most other parts of the world, by the circumstance that the slave is a variety of the human species, and is marked by physical peculiarities so different from his master, as to render future amalgamation improbable. In ancient Rome, in modern Europe generally, and, in most other countries, the slave not being thus distinguished, on obtaining his freedom, was soon lost in the mass around him; but

The limitations of Cooper's Negro characters, consequently, but imitate the limitations of the Negro's
existence. When a character, such as Caesar or Jaap,
is confined within the family group and treated as a
child, he acts as a child. When, as we shall see shortly,
a Negro accompanies a member of the family into a
less restrictive life and is granted as much autonomy as
he seems able to use to advantage, that Negro grows.
Of the childlike Negroes, Caesar is the first, but Jaap
is the most fully described. Only Jaap and the Indian
Susquesus are major figures in all three books of the
Littlepage trilogy (*Satanstoe* and *The Chainbearer* of
1845 and *The Redskins* of 1846). In the first book,
young Jaap is indulged by his master, Cornelius Littlepage, and in the last he acts like a superannuated

nature has made a stamp on the American slave that is likely to
prevent this consummation, and which menaces much future ill to
the country. The time must come when American slavery shall
cease, and when that day shall arrive, (unless early and effectual
means are devised to obviate it,) two races will exist in the same
region, whose feelings will be embittered by inextinguishable hatred,
and who carry on their faces, the respective stamps of their factions.
The struggle that will follow, will necessarily be a war of extermina-
tion. The evil day may be delayed, but can scarcely be averted."—
The American Democrat (Cooperstown, 1838), p. 175.

Modern corroboration of Tocqueville and Cooper is offered by
C. Vann Woodward, Sterling Professor of History at Yale University: "White supremacy was a national, not a regional credo, and
politicians of the Democratic, the Whig and the Republican parties
openly and repeatedly expressed their allegiance to the doctrine. To
do otherwise was to risk political suicide. . . . Far from sharing the
expansion of political democracy, the Negro often suffered disen-
franchisement as a consequence of white manhood suffrage. By 1840
about 93 per cent of the free Negroes in the North were living in
states that excluded them from the polls. By 1860 only 6 per cent
of the Northern Negro population lived in the five states that
provided legally for their suffrage. . . . Between 1832 and 1849
mobs touched off five major Anti-Negro riots in Philadelphia. Mobs
destroyed homes, churches and meeting halls, and forced hundreds
to flee the city. An English Quaker visiting Philadelphia in 1849
remarked that there was probably no city 'where dislike, amounting
to hatred of the coloured population, prevails more than in the
city of brotherly love.'"—"The Antislavery Myth," *The American
Scholar*, XXXI (Spring, 1962), 316, 318.

spoiled child; his is not an attractive character, but he is portrayed without rancor. He quite obviously, however, suffers from Cooper's desire to make a monumental figure out of the Indian Susquesus. Jaap's function is to contrast with Susquesus and to provide comic relief from the dogmatizing and warfare, particularly in *The Redskins*.

Jaap lends himself to comic treatment because he is usually wrong and always rigid; he insists that he is superior to Susquesus (or to any Indian) although everyone else recognizes his inferiority. Susquesus, by contrast, pretends to less and is granted everything. Since the reader's sympathy is unflaggingly directed to the Indian, Jaap's grumbling criticism of Indians intrudes, irritates, and makes him undeserving of compassion. As Jaap remains static and perfectly satisfied with himself, his surroundings change. *Satanstoe* pictures him as half-grown, the slave and companion (according to Dutch custom) of Cornelius Littlepage, the narrator. The temper of Cornelius' control is indulgent rather than oppressive, and Jaap's errors are innocuous. Similarly, Mari, the heroine Anneke's slave, "was a buxom, glistening, smooth-faced, laughing, red-lipped, pearl-toothed, black-eyed hussy, that seemed born for fun; and who was often kept in order by her . . . young mistress with a good deal of difficulty" (73). Jaap and Mari are often trials but never burdens. Fittingly, Cooper describes them as they attend the Pinkster, "the great Saturnalia of the New York Blacks," a frolic Cooper obviously approved both because it gave them enjoyment and because it renewed for them annually a sense of tradition and community he felt they needed. As *Satanstoe* shows, the Pinkster let the Negroes of

New York recapture or refresh, largely through dance rhythms, their sense of identity. Cooper's awareness of Pinkster's value is revealed in his comment on the denial of such festivals by the people of New England.

> There are few blacks in Connecticut, I believe, and those that are there, are so ground down in the Puritan mill, that they are neither fish, flesh, nor red-herring, as we say of a nondescript. (66)

Hating as he did the Puritan mill, which ground exceedingly small and uniform men, and preparing for the New Englanders' attempt to usurp the lands of Dutch and English settlers later in the trilogy, Cooper, like Irving some thirty-five years earlier, shows New York as commodious; New York has ample capacity for idiosyncrasy and humor. Partly as a result of this, *Satanstoe* is a pleasant book. Its main characters are young, its theme the exploration of virgin forest, its tone so buoyant that even the fall of Ticonderoga is more an adventure than a defeat. Consequently, Jaap's childlikeness is of a piece with the novel; Susquesus' composure, his "contempt" for "so complete an absence of self-command, as the untutored Negro manifested" (356), is alien.

Jaap remains in the background in the second novel of the trilogy; the labor of slaves protects the heroine's soft hands from "any of the toil that is unsuited to a gentlewoman" (154); and Jaap is something of a protective shadow at her heels when she finds it necessary to walk in the forest. Still childlike, he is relatively unimportant in the action.

The third novel, *The Redskins,* is another matter. Centered on the landlords' struggle to keep their property, the book contains many violent scenes, a few elegiac passages, and long stretches of narrative in which the tone is consistently crabbed. The monolithic integrity of Susquesus raises him above all this, but Jaap has no comparable ability. As the Littlepages' English servant remarks,

" . . . The nigger grows uglier and uglier every year, and that is the most of a change I can see in him; while I do think, sir, that the Indian grows 'andsomer and 'andsomer. He's the 'andsomest old gentleman, sir, as I know of, far and near!" (307)

Since the English servant seems to have been imported chiefly to identify the gentlemen and scoundrels in *The Redskins,* we are not surprised to find that Hugh Littlepage (the narrator of this third section of the family history) agrees that the Indian is, indeed, a gentleman. Just as obviously, Jaap is not. He has not changed, but his world has; and the world of *The Redskins* is governed by the code of the gentleman; its standards are those of propriety. Like Caesar of *The Spy,* Jaap has no sense of propriety and no understanding of the code. As James Grossman points out, this gives the slave a certain kind of freedom:

The plight of young Wharton [a gentleman in *The Spy*] does not move us deeply, because he is so fettered by the code which forbids his showing fear; the Wharton slave, Caesar, . . . is a freer man, for he is allowed to tremble at danger and act sensibly about it.[5]

Actually, however, Caesar and Jaap are free only of the code; both are still bound by racial stereotype.

[5] *James Fenimore Cooper,* p. 25. Unlike Grossman, Cooper approved the code rather than self-expression.

Cooper places Jaap at an Indian council fire where the Negro ignores peace pipe etiquette and insists on finishing the tobacco. "'Nigger is nigger, and Injin is Injin; and nigger best,'" he says. "'Don't wait, Injin; when I done, you get pipe again, I say'" (452). This high-handed rudeness is overlooked by the Indian "with the courtesy of one trained in high society"; and we are reminded of Irving's own Caesar of the *Salmagundi Papers* of October 1, 1807. Irving's "old, weather-beaten wiseacre" also loved to play the role of the "absolute lord and ruler of the soil."

What we have in *The Redskins* is less a conscientious portrayal of an individual Negro than one of those algebraic relationships that Cooper often uses as the structure supporting a book. With his unwarranted presumption to a natural superiority over the Indians, Jaap stands in relation to Susquesus as the anti-renters, unjustifiably asserting their "natural" right to the land, stand to the Littlepages. All those whose demands are importunate and unseemly are represented by Jaap.

A second equation, however, threatens to emerge whenever the smugness of Jaap's tone seems an echo, even if a burlesqued one, of the Littlepages' own self-righteousness. Much as the skirmishes of the plot disguise this parallel, dangerous as it is to Cooper's thesis, its submerged presence is a credit to Cooper's perception. For the superiority Jaap claims comes from his identifying himself with, though as an appendage of, the social position of his owners. Unlike Twain's Jim, who is delighted to discover he owns himself, Jaap feels sorry for Susquesus.

"Old Sus hab liberty all he life, and what good he get? Nuttin' but poor red sabbage, for all dat, and never be anyt'ing more. If he could be gentle'em's sabbage, I tell him, dar war' somet'ing; but, no, he too proud for dat! Gosh! so he only he own sabbage!" (444)

Jaap's pride, then, is not pride of being, but pride of being owned—by a gentleman. Both Jaap and Jim accept without question the values of their respective worlds. In a gilded age, Jim muses, "' . . . I's rich now, come to look at it. I owns mysef, en I's wuth eight hund'd dollars. I wisht I had de money, I wouldn' want no mo'.'" [6] Both find symbols for their sense of self, but Jim's reckoning is in dollars while Jaap's is in the trappings of social rank.

Jaap had brought out, as if to sun, an old livery coat of his own that he had formerly worn, and a cocked hat, in which I have been told he was wont actually to exhibit himself of Sundays and holidays; reminders of the superiority of a "nigger" over an "Injin." (332)

Neither Jaap nor Jim has a real sense of self; the one finds his security in being a gentleman's shadow and the other exists as his own market value: $800 F.O.B. the raft.

Only in New York on Pinkster day had the Negro an identity not derived from the fact of his slavery; this is the statement of Cooper's novels containing Negroes who remain on land. Far from regretting such limitations, Cooper allows Hugh Littlepage to express, in *The Redskins,* a lament that can also be found in *The Spy* (36) and *Afloat and Ashore* (507).

It is the fashion of the times to lament the disappearance of the redman from among us; but, for my part, I feel

---

[6] Mark Twain, *Huckleberry Finn*, ed. Henry Nash Smith (Cambridge, Mass., 1958), chap. viii, p. 41.

much more disposed to mourn over the disappearance of the 'nigger.' . . . I regret the 'nigger;' the old-fashioned, careless, light-hearted, laborious, idle, roguish, honest, faithful, fraudulent, grumbling, dogmatical slave; who was at times good for nothing, and again, the stay and support of many a family. But him I regret in particular is the domestic slave, who identified himself with the interests, and most of all with the credit of those he served, and who always played the part of an humble privy counsellor, and sometimes that of a prime minister. (445)

Hugh's regret is premature, at least as far as literature is concerned. Not even Melville's treatment of this type in *Benito Cereno* extinguished it. The black prime minister endures, as the Mammy figure, in the books of such writers as Carson McCullers and William Faulkner (whose Dilsey is perhaps the greatest of such characters).

If the childlike and wrong-headed Negro elicited his irritated amusement, Cooper felt affection for the "humble privy counsellor" Hugh Littlepage hates to see disappear. Yet he believed that domestic slavery must eventually end, and he created his best Negro characters by exploring in fiction various ways in which they could be educated to responsibility.[7] In *The Water-Witch*

---

[7] Cooper, like Jefferson, was for African colonization. For a more complete statement of his views, see his own *The American Democrat* and Robert E. Spiller, "Fenimore Cooper's Defense of Slave-Owning America," *American Historical Review*, XXXV (1930), 575–82. Also Max L. Griffin, "Cooper's Attitude toward the South," *Studies in Philology*, XLVIII (1951), 67–76. Cooper disliked abolitionists as a group; too many of them were also attacking landowners as well as slave owners while they left undisturbed those people who had their riches in the form of stocks and bonds.

Cooper did not believe there would be a Civil War, but one of his last statements on the subject is to be found in *Ways of the Hour* (1850) where the attorney Dunscomb says, "'As respects the northern man, the existence of slavery in or out of the District is

(1831) he dramatizes the Negro's potential by contrasting two slaves, Euclid and Bonnie. Both belong to
Alderman van Beverout, but Euclid belongs to the
New York City household and is consequently governed
closely; Bonnie, in charge of the Alderman's country
estate, is unsupervised for some four-fifths of the year.
The Alderman has been in the country for a few days
when Euclid appears one morning.

> . . . The look of the negro was guilty, dogged, and cun-
> ning. His eye leered askance, seeming to wish to play
> around the person of his master, as it will be seen his
> language endeavored to play around his understanding.
> The hands crushed the crown of a woollen hat between
> their fingers, and one of his feet described semicircles
> with its toe, by performing nervous evolutions on its
> heel. (130)

Craven, evasive, guilty, Euclid confesses that a prize
Flemish gelding that the Alderman had left in his
charge and repeatedly warned him not to ride has been,
as feared, ridden to death.

In contrast with Euclid's irresponsibility and dis-
obedience, Cooper places Bonnie's trustworthiness. He
does not, however, let the difference go as a matter of
individual variation; rather, the incident seems invented

purely a speculative question; but it is not so with the southern.
This should never be forgotten; and I always feel disgust when I
hear a northern man swagger and make a parade of his morality on
this subject."
   " 'But the southern men swagger and make a parade of their
chivalry. . . .'
   " 'Quite true; but with them there is a strong provocation. It is a
matter of life and death to the South. . . . If there ever be a separation between the free and the slave states of this Union, the wedge
will be driven home by northern hands; not by indirection, but
coolly, steadily, and with a thorough northern determination to open
the seam. There will be no fuss about chivalry, but the thing will
be done' " (172).

to allow Cooper the opportunity to state his opinions. Speaking of Bonnie, he writes,

> Responsibility and confidence had produced their effect on this negro, as on more cultivated minds. He had been used to act in situations of care; and practice had produced a habit of vigilance and observation, that was not common in men of his unfortunate condition. There is no moral truth more certain, than that men, when once accustomed to this species of domination, as readily submit their minds, as their bodies, to the control of others. . . . Fortunately . . . for the improvement of the race and the advancement of truth, it is only necessary to give a man an opportunity to exercise his natural faculties, in order to make him a reflecting, and, in some degree, an independent being. Such, though to a very limited extent certainly, had been the consequence in the instance of the slave just mentioned. (191)

Neither Negro is ready for complete liberation, but the one, given responsibility suddenly, fails and takes refuge in evasions and lies. The other, accustomed to making limited decisions, succeeds (as does the Negro foreman, Hiram, in the Wallingford saga) in caring for an estate.

As the cautious terms of Cooper's argument show, the central doubt was the extent of the Negro's mental ability. Cooper's hopes for the Negro are grounded almost entirely on the fact of his humanity, on his having an intellect. Yet Cooper suspected that the intellect might be of an inferior kind, that it "had suffered under the blight which seems to have so generally caused the African mind to wither." By contrast, the Indian's mind "had ever possessed much of the loftiness of a grand nature, left to its native workings by the impetus of an unrestrained, though savage liberty" (Redskins, 443). Yet there are two sides to the integrity and independence of Indians. Admirable as their character is when Cooper dramatizes it, they elicit the kind of response Parkman records: "Their intractable, unchanging character leaves no other alternative than their gradual extinction. . . . "[8] If, however, the Negro's mental independence could be nourished and guided, his very lack of prior ideological commitments could be a social asset and the means of survival.

The polarity of Indian and Negro is transformed, in the novels, into actions that show mutual and categorical dislike as the rule. White characters must learn that common non-whiteness does not make for a natural affinity; thus Miles Wallingford says of the Indian, Smudge, " . . . I suspected that he fancied the negroes would prove allies to himself, in the event of a struggle, rather than foes" (*Afloat and Ashore*, 226). But the Negro, Neb, has loyally adopted the white man's prejudice and advises that "' . . . no good ebber come of Injin. If you don't drown him, he sartain drown you'" (231). His alliance with the whites unrewarded, Neb is placed on the Indian's side of the color line by the inept captain, Moses Marble.

> "Let two of the 'niggers' take a turn with the end of the whip around the chap's neck," said Marble, too dignified to turn Jack Ketch in person, and unwilling to set any of the white seamen at so ungracious an office. (234)

Marble's prejudice, which is here partial proof of his unfitness for command and which he later outgrows, is rare in being expressed on shipboard; as a rule Cooper shows racial dislike as an infirmity of the land. Once a

---

[8] Francis Parkman, *The Conspiracy of Pontiac*, II, 170.

seaman, the Negro acquires a new identity that makes him eligible for judgment based on his professional abilities and personal qualities. Neb's master, Miles, is the first to recognize the difference between a Negro ashore and one afloat.

> Neb was never half as much 'nigger' at sea, as when he was on shore—there being something in his [sic] manly calling that raised him nearer to the dignity of white man. (*Miles Wallingford*, 185)

The Negro seaman becomes so much a man that fraternity is possible—even if equality is not. Two major examples of colored and white fraternal relations anticipate the pairings of Ishmael and Queequeg and of Huck and Jim. The more dramatic of these is to be found in *The Red Rover*, (1828) in which a sailor, Dick Fid, supports the Negro Scipio (most often called "Guinea") against the prejudice of a villainous sailor who protests, in a tavern argument, that it is not " 'genteel behavior to bring a nigger . . . to give an opinion in the teeth of a white man' " (39). Scipio, whose accurate knowledge has forced the seaman to use prejudice in lieu of information, "folded his arms and walked out of the house, with the submission and meekness of one who had been too long trained in humility to rebel." Dick Fid remains, however, to swear that the Negro " 'if he was fairly skinned, would be the whiter man of the two' " (40). Although the friendship of Fid and "Guinea" is a minor part of the narrative, it lasts through the novel and ends only with a melodramatic and heavily symbolic scene near the end. The Negro, dying of wounds received in a shipboard battle, is about to be thrown overboard by the victors when Dick Fid (whose own neck is already in a noose) frees his arms long enough to lash the body of the dying Negro to his own. Once they are thus firmly bound together, the commander of the conquering group orders, "'Away with them to heaven'" (455). The hanging is interrupted, however, and we do not see, as we expect, the two friends dying together at the end of the yardarm.[9]

A more detailed study of possible fraternity can be found in a two-volume novel published as *Afloat and Ashore* and *Miles Wallingford* (1844). While the narrative is chiefly about Miles' growth to maturity (see Chapter IX), it traces the adventures of Miles and his companion-slave Neb from boyhood and illustrates fully the system of slavery only sketched in the Littlepage trilogy. Miles describes the relationship by saying,

It is not easy to describe the affection of an attached slave, which has blended with it the pride of a partisan, the solicitude of a parent, and the blindness of a lover. I do

---

[9] Herman Melville reviewed *Red Rover* for the *Literary World* of March 16, 1850 (VI, 266–67). Leon Howard conjectures that this novel may have been a catalyst for *Moby Dick*. "Some of the incidents by which Cooper strove to give his book this [legendary] quality were of particular interest: the mystery of the officer in command of a vessel, whose unconventional behavior caused his superstitious crew to mutiny in the belief that he was an emissary of the devil; the sinking of the ship in the ominous presence of a blowing whale; and the almost supernatural appearance, in the middle of the ocean, of the staring-eyed corpse of a man last seen the day before. Such material as this was the stuff of romance, although the romance was tempered by occasional bits of comic realism exemplified by the agent who talked generous generalities while taking a penny-pinching advantage of a man's anxiety to serve on board his ship and by a psychological realism in its stress of the Red Rover's strong-minded personal dominance over his crew."—*Herman Melville* (Berkeley, 1951), p. 152.

The Negro "Guinea" of this book wears throughout the book a dog collar which is repeatedly mentioned and becomes the means by which Cooper effects the classical recognition scene that clears up the plot. He may well be the forerunner of Black Guinea, "'der dog widout massa,'" the Negro with the stature of a dog in *The Confidence Man* (New York, 1954), p. 8.

think Neb had more gratification in believing himself particularly belonging to Master Miles, than I ever had in any quality or thing I could call my own. (12)

Out of context and after *Benito Cereno* this is a difficult passage to read correctly; Miles's tone, however, is not smug nor is the meaning sinister. The affection described here never changes. On the contrary, it is repeatedly illustrated by the action and binds the two so closely that Neb gets a lively if vicarious pleasure from Miles's triumphs. Getting his first command just as a heavy storm begins, Miles reports,

I confess I was, at first, nearly as much depressed by the novelty and responsibility of my command, as Neb was delighted. . . . As for Neb, the harder it blew, the greater was his rapture. He appeared to think the wind was Master Miles', as well as the ocean, the brig, and himself. The more there was of each, the richer I became. (*Afloat and Ashore*, 144, 145)

If Miles's fortunes, even misunderstood, influence Neb, the opposite is equally true. Neb, Miles reports, "encouraged . . . idleness, and a desultory manner of misspending hours that could never be recalled" (12).

Neb's more lasting effect on Miles begins when the two run away to sea together. Neb's mother (something of a female prime minister herself) sends word that "no such disgrace as a runaway slave ever befel [sic] her or hers, and she says she will not submit to it" (47). This reprimand sets Miles to thinking.

. . . What was his delinquency compared to my own? He had followed his master out of deep affection, blended somewhat, it is true, with a true love of adventure; while in one sense, I had violated all the ties of the heart, merely to indulge the latter passion. (55)

With this recognition of a difference in their comparative guilt, Miles exhibits an increasing sense of responsibility for Neb. Since all the action is seen through the eyes of Miles, we are conscious of his attention to the watch Neb stands, his position and performance during storms and battles, and his progress toward becoming a first-rate seaman. Finally, after Neb has saved the ship almost single-handedly when pirates attack, Miles is driven to a lengthy analysis:

Everybody was praised but Neb, who, being a "nigger," was in some way or other overlooked. I mentioned his courage and readiness to Mr. Marble, but I could excite in no one else the same respect for the poor fellow's conduct that I certainly felt myself. I have since lived long enough to know that as the gold of the rich attracts to itself the gold of the poor, so do the deeds of the unknown go to swell the fame of the known. This is as true of nations, and races, and families, as it is of individuals; poor Neb belonging to a proscribed color, it was not in reason to suppose that he could ever acquire exactly the same credit as a white man.

"Them darkeys do sometimes blunder on a lucky idee," answered Mr. Marble [the mate] to one of my earnest representations, "and I've known chaps among 'em that were almost as knowing as dullish whites; but everything out of the common way with 'em is pretty much chance. As for Neb, however, I will say this for him: that, for a nigger, he takes things quicker than any of his color I ever sailed with. Then he has no sa'ce, and that is a good deal with a black. White sa'ce is bad enough; but that of a nigger is unbearable."

Alas! Neb. Born in slavery, accustomed to consider it arrogance to think of receiving even his food until the

meanest white had satisfied his appetite, submissive, un-
repining, laborious, and obedient—the highest eulogium
that all these patient and unobtrusive qualities could obtain, was a reluctant acknowledgement that he had "no
sa'ce!" His quickness and courage saved the *John*, nevertheless; and I have always said it, and ever shall.
(63, 64)

For all his defense of Neb, Miles never grants him
equality of intellect. Neb never knows "when it became
necessary to take in the last reef" in a storm, nor how
to stow cargo "so as to favor the vessel" (120), but he
is as expert as nine men in ten on a ship in routine
matters; and as the two mature, Neb's lack of ability
for headwork ceases to be important. Miles, who has
no brother, decides finally: "A sterling fellow was Neb,
and I got in time to love him very much as I can
conceive one would love a brother" (120).

The two have common adventures and parallel
romances, and Neb, offered his freedom, refuses it. " 'I
belong to you, you belong to me, and we belong to one
anodder,' " he says at the end of the first volume.
Throughout the perils and rescues which follow in
Miles Wallingford, each becomes his brother's keeper
so many times that the sense of responsibility can only
be seen as mutual. By the end of this book, Miles insists
on freeing Neb and his wife Chloe, but his action only
stands slavery on its head, as Miles wryly realizes. "He
has no intention to free me, whatever may have been
my plans for himself and his race" (434). Miles's own
children, at the end, are leaving Clawbonny (the family
lands), but Miles and Neb stay together. To Neb, the
"freedom" Miles offers would mean at once the end of
fraternity and the beginning of a nominal equality that

he sees as inequality. He is insulted at the idea of working for wages "like a hired man"; and since he desires
little more than his basic needs, Neb flatly refuses to
become a wage slave. The end of the joint history shows
the two men still in an emotional fraternity and a
familial economic pattern.

Neb is Cooper's most fully characterized and most
attractive Negro character. With him Cooper breaks
almost entirely with the comic stereotype who is a
household accessory; and although Neb is portrayed as
a victim of occasional prejudice, he has a chance to win
respect as an individual. He never pretends to superiority, yet proves himself superior to most of his shipmates; and if his intellect is "blighted," it does not keep
him from learning and growing until he is more able
than many of his companions. Furthermore, he is
brought from the fictional background and made a major
character in the two books; in stature he is fully the
equal of Moses Marble, Miles's other friend.

Neb's growth requires social latitude; and while he
finds his moral freedom most notably at sea, the tolerant
and commodious New York society from which he
departs and to which he returns from time to time gives
him a comfortable leeway. Influenced as it is by the
Dutch, and still retaining some of their optimism and
good humor, Cooper's slave-owning New York state
could never in a million years have produced a Simon
Legree.

IV

THE WONTERFUL WORLD OF THE DUTCH

*"We meet with wonters when we least expect 'em;
and t'at it ist t'at makes wonters so wonterful!"**

ONLY a honed and polished analytic intelligence could
reflect attractive portraits of merchants and civic officials
when the mind of the artist recoiled from a vulgar
aristocracy of money that merchants and officials were
coming to represent. Disliking as he did materialistic
values, sensing an affinity between a merchant's ethics
and expediency, and fearing that principal might well,
in a political system still cartilaginous, triumph over
principle, Cooper detested the Hamiltonian ideology
that had perverted the language and ideals of the
nation's founders. In this, as in all subsequent chapters
of this study, we cannot forget that a great part of
Cooper's fiction expands John Adams' caveat: "This
aristocracy of wealth is now destroying the aristocracy
of genius, talent, and merit too." [1]

---

* Andries Coejemans in *The Chainbearer* (367).

[1] *The Works of John Adams,* ed. Charles Francis Adams (Boston,
1850–56), IV, 354. Adams' warning is quoted by Marius Bewley in
his essay, "Fenimore Cooper and the Economic Age," in *The
Eccentric Design* (London, 1959), p. 58. Bewley's study of Cooper,
like Yvor Winters' essay in *In Defense of Reason* (Denver, 1947),
is both seminal and of perennial value. Both offer statements of
Cooper's relation to the economic and political facts of American
history. The prologue and first section of William R. Taylor's
Cavalier and Yankee include additional suggestions and helpful
quotations from American statesmen. Robert E. Spiller's *James*

Because of this fear and because Cooper wrote (in other novels) against smuggling, we might expect his disapproval to lie leaden on the New York merchant, Alderman Myndert Van Beverout (*The Water-Witch*, 1831), who connives with smugglers and values all things in terms that can be entered in his ledger. Yet Cooper wrote of him, and of other Dutch merchants, ebulliently and deftly and with a humor that precludes rancor. There are a number of reasons for Cooper's tone; none excludes the others and the sum of them probably represents the truth of his feeling about the Dutch.

Speaking of *The Water-Witch* in his biography of Cooper, James Grossman suggests that Cooper sets for himself "the private task of treating commerce, a respected institution, with amusement and contempt . . . " (73). The task was made easier since he was writing of pre-Revolutionary Dutch; the laws being broken in *The Water-Witch*, consequently, are the somewhat capricious restrictions imposed by a monarchy, while the frontier setting of the Littlepage novels removes their Dutch characters almost entirely from the law.

Furthermore, an amused and indulgent tone in writing about the Dutch had already been established in American literature by Washington Irving. Cooper adopted this, but deepened its significance. The Dutchmen of Cooper's fictional world, like those of Irving's, use their profits as means; large bank balances support a life of ease, comfort, tolerance, and affability. They

---

Fenimore Cooper (New York, 1931) and Dorothy Waples' *The Whig Myth of James Fenimore Cooper* (New Haven, 1938) are among the most valuable of the older studies of Cooper's relation to the political scene.

desire a classical leisure, which desire Cooper approves, and lack only the wisdom which should, classically, accompany it. By contrast (and the contrast was never absent from Cooper's mind or from Irving's), the New England resident was acquisitive and miserly; for the Connecticut Yankee, profits and property were ends. Cooper shared with the Dutch a hatred of New England avarice that cannot be underestimated in explaining his tolerance of *burgherlich* Dutch society. The two attitudes toward wealth are opposed throughout the Littlepage trilogy.

Cooper's friendship with Gulian C. Verplanck further explains the portrayal of Dutchmen as self-indulgent in an affable and expansive way that itself deserves indulgence. A member of the Bread and Cheese club (the New York luncheon group Cooper formed), Verplanck was interested in literature, history, and art, and wrote articles and books on law, theology, and Shakespeare. Van Wyck Brooks describes Verplanck as the "intellectual spokesman of the New York Dutch. . . . A friend of every liberal mind, Verplanck impersonated well the fading Dutch spirit of the town." [2] Cooper's friendship with Verplanck and their common admiration for Shakespeare suggest an explanation for Cooper's placing likable Dutchmen in a Shakespearean setting in *The Water-Witch*.

All Cooper's Dutch are convivial, tolerant, expansive, prone to superstition, and responsive to augury; they can be trusted in all matters not involving a fine horse (for which they have a passion). More than this we cannot say without separating the Dutch of Albany (and *Satanstoe*) from those of New York (and *The*

---

[2] *The World of Washington Irving* (New York, 1944), p. 235.

Water-Witch), for Cooper's purposes in writing the two books differed and the difference affects the characters. *The Water-Witch,* as Cooper explains in the Preface,[3] is an experimental novel. Described by Yvor Winters as "certainly one of the most brilliant, if scarcely one of the most profound, masterpieces of American prose,"[4] it is more the result of Cooper's curiosity about writing as an art than of any concern with historical narrative or social analysis. *Satanstoe,* however, and, to a lesser extent, *The Chainbearer* are meant as bases on which to build a thesis. In these, Cooper makes a disguised bid for the reader's sympathy and attempts to enrol him as a partisan of the New York landowners. Based partly on Mrs. Grant's recollections of her childhood,[5] *Satans-*

---

[3] " . . . This is probably the most imaginative book ever written by the author. Its fault is in blending too much of the real with the purely ideal. Half-way measures will not do in matters of this sort; and it is always safer to preserve the identity of a book by a fixed and determinate character, than to make the effort to steer between the true and the false" (iii). Cooper also complains, in a passage that reminds one of Hawthorne, that "the facts of this country are all so recent, and so familiar, that every innovation on them, by means of the imagination, is coldly received, if it be not absolutely frowned upon" (iii). Nevertheless, *The Water-Witch* is an interesting attempt to use in fiction what Hawthorne described as "neutral territory, somewhere between the real world and fairyland, where the Actual and the Imaginary may meet, and each imbue itself with the nature of the other."—"The Custom House" in *The Scarlet Letter* (Columbus, O., 1962), p. 36.

[4] "Fenimore Cooper, or The Ruins of Time," *In Defense of Reason,* p. 197. As Professor Winters describes the prose, "the subject is never adequate to permit the extraction from the rhetoric of its full possibilities, so that we have a species of lyricism, which, through real enough, is frequently all but verbal or even syntactical; we have something approaching pure rhetoric."

[5] Mrs. Grant, the daughter of a British officer who had been stationed in Albany, published her *Memoirs of an American Lady* (2 vols.) in England in 1808; an American edition came out in 1809. Cooper refers the reader to her book in a footnote in *Satanstoe.* See Dorothy Dondore, "The Debt of Two Dyed-in-the-Wool Americans to Mrs. Grant's *Memoirs:* Cooper's *Satanstoe* and Paulding's *The Dutchman's Fireside,*" *American Literature,* XII (1940), 52–58. Cooper's *The Water-Witch* and Paulding's *The Dutchman's Fireside* were both published in 1831, but their pictures of the Dutch

toe reads as a charming memoir of a vanished society. *The Water-Witch*, by contrast, is made of the stuff of legend.

Although the action of *The Water-Witch* begins in New York City, and returns to it occasionally, the novel's true setting is Alderman Van Beverout's estate on Long Island and the waters surrounding it. Cooper uses no supernatural machinery, suggesting rational explanations for the many seemingly supernatural occurrences in the narrative; yet he succeeds remarkably at evoking the setting of *The Tempest*: a kind of never-never island awash in the Atlantic just off the eastern coast of America. From the novel, one has no more sense of the continent that lies behind the port of New York than one has, in the play, of the continent just west of Bermuda. As in the play, the orientation of the novel is eastward to Europe—particularly to Italy. With the exception of the members of Van Beverout's household, the major characters in the story are European residents, and what we have is actually an international novel set on Long Island. Even the household of the Alderman is not "typically" American, consisting as it does of the two Dutchmen (the Alderman and the visiting Patroon of Kinderhook, Oloff Van Staats), the Alderman's niece Alida de Barbérie (herself half-

---

vary in spite of their common debt to Mrs. Grant. Paulding says the Dutch most valued "courage and prudence"; Cooper grants the former, but largely denies the latter. Paulding asserts the Dutch revered learning; Cooper insists they paid little attention to schooling. In July, 1832, Cooper wrote: "Patterson speaks of the Flemings as being among the most ignorant people of Europe, which is saying a good deal. But is not this the character of our New-York Dutch, who are descended from the Flemings rather than from the real Hollanders—" (*Letters and Journals*, II, 280.)

Paulding's portrait of Sir William Johnson is obviously indebted to Cooper's Natty Bumppo. See *The Dutchman's Fireside* (New York, 1868), pp. 136, 278.

French and attended by a French servant), and the Negro slaves (whose African origin is stressed rather than minimized). Edith Wharton never assembled, at a weekend gathering of the *haut monde,* a more cosmopolitan group.

Filled as it is with Shakespearean quotations and allusions, the book has received its share of cybernetic attention, and the Shakespearean origins seem to have been located adequately.[6] Larger relevances also deserve mention, however, and it should be pointed out that Cooper takes over, for *The Water Witch,* the central tension of *The Tempest:* a core of meaness, ugliness, and treachery is obscured by mists of enchantment, by witchery, by a relaxation of severity that we see as tolerance. As the smugglers' ship, "Ariel," flits about the island, eluding all pursuers, her masts appearing above the treetops in the moonlight, sailing noiselessly through "temporary" channels navigable only by her crew, she carries in her hold the merchandise of corruption. Her cargo is sensuous and exotic: silks, furs, brocades, laces, velvets. The smugglers have "silken" beards, rich India-shawls, caps ornamented in gold, Asiatic daggers, and as they spill bales of luxurious materials on Alida's boudoir floor they talk smoothly of Italian sunsets and the beauties of Sorrento.

So unreal is the novel, so airy and improbable, that it lifts the stout Alderman out of the corruptions of commercial New York and sets him down in an enchanted world where trade is adventure. James Gross-

---

[6] By 1940, Edward P. Vandiver had found over eleven thousand lines from Shakespeare in Cooper's works ("James Fenimore Cooper and Shakespere," *Shakespeare Association Bulletin,* XV [1940], 11–117). W. B. Gates's "Cooper's Indebtedness to Shakespeare" contains the information that 395 out of 939 chapter headings are Shakespearean (*PMLA,* LXVII [1952], 716–31).

man ascribes the Alderman's translation to Cooper's own stay at Sorrento, where he wrote *The Water-Witch* in 1830. Cooper learned in Italy, says Grossman, that

> nations in their decline, living off the accumulations of past energies, were happier . . . than nations busily accumulating in the present. American activity, viewed by an American who had learned such dangerous truths, was surely not what it seemed, and Cooper's finest effects of illusion in *The Water-Witch* are achieved not with physical but with social phenomena. It is not the ship but commerce itself that is so strange. The true romantic figure in the tale is not the conventionally daring smuggler who risks his life casually and gracefully, but his customer, the timid respectable merchant, Alderman Van Beverout.
> The Alderman is the poet of profit. His elaborate rhetoric, rich with the imagery of trade and ledgers[,] turns the entire world into gold, much as some excessively romantic lover might find his beloved's face everywhere in Nature. . . . He is above the vulgar moral pretension, so fashionable in Cooper's age, that trade is the exchange of equivalents. The beauty of life is in its unearned increments of value, its terror in the unpredictable risks of the market. (72)

The accuracy of Grossman's comment can be appreciated only with difficulty because Cooper's portrayal of Van Beverout successfully, but very narrowly, skirts two conventional types of character. The one is the placid and phlegmatic Dutchman who loves only creature comforts; the other, a man characterized by his own dialogue, which consists almost wholly of the jargon of his profession or ruling passion. The character of Van Beverout comprehends both these, but he gives the jargon of commerce so wide a metaphorical extension that it becomes equal to his aesthetic responses, his

99

affection for his niece and his geldings, his emotions—
his whole view of himself and his world. It is as though
the Alderman were a practicing nominalist who uses the
jargon of commerce to conjure a world into existence.
For example, in a passage obviously indebted to Shy-
lock's "My daughter and my ducats" confusion, the
Alderman responds to the news that his gelding is dead
and that Alida has vanished. He addresses himself
both to the delinquent slave and to Alida's disappointed
suitor:

> "She was a pleasant and coaxing minx, Patroon," said
> the burgher, pacing the room they occupied, with a quick
> and heavy step, and speaking unconsciously of his niece,
> as of one already beyond the interests of life; "and as wil-
> ful and headstrong as an unbroken colt. Thou hard-riding
> imp! I shall never find a match for the poor disconsolate
> survivor. But the girl had a thousand agreeable and de-
> lightful ways with her, that made her the delight of my
> old days. . . . This is an unhappy world, Mr. Van Staats.
> All our calculations come to naught; and it is in the power
> of fortune to reverse the most reasonable and wisest of our
> expectations. A gale of wind drives the richly freighted
> ship to the bottom; a sudden fall in the market robs us
> of our gold, as the November wind strips the oak of its
> leaves; and bankruptcies and decayed credit often afflict
> the days of the oldest houses, as disease saps the strength
> of the body; Alida! Alida! thou has wounded one that
> never harmed thee, and rendered my age miserable!" (136)

This wild association of ideas is vintage Van Beverout,
for whom life is a tempestuous whirl of values and
delights—and always has been. The Hereafter, which
lowered over the life of a Puritan, has little effect on
Van Beverout. He alludes casually to the amorous
exploits of his youth, calls his personal slave-companion
from youth "Cupid," and names his estate "Lust in

Rust"—his version of *otium cum dignitate*. Yet his past enjoyments, of whatever kind, do not cause him to worry about the future. When things are going badly, he muses,

> "Life and morality! One must quit trade at some time or other, and begin to close the books. I must seriously think of striking a final balance. If the sum total was a little more in my favor, it should be done tomorrow." (297)

Cooper lets "an English wag" characterize Van Beverout as a "man of alliteration." Thus the Alderman is described as "'short, solid and sturdy in stature; full, flushed, and funny in face; and proud, ponderous, and pragmatical in propensities'" (6). Only the p's would apply to Oloff Van Staats, the Patroon of Kinderhook, and the other Dutchman in *The Water-Witch*. Oddly disparate qualities make up the Patroon and his background, from which he is inseparable. Phlegmatic yet vital, steady yet occasionally impulsive, made a man of leisure by his weath and one of dignity by his inherited rank, Oloff is in an embarrassing position throughout the novel, and his responses to the intricacies of the plot prompt Cooper to an unusual excursion into psychological theory.

> Men of slow faculties love strong excitement, because they are insensible to less powerful impulses, as men of hard heads find most enjoyment in strong liquors. The Patroon was altogether of the sluggish cast; and to him there was consequently a secret but deep pleasure, in his present situation. (179)

Although he may not be able to analyze a situation, the Patroon can act, and quickly, under the right circumstances. At one point, when Alida is thought to be aboard the smuggler's brigantine and the British cutter and Alderman's yawl are both pursuing her, the brigantine comes close to the yawl. The Patroon is aboard the yawl, but is

> . . . too intent on the expected attack, to heed a danger [of collision] that was scarcely intelligible to one of his habits. As the brigantine glided past, he saw her low channels bending towards the water, and, with a powerful effort, he leaped into them, shouting a sort of war-cry in Dutch. At the next instant he threw his large frame over the bulwark, and disappeared on the deck of the smuggler. (257)

Yet, having made this impulsive move, the Patroon fails to improve the occasion; and when the Alderman himself boards the smuggler's brigantine a week later, he finds that Alida "looks like a nun at the mention of his [the Patroon's] name." Van Beverout reflects ruefully that "'the Patroon is no Cupid, we must allow; or, in a week at sea, he would have won the heart of a mermaid'" (297). Oxlike yet impulsive, the Patroon prefigures the more fully drawn Guert Ten Eyck of *Satanstoe*.

Cooper occasionally hints that the Patroon could have been more complex: a fortune-teller, for instance, has predicted that one of the Van Staats will marry a witch. But this suggestion is never developed and what complexity the Patroon has comes from his being assigned two different, though related, values by the Alderman and his niece. Thinking, erroneously, that the Patroon is dead, the Alderman is sorry that "'the death of the young Patroon of Kinderhook would render one of the best and most substantial of our families extinct, and leave the third best estate in the province without a direct heir'" (260). Alida, responding to jealous questioning by her British admirer, says,

> "My knowledge of the beauties of the house of Mr. Van Staats is confined to very unpoetical glimpses from the river, in passing and repassing. The chimneys are twisted in the most approved style of the Dutch Brabant, and, although wanting the stork's nest on their summits, it seems as if there might be that woman's tempter, comfort, around the hearths beneath. The offices, too, have an enticing air, for a thrifty housewife!" (271)

Oloff consequently emerges as a symbol of substance and comfort; he is not egotistical, but has a solid sense of his own worth and position. When Alida has been, for several days and nights, sailing around Long Island with the smuggler, Oloff says quietly, "'I cannot say that I wish the successor of my mother to have seen so much of the world'" (225). This tolerant judgment, which expresses his disapproval in understatement even while it insists on his rights and refuses to circumscribe Alida's, is typical of Cooper's Dutch. The statement also stresses the stability and dullness that Alida sensed would be the lot of Mrs. Oloff Van Staats.

The principal Dutch characters of *Satanstoe* are of the chronological age of Van Staats, but they behave more as Van Beverout must have acted in his youth. *Satanstoe* is a young book, and the Albany Dutch are the liveliest group in Cooper's novels. Part of this verve, as we shall find, can be traced to Cooper's own sources of information, but his purpose also contributed to a relaxation of strictness. Much as the idea would have horrified Cooper, the plan of the Littlepage trilogy is that of the old Puritan jeremiad; and he wished to

establish, in *Satanstoe,* an attractive society from which
The Chainbearer and *The Redskins* could progressively
decline.[7]

Two familiar literary themes underlie the saga of the
Littlepage family, and both need the Dutch characters
for their realization. The first is the rites of passage
from boyhood to manhood; this is clearest in *Satanstoe,*
in which the education of the young men and their
journeying forth to conquer, or be conquered by, the
wilderness justifies the action. In taking over this theme
from his literary sources, Cooper actually minimized it;
for Mrs. Grant insisted that such initiatory journeys
were an important part of the lives of Albany's young

---

[7] The structure of this trilogy expands Cooper's belief (which
also informs such books as *The Pioneers*) that there were three
stages of civilization in a new country. These were exploration,
settlement, and a final time of harvest. Life in the first is adventurous
and full of hope; in the second it is almost unavoidably crude, hard,
and vulgar, and work is essential. In the third, those who deserve
leisure because they have the ability to use it wisely could turn
their attention to the arts and their studies and live the good life.
The era of *The Redskins* should be very close to that third stage,
but it is the most strife-torn of the three. Cooper parted only reluctantly with his dream of life in the third stage, as a bitter
posthumous fragment attests. "Nevertheless, the community will
live on, suffer, and be deluded; it may even fancy itself almost
within reach of perfection, but it will live on to be disappointed.
There is no such thing on earth—. . . . "—Quoted by Robert E.
Spiller, *Fenimore Cooper: Critic of His Times,* p. 315. "On earth"
has much to do with the increasingly religious emphasis in Cooper's
last novels. The correspondence between Cooper's thought and
that of John Adams is apparent. "It is not indeed the fine arts which
our country requires [at this time]; the useful, the mechanic arts
are those which we have occasion for in a young country. . . . I
must study politics and war, that my sons may have liberty to study
mathematics and philosophy, geography, natural history and naval
architecture, navigation, commerce, and agriculture, in order to give
their children a right to study painting, poetry, music, architecture,
statuary, tapestry, and porcelain."—Quoted in *The Literary History
of the United States* (New York, 1957), p. 150.
The permanence of this particular disillusion can be suggested
by such a work as Willa Cather's *O Pioneers!* Her characters feel
they are being deprived of the life that "should be"; in Miss Cather's
novels, the initial vitalizing vision is often followed by a time of
privation and terrible labor and that, in turn, by more work,
materialism, and shoddiness.

men. James K. Paulding has also described such journeys in *The Dutchman's Fireside:*

> Previous to assuming the port and character of manhood, it was considered an almost indispensable obligation to undertake and complete some enterprise of this kind, full of privation and danger. The youth went out a boy, and returned a man, qualified to take his place among men, and to aspire to the possession of the object of his early love.[8]

Cooper's narrative, beginning with the boyish escapades of the two heroes, Cornelius Littlepage and Dirck Van Valkenburgh, in Albany, ends with the triumphant return of Cornelius and his marriage to Anneke Mordaunt. It thus conforms briefly to the pattern, but the theme obviously could not be carried on through three books; and as the Dutch are shown being assimilated by the Anglican gentry, it soon fades. It leaves an afterglow in the next two novels, however, as each begins when the young heir of the family sallies forth to claim his own.

The second underlying theme, the destruction of the wilderness (or, in its extreme terms, man's violation of Paradise), becomes, as the trilogy progresses, increasingly important and difficult for Cooper to control. In *Satanstoe*, which shows the wilderness as trackless and the protagonists as explorers, the problem is not great, for the wilderness is left unchanged; but *The Chainbearer* shows the wilderness being possessed for settlement, and its Biblical quotations and Old Testament

---

[8] *The Dutchman's Fireside*, p. 81. Paulding was also one of Cooper's friends, and Cooper read this book while in Europe; he wrote Carey and Lea (his own publishers) qualified praise of the book, but objected that Paulding's Sir William Johnson was no more like the original (who was related to Cooper's wife) than "Gen. Jackson is like your Father in God the Pope."—*Letters and Journals*, II, 150–51.

characters bring the Eden theme to the foreground. Cooper's hardest task is to show a clear distinction between two types of invaders: the Dutch (who are now allied with Anglican English) and the Yankees (who have come uninvited from Puritan New England). While he pictures the Yankees' destruction as the more wanton, Cooper cannot deny that both groups wield axes; he was, in fact, convinced that axes were necessary and even wrote an apostrophe to the American ax. Yet axes destroy the wilderness; the immediate fictional problem is to show the act of destruction as evil when performed by the Yankees and good when done by the Dutch and Anglicans.

Cooper consequently describes and analyzes the means and motives of possession. The Dutch group have purchased title to the land; the Yankees try to take over by force, by trickery, or by using their unasked labor as the basis for a claim. The Dutch want to clear the land only enough to settle down and enjoy it peacefully; the Yankees want to convert it and its forests to cash; they want to strip it, wastefully and greedily, for present profit or speculate with it in the future. Although he needed no encouragement, Cooper could find plenty of corroboration for his views in Mrs. Grant's *Memoirs* or in Irving's writings. Both earlier writers had complained of the Yankee's trickery, litigiousness, and acquisitiveness. What they largely described, however, Cooper dramatizes. By making the chainbearer a Dutchman and evoking the Dutch world created in *Satanstoe,* Cooper shows Dutch possession of the wilderness as a tidying up, a drawing of boundaries and establishing of those regulations without which the world is chaos and true freedom impossible. By using,

at the same time, Jason Newcome and Aaron Thousandacres as Yankee representatives, Cooper shows their
attempt to take possession as rapine. It is ultimately
through his characters that Cooper can show, rather
than tell, and consequently make the distinction—fine
though it is.

Dutch awareness of the shortcomings of Puritan
ethics is established at the beginning of *Satanstoe*, when
Colonel Abraham Van Valkenburgh (Dirck's father) advises against sending Dirck and Cornelius to Yale (from
which Cooper had been expelled for a prank). His
reason is that Yale has

> "too much Suntay . . . the poy will be sp'ilt by ter min-
> isters. He will go away an honest lat, and come pack a
> rogue. He will l'arn how to bray [the dialect happily
> gives the reader both bray and pray] and to cheat." (20)

The Colonel is perfectly content "that his son and heir
should know no more than he knew himself, after
making proper allowances for the difference in years
and experience" (35). As a result, the education of the
boys is desultory; yet a lack of learning does not damage
them in Dutch society, whose values are reflected in
Corny's description of his friend as a "sterling [Cooper's
favorite word for the Dutch and Negroes he approved]
fellow, as true as steel, as brave as a gamecock, and as
honest as noonday light" (47). Dirck's appearance, at
nineteen, "would have done the heart of Frederick of
Prussia good" (47); mentally, Dirck is slow but sure.

> In the way of thought, Jason would think two feet to
> Dirck's one; but I am far from certain that it was always
> in so correct a direction. Give the Dutchman time, he
> was very apt to come out right; whereas Jason [a shrewd

Yankee], I soon discovered, was quite liable to come to wrong conclusions, and particularly so in all matters that were a little adverse, and which affected his own apparent interests. (47)

The comparison of Yankee and Dutchman is relentless. Colonel Van Valkenburgh describes the Yankees as "the locusts of the West," and Cooper exerts himself to paint in words the threatened territory as calm and comfortable, yet picturesque, with little stone houses fronting on the Hudson and "noble orchards" laid out neatly behind.

Tidy and pleasant as the Dutch world is, it is not at all pastoral, being saved from placidity by the exuberance of the Dutch themselves. Like the Patroon of Kinderhook, they covet excitement, can thrill only to excess. Consequently, they drive their magnificent roadsters too hard and too fast; their sledding in the streets of Albany endangers participants and pedestrians alike, and they consider the Hudson their own magnificent, if treacherous, playground. While not callous to danger, the Dutch are sufficiently heedless to find it more often than is absolutely necessary; and while they are not cruel, they are often insensitive. They mean well—always—but lack empathy.[9] Their practical jokes are

---

[9] In one farcical scene, for instance, the Anglican minister, walking across the frozen Hudson, hears sleighbells behind him; thinking he is about to be run down by the horses, he runs ahead of the sleighs and reaches the shore "pretty well blown." His pursuers (one of whom is Guert Ten Eyck) had intended to give him a ride, but neither during nor after the chase do they sense his real fright. They content themselves with christening him the "loping Dominie" in honor of his wild gallop (*Satanstoe*, p. 162, *passim*).

The Hudson in this book is the setting for one of the most "sublime" scenes in American literature. Guert and Cornelius, who have taken their girls sleighing, are caught on the river when the Hudson's ice starts to break up. The synthesis of horror and beauty in the ensuing action is hard to equal.

Gargantuan; they steal and consume, for instance, an entire meal the mayor's servants have prepared for his dinner guests. Yet their confessions of guilt are prompt, and even the redoubtable Madam Schuyler cannot long be annoyed with such an irrepressible scamp as Guert Ten Eyck. Cornelius Littlepage tries to explain her leniency by describing Guert:

> But even the most intellectual and refined women, I have since had occasion to learn, feel a disposition to judge handsome, manly, frank, flighty fellows like my new acquaintance, somewhat leniently. With all his levity, and his disposition to run into the excess of animal spirits, there was that about Guert which rendered it difficult to despise him. The courage of a lion was in his eye, and his front and bearing were precisely those that are particularly attractive to women. To these advantages were added a seeming unconsciousness of his superiority to most around him, in the way of looks, and a humility of spirit that caused him often to deplore his deficiencies in those accomplishments which character- ize the man of study and intellectual activity. It was only among the hardy, active, and reckless, that Guert mani- fested the least ambition to be a leader. (228)

Guert and Mary Wallace, the girl he loves, are both orphans. Whereas Guert lacks, as a consequence, any government at all, Mary Wallace " 'has been taught prudence as her great protection.' " As a result, when Guert pleads at once his unworthiness and her power to make of him what she will, she shrinks from such a rash assumption of responsibility for his behavior and his fate. Both Guert and Mary are rather complex, as Cooper's lovers go, and Cooper neither interrupts nor smooths their relation with any machinery of plot; since he does not, the question of Mary's motivation is pertinent. It may be (and the narrator's slight tone of disapproval suggests this) that Mary feels Guert too glibly pleads his good intentions, too smoothly turns his inability to govern himself into a charming asset, too quickly produces the frank confession of guilt that stays reproach. Or, since the intervening voice of the narrator makes certainty impossible, it may be that Mary, like the Indian Susquesus, merely distrusts Guert's ability to acquire wisdom. "'Head too young—hand good— heart good—head very bad'" (452), says the Indian; and Guert's actions support this judgment. Rejected by Mary, and taking the advice of a fortune teller, Guert goes off to war with Cornelius and eventually accompanies him to the Littlepage land. During the ensuing actions, he is frequently posed and compared with Susquesus; both are magnificent physical specimens. Guert is, however, fatally wounded by a Huron; and Mary gives way to "that pent-up passion, which had so long struggled with her prudence" (357). When he dies, Mary feels that she has been wrong not to marry him, and the rest of the trilogy shows her living quietly, still devoted to his memory, and reminding everyone, by her quiet presence, of the loss of Guert Ten Eyck. The death of Guert extinguishes, in Cooper's novels, the youthful Dutch spirit.

At Guert's death, the Yankee Jason Newcome pushes forward; and Cooper resumes the comparison of Dutch and Yankee.

All the wildness of Guert's impulses could not altogether destroy his feelings, tone, and tact as a gentleman; while all the soaring, extravagant pretensions of Jason never could have ended in elevating him to that character. (478)

Remarks such as this brought complaints from Cooper's New England readers, to whom Cooper replied in the Preface to *The Chainbearer*:

> New England has long since anticipated her revenge, glorifying herself and underrating her neighbors in a way that, in our opinion, fully justifies those who possess a little Dutch blood in expressing their sentiments on the subject. (iv)

While Mordaunt Littlepage, the narrator of *The Chainbearer*, is only part Dutch, the titular hero, Andries Coejemans, the chainbearer, is monolithically a Dutchman. Speaking a heavy dialect, old Andries pits his stubborn Dutch honesty against not one, but two, of the Yankees. He has reasons.

> His means had once been respectable, but as he always maintained, he was cheated out of his substance by a Yankee before he was three-and-twenty, and he had recourse to surveying for a living from that time. (8)

Andries' vulnerability, clearly traceable to the casual attitude toward education that was for Cooper the great Dutch weakness, continues to affect him; having "no head for mathematics . . . he quietly sunk to the station of a chainbearer . . . " (8). As a chainbearer, he has "an unrivalled reputation," but since he cannot calculate —the pun is obvious—he is no match for Jason Newcome, who is nothing if not a masterful calculator. To reinforce the character of Andries, Cooper alludes to Washington's career as a surveyor, lets Andries speak of his admiration for Washington, and once digresses into a long expository passage in which he extolls the virtues and services of Philip Schuyler, the "presiding spirit" of the army at Saratoga even though "forced by popular prejudice" of the New England group "to retire from the apparent command . . . " (12).

If we consider about equally the needs of Cooper's thesis and his conception of Dutch character and practices, we can predict the character of Andries. Surviving fragments of Cooper's last major work, a history of greater New York, contain his summary judgment of the Dutch: "their isolated position, slowness of movement, and inattention to schools, soon lowered the standard of intelligence among their descendants."[10] With this in mind, we understand that Andries, "illiterate almost to greatness" (14), is the logical result of Dutch neglect of education. Save for his illiteracy and poverty, Andries is much like Oloff Van Staats; he has the huge frame, uncompromising moral sense, solid confidence in his own worth, and the reverence for traditions that mark the Patroon. These were the qualities Cooper found useful to reinforce his thesis, and Andries consequently stands in relation to Mordaunt Littlepage as the upright Onondago (Susquesus) stands to Hugh Littlepage in *The Redskins*. Both are innately honest and act as disinterested observers who support the Littlepage point of view. At the same time, it is they, more than the Littlepages, who are contrasted with the New England people.

Thus Andries, who has been a captain in the Revolutionary War, is shown as a good leader of men.

---

[10] James F. Beard, Jr., has reproduced manuscript pages in "The First History of Greater New York: Unknown Portions of Fenimore Cooper's Last Work," *New York Historical Society Quarterly Bulletin*, XXXVII (1953), 109–45. The quotation is from manuscript page 56 (page 142 of Beard's article).

Andries commanded respect by means of his known integrity. . . . Such a man when he has the moral courage
to act up to his native impulses, mingled with discretion
enough to keep him within the boundaries of common
prudence [here Cooper gives Andries a non-typical attri-
bute], insensibly acquires great influence over those with
whom he is brought into contact. Men never fail to respect such qualities, however little they put them in practice in their own cases. (146)

Whereas Andries leads only because followers choose
him, Jason Newcome has a demagogue's desire for
power and leads by deceit. Andries says,

"He understands mankint, he says, and sartainly hast a
way of marching and countermarching just where he
pleases wit t'ese people, makin' 'em t'ink t'e whole time
t'ey are doing just what t'ey want to do." (157)

Andries, like Susquesus, is absolutely honest; Jason is
only "law honest." As Andries tells Mordaunt, "' . . .
He swears py t'e law, and lifs py t'e law. No fear for
your tollars, poy; t'ey pe all safe, unless, inteet, t'ey haf
all vanishet in t'e law'" (158). Jason tries to maneuver
the people into restricting the community-built church
to his own sect; Andries counsels the community to
"'rememper you haf a peing to worship in t'is house,
t'at is neit'er Congregational, nor Presbyterian, nor anything else of the nature of your disputes and self-
conceit'" (146). We may question the ability of Andries'
religious tolerance to convert his speech suddenly to
standard English, but there is no doubt that he loathes
Puritan self-righteousness. On meeting the lawless
Thousandacres family, he decides they think "T'eir

godliness ist so pure even sin wilt do it no great harm'"
(301).

Although no match for Jason Newcome, Andries
opposes him ideologically; physically, he challenges the
squatters, the Thousandacres family. Since physical
violence is the only thing the squatters understand,
Cooper needed a protagonist to counter them, and (for
the good of his thesis) that man should be as untutored, landless, and friendless as they. Consequently,
old Andries fights the Littlepages' battles and argues
questions of ethics with Aaron Thousandacres until
Aaron shoots Andries and someone (undoubtedly Susquesus) shoots Aaron. Cooper arranges the joint death
scene of the two mighty men as a tableau. Its correct
title, however, would be as awkward as the situation
itself: "Dutch Honesty Slain by Yankee Avarice But
Avenged by Unfaltering Indian Justice."[11]

Old Andries Coejemans is, consequently, something
of a sacrificial ox; and while Cooper's Dutchmen have
qualities in common with oxen, we suspect that Andries
is in a sense Dutch by definition. He bears the marks
of manufacture. For the good of his thesis, Cooper had
to deprive Andries not only of a Dutch love of drink,
but of exuberance, impulsiveness, and gaiety. Land
rights were serious matters, and Andries is consequently

---

[11] Cooper's Bread and Cheese club contained more artists than
writers, and he had a keen interest in art that he somewhat dis-
concertingly expressed by dropping by friends' studios and making
suggestions about work in progress. His friendship with Horatio
Greenough, whom he rescued and started on his career, was probably
the most important to his writing. For two excellent articles on
Cooper's use of artistic techniques in writing, see Howard Mumford
Jones, "James Fenimore Cooper and the Hudson River School,"
Magazine of Art, XLV (1952), 243–51. Also James F. Beard, "Cooper
and His Artistic Contemporaries," in *James Fenimore Cooper: A
Re-appraisal*, pp. 480–95.

serious; he takes upon himself a battle which Cooper's earlier Dutch characters would either have avoided or have treated as adventure. Viewed *extra libris,* the Puritans have an additional triumph: they have cost Andries his essential Dutchness.

Cooper's last known work, the New York history mentioned earlier, shows him still unable to think of the Dutch without contrasting them with the New England people. Like Irving, he makes the point that the Dutch have a capacity for contentment (the burghers "were satisfied, provided they could smoke and trade") that the New England people lack. "Then as now," he writes in the history, the New England people "appeared never to be content with the extent of their possessions, so long as anything remained to be added to them." For a true picture of the contented Dutch, however, we must go back beyond Andries to Guert Ten Eyck, the other Dutch of *Satanstoe,* and those of *The Water-Witch.* There we get them in their full expansiveness and *joie de vivre.*

Hawthorne wrote a wonderfully wistful line in *The Scarlet Letter*: "We have yet to learn again the forgotten art of gayety." If evil is deprivation, Hawthorne joined Robinson and Cooper in charging the Puritans with the evil of extinguishing gaiety. Cooper may have been less sensitive than Hawthorne to the loss, but the Dutch of *The Water-Witch* and *Satanstoe* are his gayest Americans. Washington Irving, writing of them from the outside, caught some of their spirit but made them comic. Paulding and Mrs. Grant, like local-color writers who followed them, responded to the desire to preserve a record of mores. It remained for Cooper to integrate

the Dutch spirit with the American scene. Some of
Cooper's subjects (the Dutch view of a fresh world,
the trees now vanished, man's capacity for wonder)
recur in Fitzgerald's famous conclusion to *The Great
Gatsby*. In American literature as in Cooper's fictional
world, the Dutch have continued to mean youth and
vitality and the ability to feel, as even his most serious
Dutchman says, that "wonters" can be "wonterful."

V

THE CASE AGAINST NEW ENGLAND

The lean cats of the arches of the churches,
That's the old world. In the new, all men are priests.

They preach and they are preaching in a land
To be described. They are preaching in a time
To be described. Evangelists of what?

—Wallace Stevens*

The soldier and the priest were overpowered; and
from the Reformation downward, the monied type
possessed the world.

—Brooks Adams†

FOR COOPER, the history of American Puritanism was
one of perversion. The best proof of his sure grasp of
the economic motives at work in the Protestant Reformation is a European novel, *The Heidenmauer* (1832).[1]

---

* From "Extracts from Addresses to the Academy of Fine Ideas,"
The Collected Poems of Wallace Stevens (New York, 1955), p. 254.
Used by permission of Alfred A. Knopf, Inc.

† From *The Law of Civilization and Decay* (1896).

[1] See Marius Bewley, *The Eccentric Design*, pp. 47–58. As
Bewley correctly says, Cooper determined to analyze, in the European novels, "the dangers he believed confronted America, but to
do so in terms of a larger historical context than concentration on
the national scene would permit, for he saw that these dangers had
their roots and their counterparts in the cycle of European history"
(51). It was also more tactful to locate America's dangers abroad.
Bewley says "the point of *The Heidenmauer* is that the economic
motive is always an element of dangerous impurity, that it works
in disguises and moves toward goals which are other than the ones
professed." This is translated, in Cooper's novels, into the questions
of appearance and reality, of hypocrisy, and of the masks and
disguises assumed by the Yankees.

His overtly American novels, however, make the same statement through characterization of three types of Yankees. These are: the Saxon squatters who have taken over a religion worn so thin they seem pre-Christian; the acquisitive, provincial, hypocritical materialists like Hiram Doolittle and Jason Newcome; and the character William R. Taylor designates as the "transcendent Yankee"—the man who appears to be a Yankee but is not. Harvey Birch is Taylor's prototype for the species he describes in *Cavalier and Yankee*; and since Birch requires separate consideration as a character, any discussion of this third type is reserved for the eighth chapter of this study.

Before Cooper was born, Royall Tyler had already presented on stage a Brother Jonathan, the self-assertive bumpkin who is the comic foil in *The Contrast* (1787). Jonathan the self-righteous rube became popular on the American stage, but the closest Cooper comes to adopting the character is probably his Captain Noah Poke of *The Monikins*. Cooper's sense of humor was not deficient, but he, like the English, found the ignorant braggart a bore or a threat to society. Provincialism was, for Cooper, something to be regretted. Yet the Brother Jonathan tradition, which neither he nor his readers can escape entirely, weakens his attack on such characters as the Newcomes.

Also preceding Cooper, as we noticed in the last chapter, were Irving and the travelers and diarists who portrayed Yankee acquisitiveness. The grasping Yankee was, in fact, "the American" image for Europeans. By the 1820's, this crude and mean Yankee was being reviled also in the almanacs and papers of western America. The comic and the calculating Yankee merged in the Yankee peddler, of whom Constance Rourke says, "masquerade was as common to him as mullein in his stony pastures."[2] Cooper was not alone in distrusting —even fearing—him.

> The real Yankee, whose appearance only is given to Harvey Birch, is an unpleasant type: hypocrite, chiseler, fiend. He rarely shows his undisguised face in good company. He is an outcast of a sort, an Ishmael, whose grasping hand is turned against everyone. If the transcendent Yankee [Harvey Birch or Natty Bumppo] is kept in the woods or at sea, the real Yankee is kept in the cellar or locked up in the woodshed like an idiot kinsman. He is always apt to break out.[3]

This is the Yankee some of us, including Lawrence, sense hiding behind Franklin's *Autobiography* and the genial mask of Poor Richard. This is the ruthless manipulator of people that Cooper portrays and Miss Rourke describes. The opening scene of *American Humor* is carefully located; it is the residents of a "fertile Carolina valley" that are to be victimized by the itinerant Yankee peddler. The concept of the Yankee as a threat to "the good life" (often represented by the South) is too familiar and too large to explore here, but it permeates much of American literature and can be found in so recent a book as Edmund Wilson's *Patriotic Gore.*

---

[2] *American Humor: A Study of the National Character* (Garden City, 1931), p. 18.

[3] William R. Taylor, *Cavalier and Yankee*, p. 108. Taylor's description recalls, of course, D. H. Lawrence's warning: " . . . When *this* man breaks from his static isolation, and makes a new move, then look out, something will be happening." Lawrence is referring to the "intrinsic-most American" that is Natty Bumppo, and is concerned here with Natty as an isolate and stoic killer (*Studies in Classic American Literature* [Garden City, 1953], p. 73).

A second general approach to the Yankee as a threat can be made through psychology. When Taylor and Lawrence speak of the Yankee "breaking out," they are grounding the warning in psychological theories of repression. Cooper, of course, is pre-Freudian, but he states repeatedly that the New England Puritans' attempts to suppress normal outlets for human frailties led to violence and periodic debauchery in the New England colonies as in no others. Like Cooper, Miss Rourke connects the masked or locked-up malevolence of the Yankee with the Puritans. As she says, "emotion was stirred by the terror of the prevailing faith, yet caught within the meshwork of its tenets. Such compression with such power was bound to result in escapes and explosions" (21).

In *The Wept of Wish-Ton-Wish*, Cooper sets forth most of the latent forces that Puritanism bequeathed to the Yankee. The comprehensive action of the book is a struggle for power between Puritans and Indians. Within this, however, the book identifies three conflicting groups in the first half of the story. Set in Connecticut in the latter part of the seventeenth century, the book describes a Puritan community besieged by Indians and searched by British troops who look for regicides and try not to see the Indians. The tension thus created is artistically successful, since it deepens the novel and dramatizes the true and unenviable position the Puritans at one time occupied: surrounded by Indians, they were harassed rather than protected by unsympathetic officers of a disinterested King. By stressing the Puritans' vulnerability and by making the opposing groups (savages and Royalist soldiers) a real threat, Cooper focuses the reader's sympathies on the

Puritans even while he criticizes certain individuals and practices.

The Puritans in the first half of the book are the members of the Heathcote household and a regicide, known as "Submission," whom they occasionally harbor. Old Mark Heathcote has removed to the wilderness to escape the doctrinal contentions and schisms of coastal Puritan settlements. After a youth of "ungodliness," he has found faith; and "'rather than let go its hold, will I once more cheerfully devote to the howling wilderness, ease, offspring, and, should it be the will of Providence, life itself'" (5). The patriarchal structure and religion of the household chasten its members, but they live comfortably and not unpleasantly. Mark never asserts his right to power, but reigns by deserving the family's respect; where Mark is concerned, compliance is the only comfortable posture.

Yet compliance does not mean the family is never perplexed by Mark's behavior. Keeping the point of view outside Mark, Cooper allows other members of the household to describe its workings. The family notices somewhat uneasily that Mark combines a stern militancy with his Christian humility; his eye glitters at the sight of an old weapon once used against the Stuarts; and he explains to his grandson the ethic of a Christian soldier: "'Much of the justification of . . . combats must depend on the inward spirit, and on the temper of him that striketh at the life of a fellow sinner . . .'" (31). Mark's past and potential militancy are underscored as the British troops hunt for the regicide Mark protects. In a novel filled with allusions to Azazel, the scapegoat, Submission is somewhat ambiguously symbolic; but he is clearly the hunted man that Mark, save for the grace of God and his early removal to America, might have been. Cooper always writes leniently of Puritan behavior during the witchcraft trials; yet he never lets his readers forget that the Puritan is also a killer.

Two other traits are notable in Mark's behavior. The first is his anchoritish tendency; he builds, as a part of his establishment, a structure that is both a literal fortress against the world and a place of retreat for himself. Cooper cannot forbear stating that the latter-day descendants of the Puritans would not tolerate such "aloofness." The retreat itself is symbolic. It designates Mark as one of those who cannot commune with God or appreciate the ordering of the natural world unless he is shut off from that world and praying in a blockhouse made of the trunks of fallen trees.

In addition to being the place in which Mark can seal himself off from worldly interests and cares, the retreat becomes a prison for a captured Indian boy whose soul Mark believes himself destined to save. Still later, when the boy's tribe attacks to rescue him, the family enters the blockhouse and, so far as the Indians are concerned, departs this earth. Cooper extends the metaphysical significance of this latter scene by giving it from the Indians' point of view. Having set fire to the building, the Indians are as impressed by the silence from within as they are awed by the white family's piety. Only when the building has been reduced to rubble and ashes do the Indians leave; yet, when they (and the reader) next return to the valley, the "dead" have apparently been reborn and the Indians are ready to leave unmolested the charges of so mighty a God. Mark, however, learns of this and refuses to let the

Indians be deceived; he chooses what he considers the lesser evil and confesses that the family descended into a well beneath the ground. Even though the Indians promptly make prisoners of the family, Mark never regrets risking their lives in the interests of truth.

In addition to subordinating the interests of this world to those of the next, Mark also shares the Puritan habit of interpreting all happenings as possible signs of the will of Providence. Thus he believes that the Indian boy mentioned earlier has not been so much captured as delivered up to him for salvation. Cooper explains that "it was far from difficult for a man of his ascetic habits and exaggerated doctrines to believe that a special interposition had cast the boy into his hands for some hidden but mighty purpose . . . " (91). Yet Mark is kind to the boy, feeling a "certain occasional repugnance, which all his zeal could not entirely subdue, at being the instrument of causing so much suffering to one who after all had inflicted no positive wrong on himself" (94). Counterposing, in this way, zeal and humanity, and showing religion as a denial of humanity, Cooper makes Mark likable and prepares to contrast his humaneness to the inhumanity of the monstrous minister who appears in the second half of the book.

Cooper readies a second contrast between Mark and the minister, Meek Wolfe, in the first of the novel's two funeral scenes. Preparing to bury the dead after the Indian attack, Mark cautions his people against stirring up feelings of vengeance among the other settlers. Vengeance is the Lord's prerogative, and Mark calls instead for thanksgiving, responding to the scourge with a fervor and gratitude that Jonathan Edwards might have envied.

"The bands of the heathen have fallen upon my herds;
the brand hath been kindled within my dwellings; my
people have died by the violence of the unenlightened,
and none are here to say that the Lord is just! I would
that the shouts of thanksgiving should arise in my fields!"
(199)

The narrative breaks off soon after this scene; when
it resumes, the valley of Wish-Ton-Wish boasts a settlement near the Heathcotes' rebuilt home, and King
Philip's War is in progress. Cooper's description of
Mark, now ninety years old, again emphasizes his human
qualities. He still has "gleamings of a natural kindness,
which no acquired habits nor any traces of metaphysical
thought could ever entirely erase" (227). With this
reaffirmation of Mark's humanity, Cooper is ready to
introduce the guiding spirit of the new settlement, the
Reverend Meek Wolfe.

As his name indicates, Meek Wolfe embodies the
discordant parts of Puritan theology. He advocates submission to Providence, but acts with rapacious bigotry
and shouts for vengeance against the Indians. He
frightens his hearers as though he were Jonathan Edwards, and holds out enticements to salvation as though
he were Solomon Stoddard. And yet it is not so much
for the contradictions he represents as for the humanity
he denies that Cooper finds Meek Wolfe loathsome.
He is both a type and, in this book, a cause of those
aspects of Puritanism Cooper disliked; and the reader's
attention to what Cooper says of him is repaid by an
understanding of the clear connection Cooper saw between Puritan theological practices and later New England secular sins. In the Puritanism of Meek Wolfe

and the community of *The Wept of Wish-Ton-Wish*
are bedded the seeds that, once escaping clerical control,
sprout rankly over Cooper's America and threaten to
choke out all other ways of life.

"The Reverend Meek Wolfe was," Cooper tells us,
"in spirit, a rare combination of the humblest self-
abasement and of fierce spiritual denunciation" (273).
This same combination, translated into the social realm
of the Newcomes, becomes a pretense of humility (useful for demagogues) and fierce political denunciation.
Meek Wolfe also foreshadows the Newcomes' narrow-
ness of education and outlook; for the minister "had
abundantly qualified himself for the intellectual warfare of his future life, by regarding one set of opinions
so steadily as to leave little reason to apprehend he
would ever abandon the most trifling of the outworks
of his faith" (273). As an embattled defender of a
segment of Protestant thought, Meek Wolfe prepares
for those un-Christian militants, the Bush and Timberman families, who still carry with them the tattered
remnants of a Bible.

If Meek Wolfe's zeal is the fiercer for his faith's
being so narrowly enchanneled, it at least matches his
view of mankind. "In his eyes, the straight and narrow
path would hold but few besides his own flock" (273).
The minister's self-assurance is equalled by his flock's;
and since no person in the community is outside the
church, the group consists largely of saints whose only
doubt is whether they will eventually produce a messiah
or a heavenly kingdom on earth. In action, this assurance of election appears as a communal megalomania
that persists, outliving the faith on which it was based,

in the bumptious egotism of the Newcomes', the Anti-Renters', and the squatters' demands for a quitclaim to the American paradise.

To this same culprit tradition Cooper also traces the latter-day New Englander's invasion of personal rights. Privacy was important for Cooper (much of the value of land-owning was the privacy it insured); and yet privacy is a concept alien to his Puritan.[4] Cooper dramatizes a scene in church to make sure the reader understands the connection. When Ruth Heathcote, a blameless woman grieving for a daughter carried off by the Indians, fails to come to church, Meek Wolfe interrupts the services to demand from the pulpit the reason for her absence. Such a scene, Cooper assures us,

> was far from being extraordinary in a community where it was not only believed that spiritual authority might extend itself to the most familiar practices, but where few domestic interests were deemed so exclusive, or individual feelings considered so sacred, that a very large proportion of the whole neighborhood might not claim a right to participate largely in both. (277)

Omnipotent in the community, Meek Wolfe is shown as a monomaniac; Cooper makes him a personification of Puritan ministerial power and allows him, in the novel, no homelife, no non-ministerial function, no humane action. Drawn to him as though mesmerized,

---

[4] Cooper's reaction to prying is always irascible. In *The Sea Lions,* he writes: "It is a common boast of Americans that there are no spies in their country. This may be true in the every-day significance of the term, though it is very untrue in all others. This is probably the most spying country in Christendom, if the looking into other people's concerns be meant" (77). *Miles Wallingford* contains the funniest dramatization of the problem. Miles and his friend Moses want to talk to each other after a long separation, but the eavesdroppers on board ship finally force them to climb to the top of the mainmast to find privacy.

the people become a unified and fanatic force. The power thus assembled can be used for a good cause, as Cooper shows fairly in describing the second Indian attack of the book.

At the moment when the first of these little divisions of force [the townspeople] was ready to move, the divine appeared in its front, with an air in which spiritual reliance on the purposes of Providence, and some show of temporal determination, were singularly united. In one hand he bore a Bible, which he raised on high as the sacred standard of his followers, and in the other he brandished a short broadsword, in a manner that proved there might be danger in encountering its blade. The volume was open, and at brief intervals the divine read in a high and excited voice such passages as accidentally met his eye, the leaves blowing about in a manner to produce a rather remarkable admixture of doctrine and sentiment. But to these trifling incongruities, both the pastor and his parishioners were alike indifferent; their subtle mental exercises having given birth to a tendency of aptly reconciling all seeming discrepancies, as well as of accommodating the most abstruse doctrines to the more familiar interests of life. (284)

There is a political undertone here as Cooper is aware of how Hamilton's followers "accommodated" the language of Adams, for one, to "familiar" interests. However inadequate Meek Wolfe may be theologically, he is pragmatically a triumph; looking something like an animated Colonel Pyncheon, he leads the colonists to victory. Yet Cooper's moving portrait (and it is a judgment) is not complete until after the funeral service Wolfe preaches for those killed in the attack. The scene is obviously meant as a contrast to that earlier occasion on which Mark Heathcote asked forgiveness for the Indians, and Cooper's report of this service is fully as important to his New England as Father Mapple's sermon is to *Moby Dick*.

The appeal of the divine was in his usual strain of sublimated piety, mysterious insights into the hidden purposes of Providence being strangely blended with the more intelligible wants and passions of man. While he gave Heaven the glory of the victory, he spoke with a lofty and pretending humility of the instruments of its power; and although seemingly willing to acknowledge that his people abundantly deserved the heavy blow which had alighted on them, there was an evident impatience of the agents by which it had been inflicted. The principles of the sectarian were so singularly qualified by the feelings of the borderer, that one subtle in argument would have found little difficulty in detecting flaws in the reasoning of this zealot; but as so much was obscured by metaphysical mists, and so much was left for the generalities of doctrine, his hearers, without an exception, made such an application of what he uttered, as apparently rendered every mind satisfied.

The sermon was as extemporaneous as the prayer, if anything can come extempore from a mind so drilled and fortified in opinion. It contained much the same matter, delivered a little less in the form of an apostrophe. The stricken congregation, while they were encouraged with the belief that they were vessels set apart for some great and glorious end of Providence, were plainly told that they merited far heavier affliction than this which had now befallen; and they were reminded that it was their duty to desire even condemnation, that He who framed the heavens and the earth might be glorified! Then they heard comfortable conclusions, which might reasonably teach them to expect, that though in the abstract such were the obligations of the real Christian, there was good reason to think that all who listened to doctrines so pure would be remembered with especial favor.

So useful a servant of the temple as Meek Wolfe did not forget the practical application of his subject. It is true that no visible emblem of the cross was shown to excite his hearers, nor were they stimulated to loosen blood-hounds on the trail of their enemies but the former was kept sufficiently before the mind's eye by constant allu-sions to its merits, and the Indians were pointed at as the instruments by which the great father of evil hoped to prevent "the wilderness from blossoming like the rose," and "yielding the sweet savors of godliness." Philip and Conanchet [Indians] were openly denounced by name; some dark insinuations being made that the person of the former was no more than the favorite tenement of Mo-loch; while the hearer was left to devise a suitable spirit for the government of the physical powers of the other, from among any of the more evil agencies that were named in the Bible. Any doubts of the lawfulness of the contest, that might assail tender consciences, were brushed away by a bold and decided hand. There was no attempt at justification, however; for all difficulties of this nature were resolved by the imperative obligations of duty. A few ingenious allusions to the manner in which the Israel-ites dispossessed the occupants of Judea were of great service in this particular part of the subject, since it was not difficult to convince men, who so strongly felt the impulses of religious excitement, that they were stimu-lated rightfully. Fortified by this advantage, Mr. Wolfe manifested no desire to avoid the main question. He affirmed that if the empire of the true faith could be established by no other means, a circumstance which he assumed it was sufficiently apparent to all understandings could not be done, he pronounced it the duty of young and old, the weak and the strong, to unite in assisting to visit the former possessors of the country with what he termed the wrath of an offended Deity. He spoke of the fearful slaughter of the preceding winter [of the Indians by whites], in which neither years nor sex had been spared, as a triumph of the righteous cause, and as an encouragement to persevere. Then, by a transition that was not extraordinary in an age so remarkable for re-ligious subtleties, Meek returned to the more mild and obvious truths which pervade the doctrines of Him whose church he professed to uphold. His hearers were admonished to observe lives of humility and charity, and were piously dismissed, with his benediction, to their several homes.

The congregation quitted the building with the feelings of men who thought themselves favored by peculiar and extraordinary intelligences with the author of all truth, while the army of Mahomet itself was scarcely less influenced by fanaticism than these blinded zealots. There was something so grateful to human frailty in reconciling their resentments and their temporal interests to their religious duties, that it should excite little wonder when we add that most of them were fully prepared to become ministers of vengeance in the hands of any bold leader. (334-36)

Such people could perfectly understand President Jackson's later description of Indian extinction as "true philanthropy." They set out to exclude or exterminate the Indian, and by the end of the action not an Indian survives in or near the valley.

Latent in the Puritanism of Meek Wolfe and the rest of the community are certain tendencies and habits of mind that augur ill not only for the Indians but for the rest of American society. As Cooper describes it in *The Redskins,*

The rowdy religion—half cant, half blasphemy—that Cromwell and his associates entailed on so many Englishmen, but which was not without a degree of ferocious, narrow-minded sincerity about it, after all, has probably been transmitted to this country, with more of its original peculiarities than exist, at the present day, in any other part of the world. (398)

Susan Fenimore Cooper was correct in writing that her father "was very far from being an admirer of Puritan peculiarities, or the fruits their principles have yielded in later times. . . . "⁵ In *The Sea Lions* (1849), his last book but one, Cooper would describe another Puritan community, this one contemporary and secularized. Before that, however, he created some of his most memorable characters by recognizing the deforming power of a silent and empty tradition.

With the misshapen lives of his squatters, he calls attention to the "observances . . . clinging to the habits of thousands, long after the devout feeling which had first instilled it into the race has become extinct" (*The Redskins*, 394). For this reason the wife and daughter of the dying Aaron Timberman stand, almost grotesquely, at his bedside.

> The captious temper of self-righteousness which had led their ancestors to reject kneeling at prayers as the act of formalists, had descended to them; and there they stood, praying doubtless in their hearts, but ungracious formalists themselves in their zeal against forms. (*The Chainbearer*, 417)

Similarly, the doctrine of work once cut off from its theological source becomes only a groundless certainty that work per se is good. The narrator of *The Chainbearer* remembers,

> . . . I have often met with cases in which parties who were trespassers, and in a moral view, robbers, *ab origine*, have really got to fancy that their subsequent labors (every blow of the axe being an additional wrong) gave

---

⁵ *Pages and Pictures from the Writings of James Fenimore Cooper* (New York, 1861), p. 211. Susan goes on to claim that impartial justice was done the Puritans in *The Wept of Wish-Ton-Wish*. She obviously has in mind the portraits of the Heathcotes (not Meek Wolfe); the "less pleasing traits" may have been "softened down," as Susan puts it, because Mrs. Cooper was a descendant of the Heathcotes.

a sort of sanctity to possessions, in the defence of which they were willing to die. (268)

Losing none of the old fierce energy, but applying it to new purposes, the squatters transfer their devotion from God to Mammon without diminishing the exalted scale of their vision. The more uneducated they are, the more fervently they believe they live in Cockaigne or the land of the Big Rock Candy Mountain. Esther Bush *(The Prairie)* speaks as a true descendant of those visionaries who expected to found in America a heavenly kingdom on earth when she grandly tells her husband how to settle a quarrel with Dr. Bat: "'Give him half the prairie and keep the other half for yourself'" (413).

Similarly, Aaron Timberman is usually called "Thousandacres" because, as Susquesus explains, "'He always own t'ousand acre when he have mind to find him'" (235). For Aaron, man's estate means real estate only, and real estate demands his highest allegiance. He says, "'Let every man have as much land as he's need on; that's my religion, and it's liberty, too'" (373). (Cooper's footnote points to his violation of the Tenth Commandment.) Once Aaron takes possession of his thousand acres, however, he brings in the law and stands it on its head. Not he who invaded the land but the Chainbearer who measures it is wrong. In one display of his argumentative agility, Aaron complains that the surveyor is "lawless" since "'if there warn't no surveyors, there could be no boundaries to farms but the rifle; which is the best law-maker, too, that man ever invented'" (238). He tells the legal owners that he will not have "his" territories "'invaded by the inimy'";

and even after mortally wounding the Chainbearer, he refuses to allow medical aid: "'My family and lumber must be preserved at all risks, and no doctor shall come here'" (396).

The Bush and Thousandacres families are travesties of such a family as the Heathcotes. Both Aaron Thousandacres and Ishmael Bush are militantly patriarchal; they obey no higher authority than their own self-interest, but nonetheless cast themselves in a Mosaic role and lead into the wilderness a family bearing the Biblical names of Nathaniel, Moses, Daniel, Tobit, Enoch, Abner, Esther. Whereas Mark Heathcote ruled over a family which loved and respected him, Aaron and Ishmael govern their rebellious brood by force and faction. The solidarity of the later families is totally artificial, for the fathers, like feudal lords, use their stalwart sons as a private army in the conquest of property. At the same time, this love of possessions is the greatest threat to their unity; one of Aaron's sons comments, "'We can stand up agin almost anything better than agin a good, smart reward'" (The Chainbearer, 309).

Even their personal belongings burlesque those of the Puritans. Both families have at least one book, and the Thousandacres' copy of Pilgrim's Progress accompanies them as they wander onto another man's land, cut and sell his timber, and then demand pay for their "betterments" in having "cleared" it. They also own an old almanac and a fragment (not the whole) of a Bible. The Bushes likewise have a fragment of a Bible with them on the prairie; and as they prepare to avenge the wrongs done them, they refer to it to find the "'awful passages . . . that teach the rules of punishment'" (427). When the Bushes move off across the prairie, leaving Esther's brother Abiram (who has murdered her son Asa) standing on a ledge, roped by the neck to an overhanging limb, and thus certain to hang himself eventually, Esther reduces their tattered Bible yet once more, tearing off a portion and sending one of the children back with it as an anodyne for the condemned man.

Ishmael, significantly, cannot read the Bible; only the wives of the two squatters retain the ability to use it; and for them, who are beyond inspiration, it can be no more than an opiate. Cooper pities these women, showing them powerless before their husbands and sustained only by a fierce maternalism that he considers the unquenchable property of all females. Driven by this natural instinct, it is Esther Bush, not Ishmael, who leads a party onto the prairie in search of her missing son; it is also Esther who carries the spade and pick back to give her brother a conventional burial. Before Ishmael's rifle bullet cuts the fatal rope, they notice that "the leaves of the sacred book were scattered on the ground" (434) but do not retrieve them, and Cooper leaves the pages wafting around the prairie.

Grim as this scene is, its coldness is exceeded by that of the brutally efficient burial of the murdered son, Asa, whose body is laid in a shallow grave, covered by prairie clods, and the whole trodden back into a solid mass by Enoch and Abner, who obliterate the grave with a "strange . . . mixture of care and indifference" (163). The nearest thing to a funeral service is Esther's reminding her husband that he parted from Asa in wrath, and Ishmael's lofty rejoinder, which seems to set his own behavior as a model for God's: "'May the Lord pardon his sins freely as I have forgiven his worst misdeeds'" (164).

Old Ishmael himself is a type of the Puritans who sought to impose their own narrow version of theocracy on America. He has "cast off his own aged and failing parents, to enter into the world unshackled and free" (165), but he refuses his sons any freedom. He is actually relieved at the death of Asa, his insubordinate first-born and the most promising of his children. The remaining brothers have "terrible distrusts," when Asa is found dead, suspecting their father "as ready to imitate the example of Abraham, without the justification of the sacred authority which commanded the holy man to attempt the revolting office" (166).

They are magnificent characters, these squatters, and frightening ones, for they have no compunctions. They behave as though the dregs of their dead religion had inoculated them against decency, against any feeling whatsoever. "'It is little that Ishmael Bush regards who or what is damaged in claiming his own'" (351), Ishmael says of himself, without apology and without even the awareness that apology might be called for. In three notable ways, the squatters relate to Faulkner's Flem Snopes, and these three make up the quality of outrageousness they all share.

First, they simply assume their right to everything. They will not stoop to consider that rewards must be earned, that demands should have a basis, that even rights may need justification; the only acceptable response to their boundless but unformulated desires is the despairing cry of Faulkner's devil: "'Take Paradise!'" Secondly, so godlike is the scale on which they operate that man's feeble laws, his notions of justice, of right and wrong, do not seem to occupy the same sphere; supra-legal (or pre-legal) in their refusal to recognize the reality of law, they reduce their opponents to hysterical recognition of law's impotence. As in *The Hamlet*, they force an abdication of justice: "'I can't stand no more! I won't! This court's adjourned!'" Finally, in denying not only the brotherhood of man but their responsibility for or to anything or anyone, they discover the unanswerable power of a psychopath. The shrewd psychopath learns to use against humanity those qualities and values (love of life and of other people, the desire for resolution and repose) that are the essence of humanity. Thus Ishmael Bush, giving his brother-in-law the choice of being shot immediately or being hanged eventually, and knowing what the choice will be, transfers the responsibility for Abiram's death to Abiram himself; Ishmael rejects his rightful guilt. Abiram, pleading ("time, my brother, time!") and yielding to the human desire for life, chooses the hanging and Ishmael triumphs. "'You shall be your own executioner,'" he says sternly, "'and this miserable office shall pass away from my hands'" (412).

This ability to become inhuman oneself, this rejection of the concept of man as a responsible being, is the essence of Snopesism. It is an outrage that can be appeased only by surrender and opposed only by force. Force, in Faulkner as in Cooper, is finally used; and while it results in a wry sort of "victory" in the deaths of Flem Snopes and Aaron Thousandacres, the resolution is only temporary. Ishmael Bush, on the other hand, is allowed to vanish into a wagon train. William Wasserstrom, arguing largely from Freud's *Moses and Monotheism*, offers what seems a valid interpretation of Ishmael's actions. In committing the "mythic primal crime" that Freud considered the most "barbarous of all acts," Abiram has acted as an instrument of Ishmael's will. When Ishmael, consequently, leaves Abiram to hang himself,

> Ishmael feels that he is about to be rid of nothing less than his own concupiscence, malice, envy. This is why, in the next instant, Abiram's death cry "seemed to have been uttered at the very portals of . . . [Ishmael's] ears." Suddenly, feeling his own blood gush "from every pore in his body," he is amazed to hear "a sort of echo first . . . from his own lips. . . ." Having offered in sacrifice that part of himself, as we may say, which is guilty, Ishmael announces his own guilt, participates in Abiram's agony, achieves expiation and is reborn.[6]

Something of this kind seems to have happened to Ishmael, for his behavior at the burial of Abiram contrasts markedly with his conduct at the earlier burial of his son. Ishmael lays his hand on Abiram's bosom and says, " 'Abiram White, we all have need of mercy; from my soul do I forgive you! May God in heaven have pity on your sins!' " Esther, who has been referring to the dead man as " 'the son of my mother' " and " 'my father's child,' " now finds she can kiss her brother's corpse. Cooper adds that while Ishmael and Esther were never heard of again, some of their descendents were "reclaimed" from their lawless lives (435). The sequence established here, in which primitive violence precedes a

---

[6] William Wasserstrom, "Cooper, Freud and the Origins of Culture," *American Imago*, XVII (Winter, 1960), 435. This reading is ultimately based on Freud's phylogenic theory of evolution which explains that " 'the mental residue' of primeval times is a 'heritage which, with each new generation, needs only to be reawakened.' " Cooper knew of an early version of the same principle, according to Wasserstrom, through Condorcet and the French Encyclopedists.

religious experience, is repeated in several of Cooper's novels, most notably in *The Sea Lions* and *The Oak Openings*.

The same desires—to exploit the earth, to equate might with right, to deny responsibility—seen clearly in the primitive squatters also motivate Cooper's educated Yankees. In the latter, however, these aims are masked by a thin veneer of hypocrisy and education. They appear to be more civilized than the squatters only because they have learned to use the law and public opinion, rather than the rope and the rifle, as the instruments of their greed. Morally, Jason Newcome is as uncouth as Aaron Thousandacres, but Jason and those like him have reared on a "rustic, provincial" foundation an educational "superstructure of New Haven finish and proportion" (*Satanstoe*, p. 39). Jason measures education by its cost and values it only because it gives him access to the world where the big money is. What Cooper says of Jason, in *The Chainbearer*, is equally true of his Yankees generally: Jason is described as

one of those moneyed gluttons, on a small scale, who live solely to accumulate; in my view, the most odious character on earth; the accumulations having none of the legitimate objects of proper industry and enterprise in view. So long as there was a man near him whom he supposed to be richer than himself, Mr. Newcome would have been unhappy, though he did not know what to do with the property he had already acquired. One does not know whether to detest or pity such characters the most; since, while they are and must be repugnant to every man of right feelings and generous mind, they carry in their own bosoms the worm that never dies, to devour their own vitals. (185)

Jason's bosom serpent becomes a family motif; Opportunity Newcome, in the next generation, is likened to an "anaconda or a boa constrictor." We shall see what Cooper considers the "legitimate objects of industry and enterprise" in the next chapter; here, however, it is important to notice that Jason's gnawing acquisitiveness and envy place him in a literary line that continues through Hawthorne's writings and *The Status Seekers*.

By profession, Jason is a steward for the Littlepage family, but he secretly and silently works against his employers' interests. It is this betrayal of a trust that rankled with Cooper; and in portraying Joel Strides, the steward of *Wyandotté* (1843), Cooper made him not only a demagogue and bigot, but indirectly a murderer. Like Hiram Doolittle in *The Pioneers*, Joel betrays a trust and abuses his power but keeps clear of the havoc he causes. A third steward, Aristabulus Bragg of *Home as Found*, is characterized more leniently because a second Yankee, the newspaper editor Steadfast Dodge, is meant as the villain. Bragg, like the other stewards, serves as a kind of lay priest, guiding the people's responses and successfully exhorting them to action as though he were a more modern Meek Wolfe. Even though the religious vision, which once supported and to some extent justified intense and total commitment to action, can no longer be seen in the daylight of democracy, so frenetic is the activity Bragg engenders that no one realizes it lacks a purpose. "'The main object in this life,'" he says, is to "stir people up, and to go ahead'" (324). It does not bother him that "ahead" has neither been defined nor located; he is the political counterpart of Gershom Waring, the "movin' man" of *The Oak Openings*, who says,

". . . *Stranger* is a name I like, it has sich an up and off sound to it. When a man calls all he sees *strangers,* it's a sign he don't let the grass grow in the road for want of movin'; and a movin' man for me, any day, before your stationaries." (45)

Both men believe in action and change as catharsis and alchemy. "'In America,'" Bragg says confidently, "'we look to excitement as the great purifier'" (323).

Because of such brash attitudes, Bragg occupies the same ground as the despicable editor, Steadfast Dodge, but Cooper distinguishes carefully between the two men. Both Yankees have been harmed by "those features of caste, condition, origin, and association that characterize their particular set." This environment keeps Bragg from properly using his natural talents, but it makes a villain of a naturally evil man like Steadfast Dodge, "a hypocrite by nature, cowardly, envious, and malignant; and circumstances had only lent their aid to the natural tendencies of his disposition." Naturally evil tendencies, in short, flourish in the New England environment, and an inviolate and irresponsible press is a shield and a tool for the evil Yankee. Steadfast Dodge is, for Cooper, so thoroughly contemptible that the author vitiates somewhat, through comedy, Dodge's power to do evil. Yet, as Marius Bewley says, "the laughter dies away thinly in the recognition of the threat this kind of creature poses to American civilization."[7]

Nothing can be done to improve Dodge; but Bragg, Cooper suggests, could have become a better man if

---

[7] "Problems of the Literary Biographer," *Hudson Review*, XV (Spring, 1962), 144. Bewley is writing of Mark Schorer's *Sinclair Lewis* and notices, as other critics have, that Lewis added little, if anything, to the characterization of the Steadfast Dodge type. He goes on to say, however, that where Lewis had a "curious affinity" for Babbitt "that gradually moves towards identification," Cooper's hatred "completely framed" Dodge.

he had moved to a "better sphere." Some of Cooper's Yankees find this sphere at sea and by committing themselves thoroughly to seamen's values become no more offensive than Captain Noah Poke of *The Monikins* (1835). Captain Poke (like Captain Truck of *Homeward Bound* and *Home as Found*) is more salt than Yankee. Poke has channeled his energies into exploration, and he acquires navigational and astronomical theories rather than other men's property. Life at sea can do little, however, for the Yankee who looks on sailing as just another way of making money. Ithuel Bolt, of *Wing-and-Wing* (1842), becomes a seaman only after having been a farmer's boy, printer's devil, schoolmaster, stage-driver, tin-pedlar, housecleaner, broommaker, and anything else that appeared lucrative. On Ithuel's first trip at sea, the captain was drowned; and Ithuel, with true Yankee cocksureness, assumed command. "Whatever he undertook, he usually completed," says Cooper, "in some fashion or other, though it were often much better had it never been attempted" (48). Ithuel is so unfeeling that he once suggests they use a boatload of wounded men as a shield against British bullets (438). He lies, manages, calculates, favors smuggling (into any country but America), breaks his solemn oath, is only "law honest"; yet he prides himself on his "religious ancestry and pious education" and finds "a mode of reconciling all this to his spirituality, that is somewhat peculiar to fanaticism, as it begins to grow threadbare" (287). By contrast, the deistic pirate who is his commander is a moral giant. Ithuel, however, not only outlives his captain but prospers:

He did not appear in America for many years. When he did return, he came back with several thousand dol-

lars; how obtained no one knew, nor did he choose to
enter into particulars. He now married a widow, and
settled in life. In due time he "experienced religion,"
and at this minute is an active abolitionist, a patron of
the temperance cause, teetotally, and a general terror to
evil-doers, under the appellation of Deacon Bolt. (469)

The kind of deacon Ithuel Bolt undoubtedly became
appears as Deacon Pratt in Cooper's last book but one,
The Sea Lions (1849). As in *The Wept of Wish-Ton-
Wish*, Cooper placed the action in a Puritan community,
but two centuries have elapsed. Only the heroine
(who is Cooper's ideal Christian woman) and the hero
(Roswell Gardiner, a reworking of Raoul Yvard of
Wing-and-Wing) escape his censure. The heroine's
uncle, Deacon Pratt, is the *reductio ad absurdum* of
"seemly" New England churchmen. He is the undisputed leader of the church and the community, and
has "all the forms of godliness in puritanical perfection"
(46). Not only are these forms empty, however, but
they are a business asset:

> . . . There is a way of practising the most ruthless ex-
> tortion, that serves not only to deceive the world, but
> which would really seem to mislead the extortioner him-
> self. Phrases take the place of deeds, sentiments those of
> facts, and grimaces those of benevolent looks, so ingen-
> iously and impudently, that the wronged often fancy that
> they are the victims of a severe dispensation of Providence,
> when the truth would have shown that they were simply
> robbed. (11)

Covetousness is the Deacon's great sin, but since it is
"a vice that may be pretty well concealed, with a little
attention to appearances" (47), his status remains
undamaged.

After some vulgar maneuvering to get the maps of a dying seaman, two groups of Yankees set forth in identical boats (both named "The Sea Lion") for a secret seal rookery near the South Pole. The Deacon has financed one ship and the Daggetts of Martha's Vineyard the other; the Deacon's group has the map; and as the rival parties sail southward, the pursuing Daggett ship once aids the Deacon's out of a "characteristic admixture of neighborly and Christian kindness, blended with a keen regard of the main chance" (138) that Cooper says is typical of the Puritans' descendants. Once they reach the seals, Daggett's cupidity wins over humanity and religion both; he decides he has no time to " 'give himself up to Sabbaths and religion' " (247). He fails Cooper's favorite test of character when he refuses to take time for a stroll to admire the beauty of the scene. He explains,

> "I cannot say I have much taste for sights, unless they bring the promise of good profit with them. We Vineyarders live in a small way, and are not rich enough to take delight in landscapes." (249)

After a series of misadventures (most of them caused by greed), they realize that the only way to escape spending a winter at the Pole is to leave some of the furs and Daggett's ice-trapped ship. Uninvited in the first place, and troublesome until this time, Daggett refuses to leave his property and uses a pauper's ploy to get Roswell to stay with him. Daggett points out that he is " '*poor*, and what is more, a *cripple!*' " and snares Roswell in the latter's own sense of moral obligation. Instead of being grateful, Daggett becomes more and more perverse and greedy during the long polar winter. Cooper arranges for Daggett to die of events caused by his Yankee traits. Roswell returns with a bag of gold for the Deacon to clutch for a few minutes before he, too, dies and his heirs start fighting over his fortune.

If we juxtapose the worlds of *The Wept of Wish-Ton-Wish* and *The Sea Lions,* we can trace the decline of faith and the rise of materialism. Inflexible as Mark Heathcote is, inhumane and fanatic though Meek Wolfe may be, they are larger than life; and where they are wrong, they are at least wrong in the grand manner. There is nothing grand about the characters of *The Sea Lions.* Except for the hero and one other sailor, they are mean men further dwarfed by their surroundings as Cooper places them among the towering icebergs or hides them in Antarctic mists. They are the Lilliputians of the world Cooper referred to as the *emporium,* and a petty world it is.

In two centuries, Puritanism in Cooper's novels had come to this; and we can identify traits as they slip from the control of the church and reappear in the secular life of the Yankee. The old intolerance of those who were not within the church becomes a narrow provincialism; the old belief in the necessity for churchmen to interrogate and regulate the church's members becomes invasion of privacy and general nosiness; the respect for learning endures as vainglorious pretense based on a superficial and narrow schooling; belief that some are chosen for salvation slides into unjustified egotism; the ability to reconcile points of doctrine and accommodate abstruse doctrines to life becomes political capital, litigiousness, and "law honesty"; and the belief that God is on the side of the righteous and lends them His power is inverted so that the side having power is right. The old responsible patriarchal structure of family and church has been remodeled as the capricious tyranny of an Ishmael Bush or obeisance to such a hypocrite as Deacon Pratt.

In Cooper's world, then, the Puritan ethic leads to ruin. Even if America were Cockaigne, even if the Yankee's intolerance of everyone else could be controlled, even if Yankee enterprise located a Rock Candy Mountain big enough for everyone, the result would only be a national bellyache. The Yankee knew neither how to use his time nor the property he endlessly acquired. The way of the Yankee led clearly to what Henry James was to call the "main American formula": "Make so much money you won't mind anything." [8] If the country were not to follow to this end the declining path of Puritanism, the only alternate way broad enough to be clearly visible to Cooper was the course taken by the predominantly Anglican gentry.

---

[8] F. O. Matthiessen, *Henry James: The Major Phase* (New York, 1946), p. 111.

VI

THE MODEL GENTRY

*Of one thing I am certain; nothing is ever gained by
temporizing on the subject of principles; that which
is right had better always be freely said, since it is
from sacrifices that are made of the truth, as conces-
sion to expediency, that error obtains one half its
power.*

—Cooper*

IF THE YANKEE DESCENDANTS of the Puritans stood for
one way of life, the Anglican gentry represented quite
another. To appreciate the incompatibility of the two
requires that one understand the impossibility of reconciling not only materialism and faith but realism and
nominalism. It means also to remember that if Cooper
had one foot in the eighteenth century and the other
in the nineteenth, he stood ultimately on ancient
ideas. A refusal to trace Cooper's thought beyond the
eighteenth century vitiates much of the criticism about
his works and accounts for misunderstandings and some
of the more ingenious theories about his religious
progress, reversals of opinion, "stages" of thought, and
ambivalence of characterization. Cooper worried certain
themes and antagonisms throughout his career, returning again and again to old problems, despairing of their
immediate solution, yet refusing to admit defeat. Many

---

* *The Redskins*, 476.

apparent antitheses that express these problems can be
related within a framework of classical capacity.

Particularly as we approach his Anglican gentry is
it important to remember that Cooper and his contemporaries knew classical writers. The connection made by
a modern political scientist and philosopher is rare.
"Cooper," writes Sebastian de Grazia, "is one of the
clearest and perhaps one of the last political thinkers
to insist that a country's form of government affects its
culture. His dividing of governments follows the classic
Aristotelian three-fold distinction. . . . "[1]

Cooper's multifarious interests, like those of Jefferson
and Adams before him, come under the general heading
of a preoccupation with the good life. What was it?
Jefferson had called it, in a word, "Tranquilitas."
Webster called it "Harmony." Jefferson died three years

[1] *Of Time, Work, and Leisure* (New York, 1962), p. 291. When
the dollars in our pockets contain quotations from Virgil, it may
seem tedious to insist on the classical bent of the nation's founders.
Yet such a reminder seems necessary when E. H. Cady's *The
Gentleman in America* (Syracuse, 1949) mentions the ancients only
in connection with the English: "They [the English] could, and
occasionally some did, cite such classical writers as Plato, Aristotle,
Isocrates; Quintillian, Cicero, Horace, Juvenal, Theophrastus,
Plutarch and Ovid" (2). He does not suggest that Americans
followed even this weak lead, and writes of Cooper: "Thus Cooper
forged the odd but coherent union of ideas which made him the
determined upholder of democracy and the class of gentlemen at
the same time" (105).

A notable exception is Charles A. Brady's "Myth-Maker and
Christian Romancer," in *American Classics Reconsidered: A Christian Appraisal*, ed. Harold C. Gardiner, S.J. (New York, 1958). The
importance of classical writers is indicated also in such general
studies as F. O. Matthiessen's *The American Renaissance* and Leon
Howard's *The Connecticut Wits*. For Cooper's own formal education, see Marcel Clavel's chapter "L'Education d'un Jeune Ameri-
cain" in *Fenimore Cooper*, particularly pages 151–53, and James
Franklin Beard's introductory remarks to Vol. I of Cooper's *Letters
and Journals*. Beard reports that "William Jay, a roommate, later
remembered that he and Cooper amused themselves after lights were
out by repeating to each other from memory whole dialogues from
the *Eclogues*" (5). Cooper was twelve years old at the time.

after Cooper published *The Pioneers* and a year before
The Prairie (1827); Webster entered the Senate in
1827. Yet there is an interesting difference between
Jefferson's Latin word and Webster's English one:
"Tranquilitas" excludes problems and disparate ideas,
while "Harmony" admits them and asks for their reconciliation. Cooper's books contain both, as we shall see,
but for now the important thing is this: Only the gentry
in Cooper's America can find for themselves and others
either harmony or tranquility.

The three politically effective natural groups occupy-
ing the novels are tantalizingly like the three forms of
moral life Aristotle posited (and Aquinas adopted).[2]
The Dutch most signally enjoy the first *(apolaustikós)*,
the voluptuous life; the Yankees devote themselves to
the second *(politikós* or *praktikós)*; and the gentry try
to attain the third *(theōrētikos)*. In practice, Jefferson,
Adams, Cooper, and Aristotle all tended to see them as
successive stages of cultural development. Aristotle's rule
was: "While the *polis* comes into existence for the sake
of life, it exists for the good life" (*Politics*, I, 1252b).
Jefferson wrote, in 1825, that "literature is not yet a

---

[2] See Aristotle's *Ethics*, I, 1095, and X, 1177; Thomas Aquinas
follows Aristotle's ordering in III *Sententia Distincta*, 35 quest. a.l.;
Summa Theologica, 2a-2ae, quest. 179 a.l.; *Ethicorum Aristotelis
expositio*, I. lect. m-58-59. In *The City of God*, Augustine identified
three types of life as *otiosum, actuosum, ex utroque composito*
(XIX, 19).

Aristotle and Aquinas both agreed that the contemplative life
was the good life. In contemplation, man is most like the gods (in
Aristotle) and is exercising his highest faculty, the power to know
truth. Since, in Aquinas, perfect happiness would come from contemplating God face to face, man's nearest earthly approach to
happiness comes from contemplating God in the mind. Such contemplation is a higher good, even, than religious activity.

The relation of the contemplative life to the state is quite clear
for Aristotle; since such a life presupposed learning and leisure,
the good state must allow leisure of the learned.

distinct profession with us. Now and then, a stray mind arises and, at its intervals of leisure from business, emits a flash of light. But the first object of young societies is bread and covering: science is but secondary and subsequent." The same system governs John Adams' statement that he studied politics and war that his sons might study mathematics and philosophy and his grand-children "painting, poetry, music, architecture, statuary, tapestry, and porcelain." This is also the format, as we have seen, of the Littlepage trilogy in which *Satanstoe* shows exploration, *The Chainbearer* settlement and work, and *The Redskins* the frustration, by the Yankees, of the Littlepages' attempts to live the good life.

Religion is inseparable from this antithesis of Yankee and gentry, and again the division is ancient. Within the humble order of Francis of Assisi, who loved God's world and contemplated His works leisurely and rever-ently, arose Friar Bacon and William of Ockham—for whom the natural world became not an object of awe but a challenge to industry and ingenuity. The world of the tree-chopping Yankee is the meaningless world of Ockham, and the Yankee's insistence on fashioning the face of the earth and the lives of his neighbors according to the notions of the Yankee majority pre-supposes an arbitrary and casual universe. Cooper (and his gentry) believe in God, a demonstrable order of the universe, and the reality of universals. Their attitude toward nature and the land is, like the Yankees' insensi-tivity to nature and abuse of the land, founded ulti-mately on the division between realism and nominalism as Gilson describes it: "The God of theology always vouches for nature; the jealous God of theologism

usually prefers to abolish it."[3] Man's greatness in a
nominalistic universe lies not in contemplating that
universe but in bending it to his will. And in a world
that has no essential meaning, expediency becomes the
rule, and the voice of the people (as Cooper incessantly
complained) is mistaken for the voice of God.

Just as, consequently, the Yankee must be understood
as a product of Puritanism, Cooper's gentry have to be
related to the more catholic tradition of the Anglican
church. Cooper did not formally join the Episcopal
church until shortly before his death, but everything
his gentry believe squares with its teachings. (Unlike many other nineteenth-century American writers,
Cooper was on the side of the Roman Catholic church
wherever it was opposed to the vulgarization and
materialism Protestant sects too often represented for
him.) The gentry's vaunted "principles" are rooted in
their religion in contrast to the Yankee's "law honesty"
that hides his basic depravity. They talk less about their
religion, however, than even the Yankee squatters do,
for Cooper believed that "it is a pretty safe rule to
suspect a man of hypocrisy who makes a parade of his
religion . . . " (*Jack Tier*, iv). Part of this parade is
the strict Sabbath of the Puritans, a repressive practice
that results in brawls and tumults. Another manifesta-
ion is the "high-pressure" activity of the Puritan sects

---

[3] Etienne Gilson, *The Unity of Philosophical Experience* (New
York, 1937), p. 85. This passage is quoted by Yvor Winters in his
essay "Henry Adams, or The Creation of Confusion," *In Defense
of Reason*, p. 375. Henry Adams had lost, as Professor Winters
explains, even the God of theologism. The present chapter is also
heavily indebted to Marius Bewley's "A Sketch for an Historical
Background" and "Fenimore Cooper and the Economic Age" in
The Eccentric Design. Cooper's thought is here soundly related to
that of Jefferson and Adams.

that Miles Wallingford calls attention to. Miles later contrasts the ministers typical of each church:

"I like the preacher who is a Christian because he feels himself *drawn* to holiness, by a power that is of itself holy; and not those who appeal to their people, as if heaven and hell were a mere matter of preference and avoidance, on the ground of expediency." (*Afloat and Ashore*, p. 506)

No Episcopalian minister in Cooper's novels even remotely resembles Meek Wolfe. Well educated in the classics, the Anglican clergy tutor the sons of the country families in Latin and Greek; and their intercourse with these households is warm and frequent. Dressed in their clerical robes ("before it was considered aristocratic to wear the outward symbols of belonging to the church of God" *Wyandotté*, 53), they accompany members of their flock to fortune-tellers' homes or cockfights and one (Dr. Liturgy of *Lionel Lincoln*) is pictured cozily at home with his shoes unbuckled, pipe in hand, and a glass of cider at his elbow (268). Mild-mannered and pious men, they preach only religion from the pulpit, but privately support the political attitudes of the gentry.[4]

---

[4] The ministers in question are Mr. Woods (*Wyandotté*), Mr. Warren (*The Redskins*), Mr. Grant (*The Pioneers*), Mr. Hardinge (*Miles Wallingford* and *Afloat and Ashore*), Mr. Worden (*Satanstoe*), and Dr. Liturgy (*Lionel Lincoln*). A brief sample of the Anglican and Puritan attitudes toward pleasure is found in the last book. Dr. Liturgy has just said, " 'There are so many unavoidable evils to which flesh is heir, that we should endeavor to be happy on all occasions—indeed it is a duty—,' " when he is interrupted by a "low, growling voice." The speaker objects, " 'It's not in the natur' of sin to make fallen men happy.' " The gloomy view is taken by Job Pray, an idiot, who is known as the "Boston Calvin" and of whom it is said that " 'Old Cotton was not his equal in subtlety!' " (*Lionel Lincoln*, p. 280).

In excluding political and personal attacks from their church services, the Anglican ministers are contrasted with other preachers. Mrs. Littlepage, for instance, "was accused of an aristocratic prefer-

These ministers often remind one of Parson Adams, and none more so than *Wyandotté's* Mr. Woods. This worthy sets out to retrieve some captives from the Indians, hoping that the natives will fail to notice that the sprig of laurel in his hand is not a real olive branch, and preparing to "'call the Deity the "Great Spirit" or "Manitou"—and to use many poetical images'" (278). Scarcely more worldly, and just as impractical, is Mr. Hardinge:

> "Here was my sister dying of blighted affections under my own roof [Miles Wallingford relates]; and the upright, conscientious father of the wretch who had produced this withering evil, utterly unconscious of the wrong that had been done, still regarding his son with the partiality and indulgence of a fond parent. To me, it seemed incredible at the time, that unsuspecting integrity would carry its simplicity so far." (*Miles Wallingford*, p. 78)

"Unsuspecting integrity" well describes all these ministers. Yet, simple and innocent as they are, their tolerance and education make their church "an institution giving a tone to American life (the sort of tone which it is usually assumed that we must seek in civilizations more permeated with ecclesiasticism)."[5]

---

ence of her own family to the families of other people. . . . This attack had come from the pulpit, too, or the top of a molasses hogshead which was made a substitute for a pulpit, by an itinerant preacher, who had taken a bit of job-work, in which the promulgation of the tenets of the gospel and those of anti-rentism was the great end in view."—*The Redskins*, 403. Such peripatetic preaching was necessary, Cooper pointed out elsewhere, because the latter-day Puritans were too miserly to support a proper minister and church.

[5] This is Henry James's appraisal of what the church means in the fiction of the Cooper family. It appears in his review of Constance Fenimore Woolson's novels (*Harper's Weekly* of February 12, 1887). Constance was Cooper's grandniece and obviously agreed with the family feelings about the church and society. The James review is reprinted in Leon Edel's *The American Essays of Henry James* (New York, 1956), p. 167.

In practice, their religion supports the gentry most strongly as they battle the rule of the majority and as they define and defend their own manner of living. They find in religion ethical absolutes that make popular opinion irrelevant; and in defending the values of the gentleman, they envision something like a ladder of morality with a perfect Christian on the top rung. Charles Brady has mentioned that Cooper's distinguishing between a gentleman and a Christian antedates Newman's; the fullest exposition of the distinction is made by Mordaunt Littlepage in *The Chainbearer*.

> . . . The qualities of a gentleman are the best qualities of a man unaided by God, while the graces of the Christian come directly from his mercy.
> Nevertheless, there is that in the true character of a gentleman that is very much to be respected. In addition to the great indispensables of tastes, manners, and opinions, based on intelligence and cultivation, and all those liberal qualities that mark his caste, he cannot and does not stoop to meanness of any sort. He is truthful out of self-respect, and not in obedience to the will of God; free with his money, because liberality is an essential feature of his habits, and not in imitation of the self-sacrifice of Christ; superior to scandal and the vices of the busy-body, inasmuch as they are low and impair his pride of character, rather than because he has been commanded not to bear false witness against his neighbor. It is a great mistake to confound these two characters, one of which is a mere human embellishment of the ways of a wicked world, while the other draws near to the great end of human existence. The last is a character I revere; while I am willing to confess that I never meet with the first without feeling how vacant and repulsive society would become without it; unless, indeed, the vacuum could be filled by the great substance of which, after all, the gentleman is but the shadow. (161-62)

As a group, the gentry do not claim grace, but for all practical purposes, as Mordaunt makes clear, they are as trustworthy as if they were truly of the elect.

This concept of the gentleman as a natural leader of society should be juxtaposed with Cooper's statement that "the governing social evil of America is provincialism." The catholic attitude of the gentry contrasts sharply with Yankee intolerance.

[In New England] habit had taken the place of principles, and a people accustomed to see even questions of domestic discipline referred either to the Church or to public sentiment, and who knew few or none of the ordinary distinctions of social intercourse, submitted to the usages of other conditions of society with singular distaste and stubborn reluctance. The native of New England deferred singularly to great wealth in 1776, as he is known to defer to it to-day; but it was opposed to all his habits and prejudices to defer to social station. Unused to intercourse with what was then called the great world of the provinces [New York], he knew not how to appreciate its manners or opinions and, as is usual with the provincial, he affected to despise that which he neither practised nor understood. (*Wyandotté*, 325)

America seemed, to Cooper, to be following the lead of the wrong group. Not only did the Yankee wish to suppress anything he did not understand (and the Yankee understood little), but the inevitable result of Yankee leadership would be moral chaos. Cooper describes something like secular nominalism when he states that the American people

possess no standard for opinion, manners, social maxims, or even language. Every man, as a matter of course, refers to his own particular experience, and praises or condemns agreeably to notions contracted in the circle of his own habits, however narrow, provincial, or erroneous they may happen to be. (*Home as Found*, iv)

So far the distinctions between Yankee and gentry are clear enough and broadly sketched. The real meaning of the gentry, however, is more complex, and Cooper tried to educate his readers so that they could distinguish between a model gentleman and an apparent gentleman. (Nobody but another Yankee would mistake his Yankees for gentlemen.) For this particular analysis, he created another set of doubles; Edward and John Effingham are first cousins, were born the same day, loved the same woman, and are equally cultivated, wealthy, intelligent, traveled, and accepted as gentlemen by Europeans. (The fact that the woman they both loved, Eve Effingham's mother, married Edward immediately identifies him as the gentleman for veteran Cooper readers.) Even though they are almost identical in appearance, Eve Effingham, a talented amateur artist, cannot capture John's likeness. Her sketches of her father are excellent, but John, who looks just like Edward to the eye, eludes her pencil. The difference is also sensed by certain people they meet who instinctively avoid John and trust Edward.

The difference is explained by the two men's lives. John, if anything the wealthier and more alert of the two, "having inherited a large commercial fortune, did not own enough ground to bury him. As he sometimes deridingly said, he 'kept his gold in corporations that were as soulless as himself'" (*Homeward Bound*, 5). John's commercial interests have led him into a chain of error. First, the soulless corporations nourished his self-reliance until he became "indisposed to throw himself on a greater power for the support, guidance, and counsel all need" (339). He is thus like Signor Gradenigo (in *The Bravo*) who "was born with all the sympathies and natural kindliness of other men, but accident, and an education which had received a strong bias from the institutions of the self-styled Republic, had made him the creature of a conventional policy" (81). John's business connections have allied him with political factions and have brought him to admire British opinions. Adopting "the current errors with which faction unavoidably poisons the mind," John has acquired "prejudices that often neutralized his reason." A lengthy stay in England has partly restored his values, but "the remains of the old notions" linger as a "twilight shading on his mind" (55). It is not surprising that Eve cannot capture him in her drawing, for he "would have puzzled the skill of one who had made the art his study for a life . . . " (5).

Cooper's usual interest in the effect of environment on similar temperaments is here, of course, as is the recurrent fascination with appearance and reality. But there is more. Cooper cleverly (perhaps too cleverly, for it seems to have eluded readers) uses the character of John Effingham to attack Hamilton and his followers. The maddening thing about Hamilton and the mercantile interests he represented was their appropriating the appearance and the language and the ideals of such men as Washington, Jefferson, and Adams and using them for ignoble ends.[6] John Effingham has, by the

---

[6] Marius Bewley offers a thorough and convincing description of this perversion in *The Eccentric Design*, pp. 33–64 and Appendixes A and B. As Bewley suggests, *The Bravo*, which is ostensibly a book about the evils of Venetian aristocracy, is clearly a study of a state that follows (into and beyond the Gilded Age) Hamiltonian "aristocracy." Cooper thought that Hamilton himself would have been disabused by a trip abroad (*Letters and Journals*, II, 32).

time of the action, begun to see the evils of Wall Street and has learned the British are not worthy of worship. His money, however, is still in industry and finance, and his attitude toward his inferiors is much like Hamilton's view of "the mass of the people" as so much raw material to be used or at least checked. Thus it is John who says that

". . . of the two, I should prefer the cold, dogged domination of English law, with its fruits, the heartlessness of a sophistication without parallel, to being trampled on by every arrant blackguard that may happen to traverse this valley in his wanderings after dollars." (*Home as Found*, 226)

John is intelligent and attractive (and useful to Cooper since his cynicism comports with Cooper's sharpest criticism of American foibles); yet we are not surprised to learn, in the usual revelation of true identities at the end of the books, that he has been unprincipled in his personal life.

No such past wells darkly behind the countenance of Edward Effingham, who is precisely what he seems—a disinterested gentleman. He also laments the American "'tendency . . . to substitute popularity for the right'" (226), but believes even the "popular oppression" of America is better than any other existing form of government. Personally, his character is even more revealing; Cooper writes that he

. . . had lived many years in that intellectual retirement which, by withdrawing him from the strifes of the world, had left a cultivated sagacity to act freely on a natural disposition. . . . Enjoying the *otium cum dignitate* on his hereditary estate, and in his hereditary abode, Edward

Effingham, with little pretensions [*sic*] to greatness, and
with many claims to goodness, had hit the line of truth
which so many of the "godlikes" of the republic, under
the influence of their passions, and stimulated by the
transient and fluctuating interests of the day, entirely
overlooked, or which, if seeing, they recklessly disre-
garded. A less impracticable subject for excitement—the
primum mobile of all American patriotism and activity, if
we are to believe the theories of the times,—could not be
found, than this gentleman. Independence of situation
had induced independence of thought; study and inves-
tigation rendered him original and just, by simply ex-
empting him from the influence of the passions; and
while hundreds were keener, abler in the exposition of
subtleties, or more imposing with the mass, few were as
often right, and none of less selfishness, than this simple-
minded and upright gentleman. (*Homeward Bound*, 53)

Reason and romanticism are behind this portrait of
Edward, the gentleman who withdraws from the world
to seek truth in isolation. Cooper's father had engaged
in politics and had been killed when struck from behind
as he left a political meeting. The romanticism comes
with Edward's ownership of land and the country life
that "attached him to this world of ours by kindly
feelings toward its land and water . . . " (5). The
Antaeus myth, the sense of drawing strength from
contact with the soil, underlies much of romantic literature and is inseparable from the gentry's feeling for land.

Most important to this portrait, however, is the
classical ideal of the good life. The life Edward Effingham is trying to lead is, as De Grazia says, the one
Aristotle thought was "the only life fit for a Greek"
(21). At the earliest opportunity he removes, with his
family and a houseful of congenial friends, to the
country. There they renew their reciprocal engagement

with the land, for land is an obligation as well as a source of pleasure. In return for the renewed sense of life and the experience of nature land offers, it must be protected and cherished in kind. As a part of God's universe, land is a reminder of man's debts, the eternal verities, and the transiency of life. At the same time, it forms a visible link with the past. The Effinghams point to a tree that stood when the Conqueror first landed in England, a mass of green that "'waved there in the fierce light when Columbus first ventured into the unknown sea'" (*Home As Found*, 203). Eve, who has spent most of her life in Europe, nevertheless points out the site of Natty Bumppo's old cabin and Natty himself is spoken of as a fabulous character by the residents of the area. Though the interweaving of characters and events is far less dense in Cooper's novels than it is in Faulkner's Yoknapatawpha County, characters of one book are often alluded to in another so that the area as it once was is recalled in a tale set at a later time. These allusions are often anecdotal and sometimes irreverent; the history of the family is incidental to the history of the land, and yet the land and the lakes assert the continuum. This reverence for tradition (which Cooper stresses also in describing Indians) is thoroughly classical; Plato and Aristotle and Cooper are of one mind. A well-founded tradition, like a just constitution, is one of mankind's best bulwarks against human stupidity and error.

The final important thing to notice about Edward Effingham is the superiority Cooper asserts for him because he is disengaged. Edward is free—which includes being free from compulsion to do good. He does not meddle with the affairs of his fellows, but grants them the same privacy he desires for himself. Edward, furthermore, does not volunteer for public office; his actions comport with Cooper's statement to a Swiss friend that "it was vain to expect that either very wise or very honest men would be in the administration for any great length of time."[7]

Just as Edward is free of psychological necessity, so is he free from the necessity to work. Massachusetts had passed a law in 1633 that forbade spending time "unproffably" or "idely," but Cooper never admitted that work was better than leisure. Again, Cooper was like the nation's founders in believing that man's nobler qualities were nourished by leisure, and that man had an inalienable right not to work if he did not have to. As John Adams expressed this thought,

The great question will forever remain, *who shall work?* Our species cannot all be idle. Leisure for study must ever be the portion of a few. The number employed in government must forever be very small.[!] Food, rai-

---

[7] *Letters and Journals*, II, 321. Again, the context is classical, and the thought close to the ideals of Plato and Aristotle. In Plato's *Republic*, those who "pass every test and trial with honor and in contemplating and leisure succeed in seeing the good in its essence, 'are to take it as a model for the rest of their life and must use it in giving order to the *polis* and private persons and themselves in turn. Most of the time they will occupy themselves with philosophy, but when their turn comes they one at a time for the sake of the *polis* take over rulership, looking on it not as a gentlemanly activity but as if it were labor done out of the necessity of making a living.' "—Sebastian de Grazia, *Of Time, Work and Leisure*, pp. 416–17. See also the discussion about the relation of freedom to leisure on p. 24.

The practice of Washington, Jefferson, and Adams had been similar to Plato's conception of public duty. When called upon, these men left (and reluctantly) their leisure to serve their country. As soon as they could conscientiously do so, however, they retired—not to the plough (as the Cincinnatus mania had it) but to their books and quiet life.

ment, and habitations, the indispensable wants of all, are not to be obtained without the continual toil of ninety-nine men in a hundred of mankind. . . .[8]

Like Adams, Edward Effingham takes it for granted that some work and others do not. Cooper describes with obvious approval Edward's hiring a housekeeper, thus pleasing both the woman who needs to work and his daughter, Eve, who does not. (Cooper always objected to the manner in which most Americans over-worked women, and he often portrays wives in Platonic terms: the poor man's slave was his wife.)

Edward Effingham is not selfish; what he has (even his tranquility) he tries to share with his family and friends, and his presence always soothes and elevates. Yet he limits his society, refuses to suffer fools gladly, and resents the intrusions of the vulgar. Since he does not feel called (nor is actually requested) to serve the state, he is prepared to lead the good life—if only the neighbors would quit invading his property and his personal life. He has designs on neither nature nor man and would, if left alone, be able to live as an

---

[8] *Works*, VI, 280. Marius Bewley quotes this passage and points to the similarity with a statement in Cooper's *The American Democrat*: "The rights of property being an indispensable condition of civilization, and its quiet possession everywhere guaranteed, equality of condition is rendered impossible. One man must labour, while another may live luxuriously on his means; one has leisure and opportunity to cultivate his tastes, to increase his information, and to reform his habits, while another is compelled to toil that he may live."—*The American Democrat*, p. 32.

Acute as Bewley is on the parallel thoughts of Cooper and Adams, he misses the analytic characterization in *Homeward Bound* and *Home As Found*. By failing to notice Cooper's careful distinctions, he finds the Effinghams confusing. "Detailed analysis of the Effingham family could show that the reality they stand for in a not overly subtle fashion is a queer combination of Adams' aristocracy, Jefferson's liberal faith in the democratic possibilities of America, with more than a perceptible taint of Hamiltonian snobbishness and financial acuteness."—*The Eccentric Design*, p. 87. Edward embodies aristocracy and liberality in a classical manner; John is responsible for the Hamiltonian attitudes.

American representative of the proper Epicurean attitudes: hope for the future, gratitude for the past, and patience to endure the present. They have their charm.

"In brief, this is what we can expect of a man: that he be useful to other men; to many of them if he can; to a few, if he can but a little; and if he can but still less, to those nearest him; and if he cannot to others, to himself." Seneca's statement (in *De otio*) well describes the function of Cooper's gentry; they make themselves useful if they can. What they do, consequently, depends on the stage of the country's development. Originally, theirs was the job of youthful exploration, which often meant fighting Indians as Cornelius Littlepage had done in *Satanstoe*. We are told (in *The Redskins*) that Cornelius is honored by the Indians as a "'warrior of great courage and skill'" (297) long after his death, and he does acquit himself well. Yet Cooper at no time indulges him in the romantic clichés of action he allows such a leader as the Virginia cavalryman, Peyton Dunwoodie, in *The Spy*.

The eye of the youthful warrior [Peyton] flashed fire. Riding between this squadron and the enemy, in a voice that reached the hearts of his dragoons, he recalled them to their duty. His presence and words acted like magic. The clamor of voices ceased; the line was formed promptly and with exactitude; the charge sounded; and led on by their commander, the Virginians swept across the plain with an impetuosity that nothing could withstand. . . . (93)[9]

---

[9] For this pattern of action as romantic convention, see David Levin, *History as Romantic Art*: " . . . In battle after battle the leader 'infused his spirit' into his men, or 'animated them with his own spirit,' or 'inspired them with his own energy,' or 'breathed his own spirit into them.' This respiratory influx of grace was nearly irresistible; having received it, the People almost always won the battle" (p. 51).

Cornelius is denied such headlong heroism; he can be brave, but he must also be mature and responsible. A situation in *Wyandotté* gives the reasoning behind this and suggests that Cooper, like Twain, saw the Southern gentleman as too much influenced by what Twain called "The Sir Walter Disease." When young Major Bob Willoughby wants to go out into the open to fight instead of defending the house from the inside, his father rebukes him:

> ". . . We are here to defend this house and those it contains; and our military honor is far more concerned in doing that effectually, and by right means, than in running the risk of not doing it at all, in order to satisfy an abstract and untenable notion of a false code." (221)

In the wilderness and on the frontier, the gentleman could enjoy himself, but he was always responsible for the safety of his group. The code Cooper believed in cut far beneath etiquette and propriety. One thing, in fact, comes through in the wilderness novels with a clarity Cooper never equalled again.

Any society, even a temporary one, governed by the gentry accommodates and controls inimical factions. The exploring party Cornelius and Dirck assemble contains also another Dutchman, a Yankee, Indians, and Negroes. Although they are beyond all law, disputes are minor and the group functions harmoniously, considering the enmities it represents. One grisly incident, however, suggests what absolute freedom for each member of the party might lead to. Jaap, a Negro, when he has the opportunity (and is away from Cornelius) flogs an Indian who later escapes; still later, two white men and a second Negro, temporarily separated from the main party, are set upon by Indians and killed. Significantly, the Negro is also cruelly tortured, and the Indian guide confirms the leaders' suspicions that revenge has been taken not against an individual but against color (411). Of all the gory scenes in Cooper (such as the hanging of a Skinner by the Cow-Boys in *The Spy*, a second torture scene in *The Oak Openings*, or the discovery of the living but scalped Thomas Hutter in *The Deerslayer*) not one takes place in the presence of a member of the gentry. They see, and cause, plenty of bloodshed, and they themselves feel vengeful occasionally, but they stay the extremes of vindictiveness in their group.

In the second stage of civilization, they relinquish personal control, but try to set up laws that will similarly protect people from each other—and the land from the people. More far-sighted than those around them, they look back to the country's beginnings and forward to its future, and they become conservative. Mordaunt Littlepage, supervising the chaining of farms and trying to keep the squatters from destroying the forest, represents this era. The land, at this stage, is still a liability, but the concept of stewardship is strong; its owners conserve not for themselves but for posterity. Caught in *politikós* or *praktikós,* they are not particularly content, but their hopes for the future help them acquire the patience to endure the present.

The best example of motives and actions at this stage is Judge Temple of *The Pioneers.* Like Mordaunt, Marmaduke Temple is a transitional figure, one so close to the period of exploration that he can remember how the scene looked from a treetop on a mountain he named Mount Vision: " 'No clearing, no hut, none of the winding roads that are now to be seen, were there, nothing but mountains rising behind mountains, and the valley, with its surface of branches . . . '" (239). The scene, fixed in his memory, gives him also a vantage point in time that the other settlers lack; to his daughter's complaint of slowness in taming the "wild country," he replies, "'If thou hadst seen this district of country, as I did, when it lay in the sleep of nature, and witnessed its rapid change as it awoke to supply the wants of man, thou wouldst curb thy impatience . . . '" (235). Knowing what the country had once been, the Judge and Natty Bumppo can appreciate—even become alarmed at—the rapidity of changes, and the conservative instinct rises in them. Natty's continual complaint is that the settlers are "wasty"; the Judge, remembering when a catch of fish saved the colony from starvation, disapproves of seining the lake more for fun than for food and of killing more fish than can be used. As he says to the local syrup gatherer, Billy Kirby,

"It grieves me to witness the extravagance that pervades this country . . . where the settlers trifle with the blessings they might enjoy, with the prodigality of successful adventurers. You are not exempt from the censure yourself, Kirby, for you make dreadful wounds in these trees where a small incision would effect the same object. I earnestly beg you will remember, that they are the growth of centuries, and when once gone, none living will see their loss remedied." (232)

Billy's answer comes straight from his consciousness of status and money and shows how little he understands the Judge's viewpoint. For he says that he has heard "rich men" in the old countries like trees, even plant them, but that he prefers stumps himself. He goes right on leveling. The Judge can only console himself with the thought that " 'the hour approaches, when the laws will take notice of not only the woods but the game they contain also' " (233). He and others like him have enough power, at this time, to get such laws passed by the state.

The incident illustrates not only the Judge's function as a conservator but also his inability to curb such men as Billy Kirby. Whereas the settlers had once been completely dependent on him for food, Temple is now little more than the community's first citizen and his only power is derived from the law. As a judge, Marmaduke Temple is inflexible, deciding strictly according to the law even when it means jailing Natty (who is technically guilty but morally innocent) on the word of a troublemaker. He does so reluctantly, but has no real alternative since " 'the laws alone remove us from the condition of the savages' " (397). Actually, Temple is slightly wrong. Traditions are to Cooper's Indians what the Constitution should be to the white settlers. Furthermore, Cooper's previous novel (The Spy) had described Westchester county during a time when the "law was momentarily extinct" and the bands of marauding white men (the Skinners and Cow-Boys) terrorized the residents with "a thirst for plunder that is insatiable, and a love of cruelty that mocks the ingenuity of the Indian. . . . " These could not, Cooper says, be compared with the Indians without doing "the savages injustice" (302). Judge Temple's verdict (like Captain Vere's in Billy Budd) counters his feelings, but is rightly based on principle; to decide any other way would mean that "justice was administered subject to the bias of personal interests and the passions of the strongest" (The Spy, p. 3).

"Justice" of this kind, which to Cooper means that the law is extinct, is exactly the problem in *The Redskins* and *Home as Found*. No longer are the Littlepages or the Effinghams (descendants of Judge Temple) the magistrates of their districts; magistrates and legislators, elected by popular vote, make and enforce (or fail to enforce) laws to satisfy the interests of the "strongest"—the majority. Theoretically, "public virtue" aids law enforcement, but Mordaunt Littlepage points out that "'public virtue is never one half as active as private vice'" (*The Chainbearer*, p. 411). Cooper himself explains in the Preface to *The Redskins* that the New York Assembly has passed a bill to "choke-off" landlords by a discriminatory tax on land rents.

It is done to conciliate three or four thousand voters, who are now in the market, at the expense of three or four hundred who, it is known, are not to be bought. (ix)

Attacked by the barnburners, the Littlepages find themselves embarassed; law enforcement officials, elected by popular vote, do not protect them, and yet the law itself prevents their fighting back. Hugh Littlepage concludes that

it ought to be written in letters of brass in all of the highways and places of resort in the country, that A STATE OF SOCIETY WHICH PRETENDS TO THE PROTECTION THAT BELONGS TO CIVILIZATION, AND FAILS TO GIVE IT, ONLY MAKES THE CONDITION OF THE HONEST PORTION OF THE COMMUNITY SO MUCH THE WORSE, BY DEPRIVING IT OF THE PROTECTION CONFERRED BY NATURE, WITHOUT SUPPLYING THE SUBSTITUTE. (367)

In the context of Cooper's whole work, the tone used here, admittedly hysterical as it is, is justified by their loss of freedom. As Irving Howe has written in his study of fiction and politics, "Where freedom is absent, politics is fate."[10]

The state exists to guarantee every man the peaceable enjoyment of his own; " . . . he little understands the true spirit of democracy, who supposes that such a man is not to enjoy the tastes and inclinations, which are the fruits of leisure and cultivation, without let or hindrance" (*The American Democrat*, p. 138). Like Aristotle and Locke, Cooper believed that freedom meant life according to the Constitution; his note at the end of *The Redskins* says that Hugh Littlepage is moving to Washington to test the validity of the nation's laws; and that if the Constitution fails him, he intends to take refuge in Florence where he can "reside among the other victims of oppression, with the advantage of being admired as a refugee from republican tyranny" (506). For those who cannot flee to Europe, should the Constitution fail them, Cooper has no more doubt about it than Natty Bumppo has: Outright anarchy is preferable.

Cooper never abandoned the battle lines he drew here, and the arguments of the last book he wrote *(The Ways of the Hour)* are those found in the Littlepage and Effingham chronicles. He did, however, abandon the landowners as spokesmen; and when their opinions are again recorded, they are voiced by an eminent attorney, Dunscomb, and the victim is an innocent and periodically insane girl on trial for a murder. The arguments, of which the following is a

---

[10] *Politics and the Novel* (New York, 1957), p. 87.

fair sample, show that only the setting has been changed.

> The respectable magistrate . . . was a man to per-
> form all his duty to the point where public opinion or
> popular clamor is encountered. . . . This popular feeling
> is the great moving lever of the republic; the wronged
> being placed beneath the fulcrum, while the outer arm of
> the engine is loaded with numbers. Thus it is that we
> see the oldest families among us quietly robbed of their
> estates, after generations of possession; the honest man
> proscribed; the knave and demagogue deified; mediocrity
> advanced to high places; and talents and capacity held in
> abeyance, if not actually trampled underfoot. (253-54)

Cooper considered the Effinghams and Littlepages,
along with the framers of the Constitution, as what
W. H. Auden calls ethical heroes.[11] The battle is between greed, envy, and mediocrity, on one hand, and
wisdom, excellence, and disinterestedness, on the other.
Cooper saw nothing happy about that "general happy
mediocrity" that Benjamin Franklin had boasted of as
being peculiarly American.[12] Cooper's terms were very
different: "The curse of mediocrity weighs upon us,

---

[11] *The Enchafed Flood* (London, n.d.), p. 84. The authority of
the ethical hero "arises from an accidental inequality in the relation
of individuals to the universal truth." Two of the dangers to such a
hero are his refusing to share his knowledge (as Anaxagoras and
Archimedes had been tempted to do) or that inferior persons who
desire "ease and bodily pleasure" (a prolongation of or return to
apolaustikós) will refuse to learn from him.

[12] In fairness to Franklin, it should be said that this phrase,
which occurs in his "Information to those who would remove to
America" of 1782, referred to income groups. Yet it seems defensible
to assert that much of his popular writing encourages such an attitude generally and asks for D. H. Lawrence's charge that Franklin's
message to Americans was "Work, you free slaves, work." Franklin,
like all the rest, felt that "the culture of minds by the finer arts
and sciences was necessarily postponed to times of more wealth and
leisure."—*Pennsylvania Gazette*, 1749. Within his lifetime, however,
he optimistically announced that "these times are come."

and its blunders can be repaired only through the hard lessons of experience" (*The Water-Witch*, iv). In his monikin country of Leaplow (the United States), it is a great "offense for a monikin to know more than his neighbors" (230); and since a monikin's reason is in his tail, all tails are docked at equal lengths as a guarantee against clerisy. In *The Ways of the Hour*, when it is learned that the defendant understands three modern European languages, her lawyer has to plead that "the state can't gain much by hanging a young woman that nobody knows, even if she be a little aristocratical" (124). And a tenant in *The Redskins* "calls all that's above him in the world aristocrats, but he doesn't call all that's below him his equals" (141). No one has an ambition as mild as that of a character in George Gissing's *New Grub Street* who "did not want to be the equal of her superiors, only the superior of her equals."

The force that enthrones mediocrity is supplied by majority rule and public opinion. The main charge against the latter is that it makes truth relative rather than absolute. Thus Opportunity Newcome asserts: "'Talk's all; and if folks have a mind to make anything honorable, they've only to say so often enough to make it out'" (*The Redskins*, 421). Cornelius Littlepage contends that the "great error of democracy" is that it fancies "truth is to be proved by counting noses" (*The Chainbearer*, 13); and a subtitle in *The Crater* (labeled by Cooper "Venerable Axiom") reads: *Vox populi, vox Dei*. In short, Oscar Wilde claimed too late that England "invented and established public opinion, which is an attempt to organize the ignorance of the community, and to elevate it to the dignity of physical force." Hugh

Brackenridge (in *Modern Chivalry*) and Cooper had already stated America's priority.

> Now, no one who has not had the opportunity to compare, can form any idea how much more potent and formidable is the American "folks say," than the vulgar reports of any other state of society. The French *on dit* is a poor, pitiful report, placed by the side of this vast lever. . . . So few doubt the justice of the popular decision, that Holy Writ, itself, has not, in practical effect, one half the power that really belongs to one of these reports, as long as it suits the common mind to entertain it. Few dare resist it; fewer still call in question its accuracy. (*The Redskins*, 401)

At least one French writer accepted Cooper's decision; Stendhal closed the first chapter of *Le Rouge et le Noir* with: "Tyranny of opinion—and such opinion!—is as stupid in the small towns of France as in the United States of America."

Cooper dramatizes this belief comically in *Homeward Bound* when Steadfast Dodge, the scurrilous newspaper editor, wants to establish a society on board ship to ascertain daily, by majority vote, such facts as "the precise position of the ship" (78). The same subject is treated seriously in Miles Wallingford's defense of "aristocratic" leadership:

> . . . I have learned to feel the truth of an axiom that is getting to be somewhat familiar among ourselves, namely, "that it takes an aristocrat to make a true democrat." Certain I am, that all the real, manly, independent democrats I have ever known in America, have been accused of aristocracy, and this is simply because they were disposed to carry out their principles, and not to let that imperious sovereign, "the neighborhood," play the tyrant over them. (*Miles Wallingford*, 202)

Cooper's complaints about the "tyranny of the major-ity" are too familiar to dwell upon; some of his more unrestrained spokesmen state that if majorities deter-mine right and wrong, it is at least theoretically possible to legalize anything—even murder. The obvious alterna-tive, in Cooper as in the writings of Thoreau, Jefferson, Brackenridge, and others, is to base government on principles that reflect the absolutes of right and wrong found in divine law.

> If there was a power superior to the will of the majority, in the management of human affairs, then majorities were not supreme; and it behooved the citizen to regard the last as only what they really are, and what they were probably designed to be—tribunals subject to the control of certain just principles. (*The Crater,* 458)

Cooper's solution, then, worked out in a number of books, is the solution, the standing firm on principles embodied in the Constitution, advocated by the Little-pages and the Effinghams. These families change, through the years, giving up certain marks of caste that they themselves see as unsuitable in America, but they absolutely refuse to arbitrate right and wrong.

The other thing they refuse to relinquish is their individual integrity. Part of the gentry's reverence for integrity comes from their conception of human dignity as godlike self-containment. Part comes from their re-spect for individual differences: Being free means to have the ability to be oneself. In *The American Demo-crat,* Cooper explained to schoolchildren that the aim of liberty is "to leave every man the master of his own acts" (95). In a democracy, this integrity is most threatened by "popular sway," and Cooper warned the children that it was a "publick duty of the citizen to guard against all excesses of popular power, whether inflicted by mere opinion, or under the forms of law" (86). When people forsake their integrity and act as a crowd in Cooper's world, they act as animals. As one of the characters in *Wyandotté* says, "'Men, as individuals, may be, and sometimes are, reasonably upright —but bodies of men, I much fear, never. The latter escape responsibility by dividing it'" (239). Even the smuggler in *The Water-Witch* promises to become an officer of the customs "'when bodies of men shall feel and acknowledge the responsibilities of individuals . . .'" (108). A proper community, for Cooper, is a confederation of individuals. "Individuality is an all-important feeling in the organization of human beings into communities," he wrote in *The Sea Lions,* "and the political economist who does not use it as his most powerful auxiliary in advancing civilization, will soon see it turn round in its tracks, and become a dead weight . . . " (157).

Considering the power of an uncontrolled press (before Cooper himself, as Bryant said, put a hook in its nose and landed the Leviathan), it is doubly unfortunate that Steadfast Dodge further discourages any sense of individual responsibility.

A great stickler for the rights of the people, he never considered that this people was composed of many integral parts, but he viewed all things as gravitating towards the great aggregation. . . . So much and so long had Mr. Dodge respired a moral atmosphere of this community character, and gregarious propensity, that he had, in many things, lost all sense of his individuality. (*Homeward Bound,* 87)

A majority, excited by such a molder of public opinion as this or by a demagogue, soon becomes a mob. And as Jefferson had said, "The mobs of great cities add just so much to the support of pure government, as sores do to the strength of the human body."[13] Cooper felt much the same way, and the ugly mobs of *The Redskins, Lionel Lincoln, The Spy,* and *Wyandotté* are sores on the body politic.

Rather than Steadfast Dodges and demagogues, what the people obviously needed were models. In a country going "from the gristle into the bone," as Cooper described it, there was a growing concern with national character. Webster, addressing a group of merchants on the needs of the country in 1831, put at the head of a list containing such predictable items as "systematic finance" and "public credit" the most surprising need of all—national character.[14] The want of models to emulate at home (since Americans were imitating what they construed as British and French customs) had concerned Brackenridge and Tocqueville. Emerson had to listen to Wordsworth's worries about the lack, and Parson Weems had made a fortune from it. Why, then, did the Effingham novels end in libel suits rather than national gratitude?

Three main reasons seem pertinent. The first is that the nation was in no mood to be criticized. Susan Fenimore Cooper tells, in *Pages and Pictures,* of her father's mentioning, at a dinner party, that "the Alps

---

[13] *Writings,* III, 269, as quoted by Bewley, *Eccentric Design,* p. 44. Bewley describes this as a "ritualistic gesture of dissent from the industrial philosophy that was taking over."

[14] See William R. Taylor, *Cavalier and Yankee,* p. 101. It was in response to this concern, Taylor contends, that the legendary or "transcendental" Yankee made his appearance in American fiction; Cooper's Harvey Birch was the prototype.

were some ten thousand feet higher than the White Mountains, and covered with perpetual snow. A severely reproving salutation, the next day, from those who had sat at table with him, was the consequence" (300). As Bryant pointed out in his memorial discourse, adverse reaction to criticism was so general that even newspaper editors forgot that Steadfast Dodge was "a satire only on those to whom it bore a likeness" (p. 59).

The second problem is ancient: How does one show virtue in action? In the frontier novels, Cooper succeeded rather well with the gentry. *Apolaustikós* calls not for abstract virtues but for action, and Cooper himself describes this first stage as one in which

> good-will abounds; neighbor comes cheerfully to the aid of neighbor; and life has much of the reckless gayety, careless association, and buoyant merriment of childhood. It is found that they who have passed through this probation, usually look back to it with regret, and are fond of dwelling on the rude scenes and ridiculous events that distinguish the history of a new settlement, as the hunter is known to pine for the forest. (*Home as Found*, p. 163)

While Cooper recognizes, acknowledges, and uses the appeal of this primal or pastoral stage in his fiction, he is (unlike some American writers and critics) too intelligent to believe one can return to it. The second, practical or political, stage must be borne.

> To this period of fun, toil, neighborly feeling, and adventure, succeeds another, in which society begins to marshal itself, and the ordinary passions have sway. Now it is that we see the struggles for place, the heart-burnings and jealousies of contending families, and the influence

of mere money. . . . This is perhaps the least inviting condition of society that belongs to any country that can claim to be free, and removed from barbarism. (*Ibid.*)

This stage is the last described in any of his novels about community life in America. Cooper was ready for the third, *theōrētikos,* and explained rather hopefully that perhaps the migratory habits of Americans were keeping society unsettled an unnaturally long time. Until Americans desired to go beyond this stage, however (and excellence must be sought; it does not plop in one's lap), his gentry could not be useful. They were more than a little like figures in an allegory as they stood waiting to be recognized as models of principled and pious Intelligence, Cultivation, Liberality, and Integrity. The time for fighting had passed; and although they have patience, if the State does not protect them as it should, they may not endure. For the good of the country, they should be cherished since they are

the natural repository of the manners, tastes, tone, and, to a certain extent, of the principles of a country. . . . If the laborer is indispensable to civilization, so is also the gentleman. While the one produces, the other directs his skill to those arts which raise the polished man above the barbarian. . . . Were society to be satisfied with a mere supply of the natural wants, there would be no civilization. The savage condition attains this much. (*The American Democrat,* p. 91)[15]

---

[15] Cooper's thought is much like Aristotle's: "There are men born to toil and others born to live the life of leisure. If the two groups are linked by a moral bond as in the family or household, then even those who work receive the benefits of those who do not. . . . [The worker] is brought into a life more human, more refined, than ever he could have reached himself."—Sebastian de Grazia's paraphrase in *Of Time, Work, and Leisure,* p. 36.

The third reason for the poor reception Cooper's gentry received seems closely allied to the second. Critic after critic (British critics in particular) complains that American literature seems obsessed with the frontier experience; it makes up too large a part of our "usable past." Such studies as De Grazia's answer that Americans have "refused" to move beyond frontier thinking; "they have acted as if there were a wilderness yet to conquer, some great work yet to do that keeps them from the second [Aristotle's third] stage."

What would this third stage be, described in simple, secular, and widely available terms? The best brief description of the life Cooper seems to have wanted is probably Ben Jonson's translation of Martial's "Vitam quae faciunt beatiorem" (X, 47).

> The things that make the happier life are these,
> Most pleasant Martial; Substance got with ease,
> Not laboured for, but left thee by thy Sire;
> A soil not barren; a continual fire;
> Never at law; seldom in office gown'd;
> A quiet mind, free powers, and body sound;
> A wise simplicity; friends alike stated;
> Thy table without art, and easy rated;
> Thy night not drunken, but from cares laid waste,
> No sour or sullen bed-mate, yet a chaste;
> Sleep that will make the darkest hours swiftpaced;
> Will to be what thou art, and nothing more;
> Nor fear thy latest day, nor wish therefore.[16]

---

[16] Ben Jonson, *Works* (London, 1903), III, 388. This epigram has also been translated by, among others, Cowley, Fletcher, Surrey, Lope de Vega, and imitated by Ronsard, Herrick, and Pope.

Martial's epigram, or parts of it, has appeared in the *Rambler*, a sermon by Taylor, the *Biglow Papers*, a sixteenth-century German religious tract, and the writings of Bacon, Samuel Johnson, Dryden, Racine, Montaigne, and Martin Luther. Its remarkable endurance suggests that it defines, for men of many countries and ages, the good life. This is the life, for Cooper, that lies beyond "struggles for place" and "the influence of mere money." Between the present he saw and the future he envisioned intervened not only Steadfast Dodge, Hamilton's Bank, and smokestacks, but also the perversions of tumbrels and Twickenham.

VII

THE UNSTABLE ELEMENT

. . . Vous monsieur, qui avez créé le "roman mari-
time" d'une manière si originale et si puissante, et
qui partagez avec Goethe et Scott le rare et précieux
privilège d'être un des "types" de la littérature
étrangère contemporaine.

—Eugène Sue*

. . . He loved the sea and looked at it with consum-
mate understanding. In his sea tales the sea inter-
penetrates with life; it is in a subtle way a factor in
the problem of existence, and, for all its greatness, it is
always in touch with the men, who, bound on errands
of war or gain, traverse its immense solitudes. . . .
He knows the men and he knows the sea. His
method may be often faulty, but his art is genuine.
The truth is within him.

—Joseph Conrad†

SO FAMILIAR TO US NOW are the great sea novels in
which the sea "inter-penetrates with life" that it is
difficult to realize that Cooper's *The Pilot* (1823) was
greeted as the first book in a new literary genre.[1] The

---

* To Cooper, Preface to *Atar Gull* (1831).
† In "Tales of the Sea" (1898).
[1] See Marcel Clavel, *Fenimore Cooper and His Critics* (Aix-en-
Provence, 1938), pp. 183–263. The *American Quarterly Review* and
the *North American Review* in this country; *Blackwood's*, Marryatt's
Metropolitan Magazine, and the *Foreign Quarterly Review* in Eng-

sea offered Cooper both sublimity of scene and almost infinite variation of adventure. In his novels, as in Rachel Carson's *The Sea Around Us,* the sea is an entity that corresponds to fact: the earth is a water-world in which continents are casual (and, in Cooper, dangerous) intrusions. Thus Cooper's seamen regard the world, and at least one (a cabin boy, Zephyr) has never touched land. He can only speculate about what going on shore would be like.

> "They say one can hardly walk, it is so steady! They say the ground is rough and difficult to walk on; that earth-quakes shake it, and make holes to swallow cities; that men slay each other on the highways for money, and that the houses I see on the hills must always remain in the same spot." (*The Water-Witch,* 163)

Land is to the sailor, like the settlements to Natty Bumppo, a place of danger, crime, and immobility. Land is an aberration; the sea, reality. This attitude is important, for such a sea is like a universe ordered by Providence; it has its own ways and its own reality, and forces man to come to terms with it. The ships he

---

land; and Eugène Sue in France are among those who give Cooper credit for inventing the sea novel.

Thomas Philbrick's *James Fenimore Cooper and the Development of American Sea Fiction* (Cambridge, 1961) contributes to Cooper studies by placing his sea novels correctly with relation to his immediate predecessors and contemporaries who wrote of the sea.

The Headsman offers proof of Cooper's own consciousness of the ship as a microcosm: "The crowded and overloaded bark might have been compared to the vessel of human life, which floats at all times subject to the thousand accidents of a delicate and complicated machinery; the lake so smooth and alluring in its present tranquility, but so capable of lashing its iron-bound coasts with fury, to a treacherous world, whose smile is almost always as dangerous as its frown; and, to complete the picture, the idle, laughing, thoughtless, and yet inflammable group that surrounded the buffoon, to the unaccountable medley of human sympathies, of sudden and fierce passions, of fun and frolic, so inexplicably mingled with the grossest egotism that enters into the heart of man. . . . " (58)

builds, the skill with which he sails them, even naval discipline and rank are parts of the price he pays to stay afloat and alive on it.

R. W. B. Lewis has said that "for Cooper the forest and the sea shared the quality of boundlessness; they were the *apeiron*—the area of possibility." [2] In a general sense, Lewis is right; by going to sea man escapes, if he wishes, those facts of his biography which would have determined his character on land. Yet Richard Poirier's designation of Twain's raft, Melville's *Pequod*, and Faulkner's woods (of "The Bear") as "places of removal" comes even closer to the meaning of Cooper's sea. As Poirier remarks,

> Each of these places of removal sets the stage for a re-ordering of the social hierarchies which exist outside it. The reordering is accomplished in terms of aspirations and achievements which connot express themselves in a society based upon practical utility and traditional manners. [3]

Poirier's "reordering of social hierarchies" stresses the societal nature of life at sea. Cooper's shipboard functions much as the Marxist's ideal society; it is a synthetic community in which each man can fulfill his potential and where artificial and arbitrary distinctions can be minimized or escaped altogether. Here, if anywhere, the Negro Neb can succeed; Roswell Gardiner *(The Sea Lions)* can here be most easily awed out of his hubris; national enemies and temperamental opposites such as the British Captain Cuffe and the French Raoul Yvard *(Wing-and-Wing)* can here feel mutual respect. Merit, or the lack of it, is more quickly visible at sea than on

---

[2] *The American Adam* (Chicago, 1955), p. 99.
[3] *The Comic Sense of Henry James* (New York, 1960), p. 34.

shore, and a man who places his own interest above that of the society of the ship creates a dramatizable danger. At the same time, merely prudish restraints can be cast off with the mooring lines. Captain Truck explains how this applies to freedom of speech, for instance.

"Those fellows, after they have been choked off and jammed by the religion ashore for a month or two, would break out like a hurricane when they had made an offing, and were once fairly out of hearing of the parsons and deacons." (*Homeward Bound,* 243)

At sea, in short, Cooper's theories about the nature of man and society could be objectified; staved hulls, jagged reefs, ingenious escapes, and navigation—whether by stars, instinct, or wild theory—all become ways of talking about men.

Furthermore, the seaman's language furnishes the vocabulary. Becoming more than just salty sayings used and misused to characterize the sailor at least since Smollett's novels, seamen's terms are often metaphors. Some are as fancifully inflated as Trysail's comment in *The Water-Witch.*

"I have often thought, sir, that the ocean was like human life,—a blind track for all that is ahead, and none of the clearest as respects that which has been passed over. Many a man runs headlong to his own destruction, and many a ship steers for a reef under a press of canvas. Tomorrow is a fog, into which none of us can see; and even the present time is little better than thick weather, into which we look without getting much information." (245)

At its most commodious, the metaphor fills a whole novel, and four books are metaphysical voyages that discover mature values *(Afloat and Ashore)*, the relation of man and society *(The Crater)*, society's errors *(The Monikins)*, and religious faith *(The Sea Lions)*.

Cooper's water world is morally neutral. And while the sea does, as Conrad said, interpenetrate with life, Cooper's portrayal of the sea and seamen's lives is affected by his interest in man's psychological and political nature. Thus we find that the sea offers Americans roughly the same kind of opportunity that America itself promised the European immigrant.[4] Some characters, like some immigrants, ship their cultural baggage with them, and for these the free (but ordered) life at sea can do little. Ithuel Bolt and Daggett are such characters; they remain essentially Yankee landsmen even while they venture forth briefly to harvest the sea. Still other characters bear aboard the psychological chains that keep them from profiting from the sea's freedom. To any man willing to start anew, however, the sea offers a second beginning. The history of one such, comparatively wealthy, character is told in the picaresque tale that runs through the two volumes of *Afloat and Ashore* and *Miles Wallingford* (see Chapter IX). As for the less well educated, Cooper suggested in his first sea novel that the sea was one place in which a man might be common without being mediocre.

Of the many common seamen in Cooper's novels who make no pretense to superiority but whose skills earn privileges and respect, *The Pilot's* Tom Coffin is the most familiar. He and Natty Bumppo appeared in the same year (1823), and Tom is as much a marine

---

[4] Cooper thought this was as it should be; and *Jack Tier* contains a bitter protest at the government's neglecting long and meritorious service in order to "extend the circle of vulgar political patronage" by appointing "strangers" over men who had earned promotions (363).

animal as Natty is a native of the forests. Born on a "chebacco-man" and trained at sea, Tom considers land useful only for raising vegetables and drying fish; otherwise it is a hostile element, the sight of which makes him uncomfortable (12) and on which he is impotent: "'I never could make any headway on dry land'" (193). So very salty is Tom that Grossman's objection of "mechanical extravagance" is justified. Tom's speech is too thickly brined with such aphorisms as "'a tumbling sea, with a lee-tide, on a lee-shore, makes a sad lee-way'" (283).

Much like the aging Natty Bumppo, Tom laughs silently (thus showing his caution and self-control), worries about "waste" (of an eighty-barrel whale being eaten by sharks), and has strong prejudices based on his experience. What Mingos are to Natty, soldiers are to Tom, who ranks "'a messmate, before a shipmate; a shipmate, before a stranger; a stranger, before a dog— but a dog before a soldier'" (259). Like Natty, he is proud of his family's talents: "'My father was a Coffin, and my mother was a Joy; and the two names can count more flukes than all the rest of the island [Nantucket] together'" (268). He is also like Natty in being privileged because of his special skills. His opinions, Cooper tells us, "in all matters of seamanship, were regarded as oracles by the crew, and were listened to by his commander with no little demonstration of respect . . . " (199).

Tom's physique, skills, and inclination separate him from the rest of the crew, and his essential identification is with his nine-pound gun just as Natty is linked with his rifle. Like Natty, Tom divides phenomena into two categories; some things call for an exertion of skills (the winds and weather "'are given for a seafaring man to guard against, by making or shortening sail'" 282), while others are Providential and demand submission ("'It is never worth a man's while to strive to dodge a shot; for they are all commissioned to do their work'" 282).

Tom becomes, for the rest of the characters, a human link with the natural world. His training and instincts let him be the first to detect a northeaster; and he is in a limited sense the superior of his captain, to whom he explains that none get to know the signs of the weather "'but such as study little else, or feel but little else'" (245). By thus limiting his very life to that of the ship and its environment, Tom qualifies for his oracular and symbolic functions. When he is lost overboard and presumed dead during a battle, his loss strengthens the crew's efforts; they are still avenging him when he reappears in time to end the fray.

. . . A wild-looking figure appeared in the cutter's channels at that moment, issuing from the sea, and gaining the deck at the same instant. It was Long Tom, with his iron visage rendered fierce by his previous discomfiture, and his grizzled locks drenched with the briny element from which he had risen, looking like Neptune with his trident. Without speaking, he poised his harpoon, and, with a powerful effort, pinned the unfortunate Englishman to the mast of his own vessel. (205)

Tom himself identifies his life and fortunes with those of the "Ariel," and he reacts strongly to a vision of her sinking. "'I thought I saw her a wrack,'" he says, "' . . . and, I will own it, for it's as natural to love the craft you sail in as it is to love one's self, I will own that my manhood fetched a heavy sea-lurch at the sight'"

187

(284). When Tom's premonition proves correct, his refusal to leave the ship and his unwillingess to outlive her make his death a suicide. The crew reports that he "'always thought it sinful to desert a wreck, and that he did not even strike out once for his life, though he has been known to swim an hour when a whale has stove his boat'" (297). Consequently, even though Tom verbally committed his life to Providence shortly before the "Ariel" sank, he required Providence to save him, if it meant to, in spite of his own willful refusal to swim. His body is never found; "with reason," Cooper adds, "for the sea was never known to give up the body of the man who might be emphatically called its own dead" (298).

Long Tom Coffin sets a standard for the American sailor. Casting off his connections with the shore, he ships aboard the "Ariel" everything worth living for and rises to be captain of a gun. He desires no further promotion, but fills comfortably a berth fit for a man who believes

"... riches and honor are for the great and the larned, and there's nothing left for poor Tom Coffin to do, but to veer and haul on his own rolling-tackle, that he may ride out the rest of the gale of life without springing any of his old spars." (210)

His unquestionable merits do not indicate that he has been unjustly denied command; Tom fits his station as naturally as a line-tub fits a whale-boat. Like Wallace, the second lieutenant in *Jack Tier,* or Stephen Stimson, a religious seaman in *The Sea Lions,* he is wise enough to recognize his limitations. As though he were consci-

ously obeying the Delphic mottoes, "Know yourself"
and "Nothing too much," Tom finds at sea the highest
contentment of which he is capable.

When professionally competent and honest men
remain contentedly as minor officers in a ship, we
begin to look among Cooper's characters for the qualities which fit a man for command. He needs, it seems,
an extraordinary vitality, high intelligence, superior skill,
and the ability to become (to use Melville's image) a
keel along which the isolatoes that form the crew can
federate. With the exception of Peyton Dunwoodie as
seen on the battlefields of *The Spy,* Cooper does not
give us, on land, characters to match his sea captains.
They can be found, however, in nineteenth-century
American histories, and Prescott's Cortez is such a man.

The most memorable of Cooper's commanders have
the romantic historical hero's ability to inspire and control men even while the leader's responsibilities, recognized and willingly accepted, isolate him from the crew.
The captains of Cooper's merchant or government ships
must reconcile their orders with their own consciences,
with their responsibility for the crew, and with the
occurrences of the voyage. The free-booters, supranational and beholden to none, need satisfy only their
own and their crews' demands. These latter, more
colorful, leaders owe much to such Byronic figures as
the Corsair, Lara, the Giaour, or Childe Harold; they
are also indebted to such actual pirates as Sir Harry
Morgan, whose becoming governor of Jamaica made
piracy almost as respectable as it was glamorous.

There is, however, one important difference between
Cooper's pirates and Byron's. Byron's characters are a

throb of reaction; if they are, as he would have us believe, the last link in a chain of experiences, the chain itself has disappeared. By contrast, even the most romantic of Cooper's captains set to sea with orders or ideas, and Cooper attempts to analyze their reconciliation of these with the experiences of the tale. As a result, a Byronic figure may be the hero of a novel which makes an anti-romantic statement.

The mysterious "Mr. Gray" who is the titular hero of *The Pilot* (1823) is only a volunteer American, but he is worth a moment's consideration because he is the most purely Byronic of Cooper's naval commanders. The character incorporates as many characteristics of the romantic hero as Cooper could reconcile with the historical figure of John Paul Jones. No one was satisfied with the amalgam.[5] The Pilot's complaints are those of Childe Harold; he feels his country has failed him (145) and asserts, usually speaking "proudly" or "scornfully," his right to a buccaneer's supranational freedom. "'I was born on this orb, and I claim to be a citizen of it. A man with a soul [is] not to be limited by the arbitrary boundaries of tyrants and hirelings . . .'" (148). His skill is superb, but his ego is even more outstanding; "'This it is,'" he says, "'to be marked, among men, above all others in your calling'" (379).

Although Jones's superior skills let him move about more willfully than most men can, he is denied freedom.

---

[5] See Marcel Clavel, *Critics*, pp. 183–263. Susan Fenimore Cooper later wrote that Cooper himself was dissatisfied with the character. "It was not sufficiently true to reality. The pilot of the frigate was represented as a man of higher views and aims, in a moral sense, than the facts of the life of Paul Jones would justify."—*Pages and Pictures* (New York, 1865), p. 77. The *North American's* reviewer (April, 1824) gave Cooper credit for having invented here a character to replace, in modern literature, "the gods of ancient writers and the witches, fairies, and other supernatural beings" who both created and resolved improbable situations.

Fame is a psychological necessity for him, and he is, consequently, a driven man and a slave to his own obsession. The tale suggests a correspondence between Jones's psychological state and his political activity. He is portrayed as something of a professional revolutionary dashing from one troubled spot to another and perverting his superior abilities to serve a tawdry goal. His motivation is that of the mercenary except that Jones asks to be paid in glory. Griffith, the American officer who speaks Cooper's mind, suggests the antidote to such "romantic notions" as those Jones is possessed by. Jones should have

> "lived in a time and under circumstances when his con-
> summate knowledge of his profession, his cool, deliberate,
> and even desperate courage could have been exercised in
> a regular and well-supported navy, and the habits of his
> youth [should have] better qualified him to have borne,
> meekly, the honors he acquired in his age. . . ." (442)

As it is, however, Jones's obsession with glory makes him miserable as a man and prevents his becoming a hero.

There is no apparent connection between a man like Jones and the villainous Stephen Spike, a captain in *Jack Tier;* Spike is ugly, aging, insecure, greedy—mean in every ungolden sense of the word. Whereas Jones is a victim of his own "romantic notions," Spike is naturally evil and acts "under impulse of the lowest and most grovelling nature." Yet the two men have much in common; both are extraordinarily competent commanders, and what Cooper says of Spike is also true of Jones. He is "only great in a crisis and then merely as a seaman" (51). Both are morally unfit for command; but since Jones is only a pilot and is consequently restrained by officers of the navy, the damage he can do to others is slight. Spike, however, is a captain and that for one reason only: he owns the ship. His purchased power and unchecked evil nature destroy his subordinates and endanger his passengers. Spike's abuse of power, shown in some of the most brutal scenes Cooper ever wrote, clearly relates to Cooper's political concerns. Given an evil captain, the whole structure of government (here naval discipline) works for evil and even the good men in the crew find themselves involved in smuggling ammunition to America's enemies (the Mexicans) and murdering the passengers. Believing that no man was perfect and that some were thoroughly evil, Cooper tried to get Americans to understand that "the true practical secret of good government" consisted of "preventing vicious and selfish" leaders "from doing harm." [6] Cooper seems to have thought that men like Jones and Spike should be kept in subordinate positions; as junior officers, they could use their excellent training even while their flawed natures were controlled by their superiors in rank and morality. It would be interesting to know if Melville's *Billy Budd* deliberately challenges Cooper's optimism; Melville grants all Cooper's conditions, then shows that they are not enough to restrain evil.

One of Cooper's most popular sea captains (the titular hero of *Red Rover,* 1828) has certain of Jones's romantic characteristics but is the direct opposite of a commander like Stephen Spike. Red Rover is a typical swashbuckler (naturally good but apparently evil) whose basic character Cooper was to rework as Tom Tiller and the Skimmer of the Seas (pirates in *The Water-Witch,* 1831) and as the Frenchman Raoul Yvard (*Wing-and-*

---

[6] *Letters and Journals,* II, 321.

Wing, 1842). The Rover is also closely related to the amphibious outlaw who is the Italian hero of *The Bravo* (1831). "Red Rover" is the pseudonym of a Captain Heidegger, a native of the American colonies, who (like Jones) presents himself as a victim of English injustice and who has also become a citizen of the world. Unlike Jones, however, he is alienated for a real, not fancied, reason; he has wounded (presumably killed) a British officer who cursed the colonies. Consequently, his heart has a home even though his humor chooses the flag his ship flies.

Red Rover's crime suggests his weakness; he controls only with great difficulty his impassioned "fearful nature." Unsupported by religion or allegiance to the institutions of a settled homeland, he cannot know, much less trust, himself. He confesses his torment at one point:

> ". . . the innocent pillow their heads in quiet! Would to God the guilty might find some refuge, too, against the sting of thought! But we live in a world, and in a time, when men cannot be sure even of themselves." (329)

Not Red Rover himself, but the cabin-boy Roderick, pays the full price of the older man's psychological chaos. Identifying his life with the Rover's, and sensitive to each shifting mood, the boy refuses to leave the pirate and eventually goes mad. He is last seen alone with the Rover on the decks of the burning ship, gliding "like a lessened shadow of that restless figure" (461).[7]

---

[7] Melville reviewed this novel for the *Literary World* in 1850 and seems to have found in it suggestions not only for Pip but for other scenes and the character of Black Guinea. (See Chapter III.)

Red Rover, like Paul Jones, has his observers also. In addition to the heroine and her mature female companion, Cooper uses a Griffith-like naval officer named Wilder as an analyst. The two men display the author's interest in human doubles; Cooper shares with Twain that curiosity about the effect of environment on personality that inspired Twain's human philopena in *Pudd'nhead Wilson* and *The Prince and the Pauper*. This is not the psychological duality of Wyandotté, but rather a comparative study of two men of almost identical temperaments. Wilder proves to be an officer of the regular navy and has strong religious precepts that restrain his pride and passions. Wilder is only temporarily on leave from the ship Cooper describes as having "the repose of high order and perfect discipline." Otherwise, they are much alike; crews respond to them, often like "mettled chargers," and they are both young, handsome, quick to volunteer for action or responsibility, quicker still to understand men and events. At one time each commands a ship and an impromptu sailing match is described from Wilder's point of view.

> To him [Wilder] there was neither obscurity nor doubt in the midst of his midnight path. His eye had long been familiar with every star that rose from out the dark and ragged outline of the sea, nor was there a blast that swept across the ocean, that his burning cheek could not tell from what quarter of the heavens it poured out its power. He knew, and understood, each inclination made by the bows of his ship; his mind kept pace with her wanderings; and he had little need to consult any of the accessories of his art, to tell him what course to steer, or in what manner to guide the movements of the nice machine he governed. Still he was unable to explain the extra-ordinary evolutions of the stranger [the "Dolphin,"

sailed by Red Rover]. The smallest changes he ordered seemed rather anticipated than followed; and his hope of eluding a vigilance that proved so watchful was baffled by a facility of manoeuvring, and a superiority of sailing, that really began to assume, even to his intelligent eyes, the appearance of some unaccountable agency. (225)

This treatment of the two men is typical of Cooper; one romantic hero is described at length but is, in turn, confounded by the hyper-romanticism of a second. The match continues until "the dim tracery of the stranger's form [the pirate ship] had been swallowed by a flood of misty light, which, by this time, rolled along the sea like drifting vapor, semi-pellucid, preternatural, and seemingly tangible" (227).

Although Red Rover and his ship may be here something of an ontological riddle to Wilder, the two men are hard to distinguish when aboard the same ship. Wilder is, however, the more controlled, and is consequently awarded the heroine, restored to his long-lost family, and made a hero in the American Revolution. Red Rover, too, is revealed, at the end of the book, as an American patriot; James Grossman protests that this attempt to redeem "the reader's morality" destroys "one of the serious and ironic themes of the novel, our own delight in the spectacle of polite wickedness." [8] This objection points out the most important difference

---

[8] James Grossman, *Cooper*, p. 59. Grossman considers the book's subject "the ability of decent attractive people to engage in an evil life" (59). Philbrick's thesis is that Cooper's sea novels are the outcome of his "maritime nationalism and romanticism" (*James Fenimore Cooper and the Development of American Sea Fiction,* p. 42). Grossman is the more correct; Cooper was interested in character rather than chauvinism. Yet Philbrick offers a needed qualification. The point of Red Rover's history is this: when decent attractive people are neglected in their youth and can find, in their maturity, no occupation which allows them to exercise their natural morality, they must exist outside society until they are given a chance to participate in a just action (the Revolution).

between Wilder and Rover, for the themes of the novel intersect in the character of Red Rover. The exterior mystery and inner turmoil of the pirate allow Cooper to give him metaphysical extensions that cannot arise from the more circumspect behavior of Wilder. Beneath the surface story of adventure Cooper submerges his interest in American government and in appearance and reality.

The "Dolphin," Rover's ship, like the colonies has no real identity. It is noted for its speed and for its sudden ability to change colors. (It is frequently repainted to suit the occasion.) One of Rover's marvelous ironies is his painting the "Dolphin" black and disguising her as a slaver, in order to berth her safely in a New England harbor and assure the townspeople's warm welcome to his crew. The crew itself, suitably for a ship that carries the flags of all nations, is chosen "from among all the different people of the Christian world" (372). Like the community in *Wyandotté*, the "Dolphin" contains American Indians as well as representatives of every other nation or continent that had furnished a part of the colonies' polyglot population. In one of the most interesting scenes of the novel, Rover analyzes for Wilder those racial characteristics that make his "a most dangerous and (considering their numbers) a resistless crew" (372). Their success, however, depends primarily on their being "directed by the mind [Rover's] which had known how to obtain and to continue its despotic ascendency over their efforts . . . " (372). Rover can rule them successfully because he identifies accurately and then indulges their temperamental peculiarities. Even better, he makes their racial weaknesses into assets by placing the men at posts that allow them to express their natural tendencies. He does not personally like certain of the men, but he gives each credit for his particular abilities and is tolerant of all. So long as his catholic attitude rules, even the natural antagonists among the crew can coexist harmoniously.

The crew, however, does not realize it is being superbly governed; the men only know that they cannot succeed without the Rover's superior intelligence and knowledge. Like Odysseus, Rover can communicate with the higher spheres, and so long as the crew remembers his ability it obeys. Threatened mutiny is based on materialism; just as Odysseus' crew unleashed the winds when they thought the bag held gold, Rover's fractious companions rebel when they have lost a prize and are quieted only by Rover's superior skills and his reminding them that without him all prizes will be lost. (303) At the end of the central action, Rover buys freedom for Wilder and the women by giving all the ship's booty to the crew. When everyone is satisfied, the Rover is left to pace the decks of his burning ship.

Having chosen this restless but superior individual as the central character, Cooper has little difficulty in creating an atmosphere of illusion. A moral pirate who governs successfully a shipload of men unable to govern themselves is already more than human; his own skill and seamen's superstitious beliefs make him ubiquitous as well. Cooper places the whole tale as close as possible to that hypothetical meridian where romance becomes myth. As seen by landsmen or other seamen, commander, crew, and ship seem unreal; and the myth of the Flying Dutchman is mentioned frequently. Various persons suggest that all aboard the "Dolphin" are leagued with the devil and receive supernatural aid.

Throughout much of the book, consequently, the real meaning of this floating community is in doubt. Sometimes all those aboard the "Dolphin" seem to be the liberated; supranational and mobile without limit, they transcend petty distinctions and confining cultures. At other times (particularly when Wilder, the women, and a regular navy are the standards), they seem so much human waste tragically adrift on an indifferent sea. The reason for this ambivalence is that Rover is moral while his crew is not; evil (here presented as materialism and intolerance) is to be found on shore and in the crew of the "Dolphin." The supernatural qualities belong properly to the ship and commander only; both are superior; but until the world offers them a proper place, they can only roam, like tormented spirits, endlessly at sea.[9]

When isolated for examination, such a captain as Red Rover seems extravagantly romantic; he would even seem so in the novel had Cooper limited his own perspective to the ship and used its decks as a stage. Joseph Conrad saw immediately how Cooper turned potential melodrama into meaningful statement:

---

[9] A certain amount of Red Rover's ambivalence (like Natty Bumppo's) may be due to Cooper's sympathy with the good man who has been driven from his natural home. *Red Rover* was published before Cooper felt the full brunt of his country's disaffection, but he wrote Horatio Greenough in July, 1832, that "I go home, if home I do go, Master Greenough, to take a near view for myself, and to ascertain whether for the rest of my life I am to have a country or not. The decision will be prompt, free from all humbug, and final. It is time that we understand one another. I am tired of wasting life, means, and comfort in behalf of those who return abuse for services, and who show so much greater reverence for fraud and selfishness than for any thing else. I can never change my principles except on conviction, but I should be a very dog to fawn on those who spurn me. I am heart-sick and will say no more on the ungrateful subject."—*Letters and Journals*, II, 268. See also Cooper's letter to William Dunlap, *ibid.*, II, 360.

For James Fenimore Cooper nature was not the framework, it was an essential part of existence. He could hear
its voice, he could understand its silence, and he could
interpret both for us in his prose with all that felicity and
sureness of effect that belong to a poetical conception
alone. . . . His descriptions have the magistral ample-
ness of a gesture indicating the sweep of a vast horizon.
They embrace the colours of sunset, the peace of star-
light, the aspects of calm and storm, the great loneliness
of waters, the stillness of watchful coasts, and the alert
readiness which marks men who live face to face with
the promise and the menace of the sea.[10]

The menace as well as the promise of the sea means
that these commanders live temporally in a series of
crises and spatially in a world where waves sweep the
decks, where wind and tide sometimes seem to conspire
to smash them on reefs, and where a sound like a gun-
shot may be an attack or a broken mast. It is a world
in which human life is expendable and the conservation
of anything at all surprising. Almost every one of the sea
novels has at least one Gothic spectacle: Dillon's body
washes ashore in *The Pilot*; a seaman is eaten alive by
sharks in *The Water-Witch*; in *The Red Rover*, the
survivors of a sunken ship look upon a sight that foreshadows Melville's Fedallah.

A human form was seen, erect, and half exposed, advancing in the midst of the broken crest which was still
covering the dark declivity to the windward. For a moment it stood with the brine dripping from the drenched

---

[10] "Tales of the Sea," p. 55. Conrad acknowledges his indebtedness to Cooper in a letter to Arthur Symons (and apparently in
answer to something Symons had written): "F. Cooper is a rare
artist. He has been one of my masters. He is my constant companion."—*Joseph Conrad: Life and Letters* (New York, 1927), II, 73.

locks, like some being that had issued from the deep to turn its frightful features on the spectators; and then the lifeless body of a drowned man [drowned the day before] drove past the launch. (264)

The violence of Cooper's sea world supports the excesses of his heroes just as Malraux's terrorists are sustained by the world of *Man's Fate* while old Gisors, quietly smoking his pipe, seems anomalous. There is, on Cooper's sea, no resting place.

To go to sea in these novels is not to engage in any rite of purification; yet "sea change" is a valid phenomenon for Cooper. He wrote in *Jack Tier* that only the experienced seaman could "think, read, and pursue the customary train of reasoning on board a ship" (174) that he practiced ashore. The key word here is "customary," for the act of embarkation prompts man to reassess his experience at the same time that he becomes more sensitive and responsive to it. Cooper describes, in *Red Rover,* the psychological effect of going to sea:

> One hour of the free intercourse of a ship can do more towards softening the cold exterior in which the world encrusts the best of human feelings, than weeks of the unmeaning ceremonies of the land. He who has not felt this truth, would do well to distrust his own companionable qualities. It would seem that man, when he finds himself in the solitude of the ocean, most feels his dependency on others for happiness. He yields to sentiments with which he trifled in the wantonness of security, and is glad to seek relief in the sympathies of his kind. (195)

As the references to encrusted feelings and wanton security suggest, going to sea strips off hampering custom but exposes the nerves at the same time. As a consequence, the act prepares a man for an intensification of experience.

Considered in time, this intensification takes the form of an acceleration of processes. The formation of friendships or testing of character that might take years on land are possible, at sea, in the action of moments. Yet the results of such tests are valid. Deserving characters profit by this quality of sea life; the Negro Neb and a plain sailor like Tom Coffin earn at sea personal recognition that a lifetime of patient toil on land would not obtain for them. Conversely, the cowardice and greed of an Ithuel Bolt, or the desperate acquisitiveness of a Stephen Spike or Daggett are here quickly revealed. Where processes are concerned, the stability of the land exerts a braking action that, as compared with the sea, postpones rewards due and too long protects the meretricious.

Qualitatively, the intensification of experience functions much as Cooper's other devices of showing a character in crucial action, on his death bed or in old age. Such situations dissolve masking forms and reveal the essence of a man. The most complex analyses are made of European, not American, commanders caught in a conflict of principles, rigid institutions, and personal loyalties. Cooper's American captains have no complex social structures to battle since they are in the pre-Revolutionary or Revolutionary Navy or post-Revolutionary merchant marine. Consequently, they have enough latitude to succeed by seeing clearly, thinking honestly, and grounding their decisions on broad international law. Captain Truck's beloved Vattel is for him the same universally valid system based on natural law that the Constitution is for the gentry.[11] Personally, the plain commanders (like Captains Barnstable, Truck, Woolston, Poke, or Gardiner) share with the romantic ones a "parental responsibility from which the sea commander is never exempt" (*The Pilot*, 286). Under their firm but benevolent paternalism, as under the gentry's, men can coexist in harmony and safety and can expand because protected from their own and their shipmates' natural weaknesses. When ruled by a good captain, the ship is, as we have said, an ideal community.

At the same time, however, Cooper denies this community any real sense of permanence. The seaman is denied the continuity that land represents for the gentry. For the unstable sea itself discourages plans for an earthly future and emphasizes the impermanence and sterility of shipboard life. Life's transiency, with all its promises and menace, is a recurring theme in Cooper and more than any other community the men of a ship realize fully that life is largely a striving and Heaven is the home of perfection. Thus it is a seaman who recognizes both a proper goal for society and the impossibility of its earthly attainment: "Content," he says, "is like the North Star—we seamen steer for it, while none can ever reach it" (*The Heidenmauer*, 65).

As individuals, Tom Coffin and a few others like him are exceptional; they are common men who become uncommon by submerging the self in the sea and whose life ends when the ship dies. Most of the seamen, however, return eventually to the land; the ship is only

---

[11] Emerich de Vattel, a Swiss philosopher and jurist, wrote a book translated in 1760, as the *Law of Nations*, that illustrated a growing concept of international law as resting on natural laws. Captain Truck, the American packet skipper of *Homeward Bound* and *Home as Found*, relates his every decision to Vattel.

temporarily a place of removal. If we let actions speak, as actions do in Cooper, these men fit D. H. Lawrence's description of Americans as "a vast republic of escaped slaves. . . . And a minority of earnest, self-tortured people." Long before Lawrence, Cooper had dramatized in fiction the question Lawrence then asks: "Which will win in America, the escaped slaves, or the new whole men?" [12]

[12] *Studies in Classic American Literature*, pp. 15, 18.

VIII

HIMSELF ALONE

Thus not only does democracy make every man forget his ancestors, but it hides his descendants and separates his contemporaries from him; it throws him back forever upon himself alone and threatens in the end to confine him entirely within the solitude of his own heart.

—Alexis de Tocqueville*

THE ALIENATED INDIVIDUAL that Tocqueville predicted and some of Cooper's novels portray was to become familiar in the American literature that followed. Philip Rieff may claim too much in saying that Tocqueville's is "perhaps the greatest single passage describing modern man,"[1] but his suggestion helps to explain the vitality and pertinence of certain of Cooper's characters.

We have seen that Cooper's America is composed largely of communities which are entities because they share something: a race, a religion, a sex, an occupation. An individual's physical separation from his true community is not important. The Scotchman working in a garden in *Wyandotté* may be hundreds of miles from another Scottish immigrant, but they share the same community. In any deep sense of attachment, they

---

* *Democracy in America*, Vol. II.
[1] "The Analytic Attitude," *Encounter*, XVIII, No. 6 (1962), 23 n.

"belong" to the community of Scots rather than to the random group accidentally co-existing within the stockade at the Hutted Knoll. When such groups clash, the result is warfare, destruction of settlements, or new laws. Furthermore, the group with the most power wins. In Cooper's world, might may not make right, but it certainly determines mores. The story of the groups that lose this battle in which government and culture conjoin is the story of extinction; the Indians, the Dutch, and the gentry are all vanishing Americans. Seamen, women, and Negroes lose personal identity and submit to the prevailing culture, and the culture which triumphs everywhere on land is that of the Connecticut Yankee.

Cooper shows one alternative to extinction or submission—detachment from society. When a lone man, estranged from all groups, approaches one of them in the novels, the resulting collisions, evasions, and adjustments become judgments. The individual has no pattern for his life, and life becomes for him a series of problems to be defined and answers to be found through experience. Mobile and plastic, he has to learn the hardest lesson about freedom: that it is more easily won than wisely used. For him, as for many moderns, there are few lines more forlorn than Milton's description of Adam and Eve: "The World was all before them, where to choose/ Their place of rest" (*Paradise Lost*, XII).

Cooper seems to have arrived at this theme, the individual's search for a resting place, almost by accident. Convinced that he could not be satisfied with imitation of drawing-room novels, and wanting to write a book that "should be purely American," he based his second novel, *The Spy*, on a tale John Jay told him. The central character, the setting, and the historical back-

ground of the novel are "purely American," but we
recognize also much that is derivative. The no man's
land between the British and colonial lines functions as
Scott's border served Rob Roy. The secluded heights
from which Washington and Harvey Birch look down
on the world would be familiar, even did they not exist,
as the brooding places of the romantic poets. Katy
Haynes's view of Washington, a cloaked figure looming
just outside her door, is suited equally to the Gothic
novel and to the epic technique of showing great men
as larger than normal size. Among the minor characters,
there are such resemblances as that of Dr. Sitgreaves to
Smollett's surgeons, and of Betty Flanagan to Miss
Edgeworth's Irish. (Miss Edgeworth herself thought
Betty "incomparable" as a character.) [2] Also among the
minor characters, however, we find the Negro Caesar
who was an "original" in American fiction.

Cooper's handling of the character of Harvey Birch
is the most significant thing about the novel. Given the
facts of the tale, Cooper began to look for motivation
that both he and his readers would accept. He suggests
in the Preface that the meanness of Harvey's circumstances may explain his willingness to detach himself
from the society and approval of other men.

> This man . . . belonged to a condition in life which
> rendered him the least reluctant to appear in so equivocal
> a character. He was poor, ignorant, so far as the usual
> instruction was concerned; but cool, shrewd, and fearless
> by nature. (iv)

Having asserted Birch's noble nature, and suggested he
had little to lose, Cooper, as though bothered by Birch's

---

[2] Letter to Mrs. Ruxton, July 8, 1822, as quoted by Marcel Clavel,
Critics, p. 114.

remaining ignobility, suggests that a love of country has "purifying consequences," particularly in times of national peril. This was one of John Jay's favorite theories, and both he and Cooper hoped that the ship of state could command a loyalty equal to the seaman's traditional feeling for his ship. Still a third reason for Birch's behavior is inserted in the novel itself; Cooper says the "superior intelligence" of Harvey's father makes the neighbors think "they had known better fortunes in the land of their nativity" (27). This hint, that the Birches may be gentlemen who have fallen on evil times, makes Harvey more understandable to Cooper and to those of his contemporaries who were capable of understanding gentlemen.[3] Yet Cooper never seems completely at ease with his heroic commoner; fortunately, the character that emerges from the novel is more consistent and credible than the one Cooper tries to explain.

As usual, action and point of view are important. Harvey is seen, usually, by other characters. This has the effect Elizabeth Bowen describes: "Certain charac-

---

[3] Henry Nash Smith has an interesting discussion of this problem. He suggests that Cooper, like his contemporaries, could not really accept the rise to gentility of the common man, and that the writers attempted rather to promote individuals out of their true class. (See *Virgin Land*, pp. 156–57.) The danger is that these discussions about "gentility" bring us perilously close to snobbishness (pride of status rather than pride of function or character).

How unfair such a reading would be to Cooper and his circle, Bryant's description of Harvey Birch may suggest. Bryant says of Harvey's creator that along with "extreme circumspection, fertility in stratagem, and the art of concealing his real character,—qualities which, in conjunction with selfishness and greediness, make the scoundrel, he has bestowed the virtues of generosity, magnanimity, an intense love of country, a fidelity not to be corrupted, and a disinterestedness beyond temptation." —*Memorial of James Fenimore Cooper* (New York, 1852), p. 44. These qualities go deeper into time and morality than "gentility" does.

ters gain in importance and magnetism by being only
seen; this makes them more romantic, fatal-seeming,
sinister." [4] This method, used here with Harvey Birch,
is also used with all the isolated men except Miles
Wallingford. They reveal themselves only in their
actions and dialogue. The other characters, who do the
seeing, represent the values and desires of their own
static groups. Harvey's housekeeper, for instance, being
a woman, thinks Harvey should marry her and settle
down "like other men of his years and property" (4).
She tells Washington that Harvey is willful and errant—
which he is so far as she is concerned. " 'Harvey Birch
will have his own way, and die a vagabond after all!' "
What to Katy Haynes is vagabondage, is to Harvey
freedom; and here, long before Conrad or Faulkner,
woman is conformity's lure and a threat to a man's
"own way."

Katy also suggests something else about Harvey. She
complains that she " 'can hardly remember his face.' "
Harvey's lack of recognizable identity becomes a motif;
only his essential being, which is unseen and inflexibly
given to his duty, remains stable. His exterior is an
exercise in shape-shifting. He is seen as a dromedary
and as a devil; he is heard as a whisper and a shout. In
several disguises, he becomes also Betty Flanagan and
a Puritan zealot. Cooper himself describes Harvey in
terms that challenge sense perception; "at first sight" he
does not seem strong, but he throws his heavy pack
about "with great dexterity." "His eyes were grey,
sunken, restless" and "seemed to read the very soul"

---

[4] "Notes on Writing a Novel," *Orion*, II, reprinted in *Modern
Literary Criticism*, ed. Irving Howe (New York, 1958), p. 58.

of those he views in "flitting moments." His face can be either "lively, active, and flexible" or "abstracted and restless."

Harvey's profession supports this quality of elusiveness. To those he deals with, he is more spectral than human; they do not know his origin or his end; and when he is not before their eyes, he does not exist. There is something sinister about a character who simply appears and vanishes, apparently at will; society cannot label him, and what they cannot label they distrust.[5] How much the character of Harvey Birch influenced Constance Rourke's description of the Yankee peddler we cannot know, but she says, "He was a myth, a fantasy. . . . Masquerade was as common to him as mullein in his stony pastures. He appeared a dozen things he was not."[6] In Miss Rourke's description, as in Cooper's novel, the peddler's approaching figure is felt as a threat by members of the communities he invades. He is so mobile as to be almost ubiquitous: "glances at him were uncertain and fleeting. The intermediate time no eye could penetrate. For months he disappeared, and no traces of his course were ever known" (125). Yet "many a sentinel, placed in the gorges of the mountains, spoke of a strange figure that had been seen gliding by them in the mists of evening" (125).

Unable to tolerate him as a mystery, these people impose on Harvey some explanation that lets them be comfortable about his freedom—or which in effect denies his freedom. They suggest compulsions that might drive him to be other than they are. Thus Katy, unwilling to grant him immunity from marriage, snares him with

---

[5] Cooper's last novel, *The Ways of the Hour* contains an attorney who realizes he was mistaken in not giving the local townspeople a motive they can understand for his defending an accused girl. Defense of the innocent per se is incomprehensible to them.

[6] *American Humor*, pp. 17–18.

another category. He is a "vagabond" by nature. Others believe him gripped by the ruling passion of avarice. Cooper warns that it is the "superficial observer" that so decides, but most of the people in the novel think him greedy. Harvey recognizes and takes advantage of their error.[7]

The price of Harvey's freedom, in the novel, is letting himself be misunderstood. Only by allowing society to attribute to him the values it understands, can he get it to relax its vigilance against him. He takes on, consequently, the character expected by others. When Betty Flanagan, drunk, staggers into the hut where he is held prisoner, the sentinels expect Betty to emerge, and Harvey appears disguised as Betty (Chapter XVII). The outlaw band of Skinners do not fear Harvey, but they do fear the cavalry of Captain Jack Lawton; and it takes only a shout, " 'This way, Captain Jack—here are the rascals 'ating by a fire—,' " to rout them. Sergeant Hollister believes Harvey is the devil, so Birch rouses him with cryptic exhortation and makes no attempt to explain. He gets his chance to rescue Henry Wharton by using the zealousness of the aunt, Miss Peyton. Disguised as a fanatic minister, Harvey gets the woman out of the way by mentioning, among other things, that " 'humility becometh thy sex, and lost condition.' " And he escapes those who first mistake him for a dromedary and who hunt him " 'like a beast of the forest!' " (115)

---

[7] William R. Taylor (*Cavalier and Yankee*) suggests the potential duality of the Yankee figure by referring to a "transcendent" Yankee who only *seems* ignoble. His thesis is largely supported by the character of Birch, of whom he says: "The real Yankee, whose appearance only was given to Harvey Birch, is an unpleasant type: hypocrite, chiseler, fiend. He rarely shows his undisguised face in good company. He is an outcast of a sort, an Ishmael, whose grasping hand is turned against everyone. If the transcendent Yankee is kept in the woods or at sea, the real Yankee is kept in the cellar or locked in the woodshed like an idiot kinsman. He is always apt to break out" (p. 108).

by responding with animal fleetness and a wild thing's familiarity with the terrain.

Because of all this shape-shifting, Harvey can be understood at only a few moments in the action. The earliest scene which reveals his basic goodness is that in which his dying father blesses him.[8] His father predicts that Harvey will be "'a pilgrim through life. The bruised reed may endure, but it will never rise'" (130). Once his father is dead, Harvey reflects bitterly:

"The valley is lovely and the people like all the race of man. But to me it matters nothing; all places are now alike, and all faces equally strange." (182)

The sense of alienation, of being misunderstood by everyone, wounds Harvey beyond all else. As he rescues Henry Wharton, he lapses for a few moments into self-awareness and tells Henry what it is like to await hanging as a spy. On this rare occasion, Harvey speaks his thoughts (as Natty Bumppo often reveals his own) in a musing monologue.

"It is hard to die at the best, Captain Wharton; but to spend your last moments alone and unpitied, to know that none near you so much as think of the fate that is to you the closing of all that is earthly; to think that, in a few hours, you are to be led from the gloom, which as you dwell on what follows, becomes dear to you, as if you were a wild beast; and to lose sight of everything amidst the jeers and scoffs of your fellow-creatures—that, Captain Wharton, that indeed is to die!" (359)

Remembering this feeling of having been deserted by all humanity, Birch confesses that he thought HE had

---

[8] The dying father's blessing of the loyal and misunderstood son is here given early in the novel, but it is reserved in *The Bravo* as one belated proof of the Bravo's real innocence (373).

also forgotten. The "he" referred to is Washington, who alone knows Birch's true function. Only he can be expected to understand, though one other character learns something about Birch. Captain Lawton of the Virginia cavalry is less inclined than the others to indulge in aprioristic speculation. He is consequently more perceptive than the rest, and less easily maneuvered by Birch, who says of him, "'the devil can't deceive him; I never could but once!'" (51). Lawton, having learned from one experience not to prejudge Birch, concludes eventually that "'either avarice or delusion has led a noble heart astray'" (279). Lawton never knows that Birch is on his, and not the enemy's, side. In mentioning delusion, he is close to the emotional truth, for the patriotism that Cooper and Jay saw as "purifying" is a driving force of obsessive power.[9]

Lawton is killed in action, and never understands Birch. The other man, Washington, is heavily depended on for understanding, but shows finally the horrifying depth of cleavage between the alienated individual and the accepted and familiar values of society. If Harvey's story is tragic, its final measure is in Washington's own betrayal, quite inadvertently, that he, too, is one of the "Others." Once the war is over and Harvey appears for an interview, Washington begins well enough by saying

> "You have I trusted more than all; I early saw in you a regard to truth and principle, that, I am pleased to say, has never deceived me—you alone know my secret agents in the city, and on your fidelity depend, not only their fortunes, but their lives." (418)

[9] Carl Van Doren compares Harvey's motivation with the daemonic impulses of Brockden Brown's characters. "Patriotism drives Birch relentlessly to his destiny, at once wrecking and honoring him."—*The American Novel* (New York, 1940), p. 25. Whether Harvey is "wrecked" or not depends, of course, on other values.

Harvey responds by gradually raising his head during
Washington's praise until he stands upright. But Washington then offers a bag of gold, apologizing that there
is not more; and when Harvey moves back in refusal,
Washington thinks that the pay is too small. Harvey
can only ask, "'Does your excellency think that I have
exposed my life, and blasted my character, for money?'"
Washington answers, "'If not for money, what then?'"
(419). This final thrust makes Harvey's estrangement
complete; the one man who should understand does not.
Washington then deepens the wound by asking how
the others, whose identity Birch must continue to conceal, can have a pledge of his fidelity. Birch turns out
to understand honor more thoroughly than anyone else
as he explains to Washington that his refusal of the
gold is in itself the best pledge of his secrecy. Much too
belatedly for the good of his own character, Washington
then says, "'Now, indeed, I know you.'" He pledges
his secret friendship, and, as though speaking with a
mouthful of eagle feathers, delivers his own benediction:

"That Providence destines this country to some great and
glorious fate I must believe, while I witness the patriotism
that pervades the bosoms of her lowest citizens." (421)

When the fictional Washington fails Harvey at the
last, his act throws a retrospective gloom over the book;
the distinctions he makes about classes seem tactless, to
say the least. Cooper is being unjust to the real Washington (who, unless we have been badly deceived,
would have understood disinterestedness); yet Washington's obtuseness succeeds in its artistic effect on the
characterization of Harvey. In Cooper's later novels,

heroes have a natural affinity. A similar situation in *Wing-and-Wing* arises from a misunderstanding when the British commander, Captain Cuffe, tries to get the Frenchman, Raoul Yvard, to trade his ship for his life. Raoul's answer is, "'. . . I forgive you, Monsieur, if you can forgive yourself. . . . '" Finally recognizing each other as men of honor, they "know" each other. As Raoul says, "'Brave men can understand one another, all over the world.'"

Cooper regretted the characterization of Washington and used historical figures more charily after this, but the character of Harvey is successful in spite of some confusion. His plasticity is superficial, however, his shape-shifting a matter of conjuring; at the core he is solid and sufficient. His dedication and his integrity are inseparable, yet it is these that separate him from the static groups in society and force those who question him to reveal themselves. One of Cooper's great virtues was his refusal to oversimplify history; and through this single-minded peddler who masquerades as a troop, he conveys something of the moral dilemma the Revolution represented for many colonists.

At the same time, Harvey, the first of the lone characters in Cooper, achieves an affinity with Nature that none of the persons in society possesses. He knows more about the forest than anyone else; he can see farther, better, and more truly than the others. He is more sensitive to whether the night will be light or dark, and the nights (as though appreciating his interest) often cast shadows and produce storms that match or cloak his actions. The interrelation of emotion, character, action, and physical phenomena is so close that Brady has described him as "the first of Cooper's guardian presences, a mythopoeic emanation, almost, of the American landscape." [10]

At the same time, Harvey's rapport with "unhand-selled savage nature" (to borrow Emerson's phrase from "The American Scholar") establishes him as a counter-hero to the actual hero of the American public. At the time of the book's appearance, Harvey was considered "unmotivated" by at least one critic who was not at all worried about "an absorption in money-making and material things" that threatened to "replace the intel-lectual and spiritual heritage" [11] Americans had proposed as the standards for their country. Few of the profes-sional reviewers showed more intelligence, and many complained that the book had no hero at all.

Cooper, nevertheless, had the wit to see that, as Melville was to say, "Something further may follow of this Masquerade." He relied, again and again, on the methods he worked out for Harvey's characterization; they underlie Natty Bumppo's character, obviously, and set a pattern as well for the series of sea captains who are, like Harvey, caught in mid-life and provided with a plausible reason for disaffection with society. Like

---

[10] "Myth-Maker and Christian Romancer," p. 72. Harvey is, of course, the first character with whom Cooper achieves that inter-penetration of setting and life that Conrad so much admired in his sea novels.

[11] William R. Taylor, *Cavalier and Yankee*, p. 18. There is a great deal of truth in Taylor's later comment that Cooper "had dis-covered that the most 'heroic' thing an American could do was to give up money, a kind of renunciation deemed almost more praise-worthy than the sacrifice of one's life" (105).

Susan Fenimore Cooper reports that a "prominent Wall Street merchant" accosted Cooper on Broadway to say how much he ad-mired *The Spy*, but complained: "Of course I thought until the last page, that he would be well paid for his services; but just as I expected to see it all settled he refuses the gold. There was your great mistake. You should have given Harvey some motive."— Susan Fenimore Cooper, "A Glance Backward," *Atlantic Monthly*, LIX (February, 1887), p. 205.

Harvey, the pirate Red Rover is obsessed with patriotism; the Skimmer of the Seas is repelled by governmental injustices and dishonesty. These occupy, however, a shipboard society that cushions them against absolute loneliness, and the reasons for their leaving the land are not actually crucial to the novels. Often their motivation seems an excuse to ally buccaneering adventure with a moral cause.

In the saga of Miles Wallingford, however, Cooper tried something completely different. Whereas Harvey does not change, but is variously seen from the outside, Miles Wallingford is himself the point-of-view character; and the character changes in response to his experiences on shore and at sea. It is the nearest thing to a fictional autobiography that Cooper ever wrote, and it is his only serious attempt to reconcile the isolated individual with society. It ends with a compromise, but the two volumes in which the hero's growth is detailed contain another story of willful estrangement from an original society and the ensuing experiences of an alienated consciousness.

IX

HISTORY AND HYPOTHESIS

IN PHRASING THE QUESTION, one realizes how inevitable it was that Cooper would write the story: What would happen to a young landed gentleman who left home and cast his lot equally with all the other men who were forming new societies aboard the ships of the American merchant marine? Cooper answered in a picaresque double-length novel, *Afloat and Ashore* and *Miles Wallingford*, published in 1844.[1] Much of the history of Miles Wallingford, the hero, is the might-have-been of Cooper's life, particularly the general pattern in which Miles returns again and again to sea— as Cooper at times threatened or wished to do. Perhaps for this reason Miles seems to have been less shaped by the author than projected from him, and he inhabits simultaneously a multiplicity of spheres. Geographically, he moves through most of the world (ranging even more widely than Cooper himself); socially, he breaks away from his original group and, after starting at the bottom, rises to a responsible position as a sea captain; psycho-

---

[1] While *Afloat and Ashore* and *Miles Wallingford* were published as companion novels (like *Homeward Bound* and *Home as Found*), the two are really one book, the first ending with the rescue of Miles and Andrew Drewett from drowning and the second beginning with the attempts to revive Andrew. They are commonly considered as parts I and II of a single work and page references here are given accordingly.

logically, his moods fluctuate with his fortunes and color the world he sees until he returns to the land and equanimity at the end of the second volume.

Clearly an experiment in social mobility, Miles is also the product of Cooper's experimentation with novelistic techniques. The narrative is told in the first person by Miles himself, but Miles is an old man at the time of the telling; the method allows a mature judgment to comment on, and sometimes undercut, youthful opinions. As James Grossman has pointed out, the technique lets Cooper intrude on the adventure story and make "the intrusion a profitable part of the adventure." Cooper's earlier experiments with first person narrative had been of a different kind, or rather of several kinds. In *The Monikins*, Giles Goldencalf had recounted his own adventures in a prose Yvor Winters has described: "The cold and formal irony of the prose achieves at times a metaphysical violence which puts one in mind of Pope." [2] Cooper could not sustain the effect throughout the book; but while it lasts (and particularly when it is applied to English nobility and the "social stake" theory), it is devastating. Eight years later, in 1843, he wrote two biographical studies in the first person: *Le Mouchoir* and *Ned Myers*. The first of these, an "autobiographical romance," is really another experiment in social satire.[3] By adhering to the point of view of an extremely well-educated pocket handkerchief, Cooper achieved a fresh approach and avoided

---

[2] *In Defense of Reason*, p. 184.

[3] Cooper probably used, as a model, Charles Johnstone's *Chrysal, or the Adventures of a Guinea* (1760–65); the method combines a picaresque pattern with a non-human point of view in order to produce social satire. Smollett's *Adventures of an Atom* is also indebted to this method, as are numerous other English and French tales; Apuleius' *The Golden Ass* seems to be the original.

the most damaging conventions. He described even the heroine drily and strangled the same old *bêtes noires* with quiet efficiency: being a Yankee became merely "the only subject of self-felicitation with which I am acquainted that men can indulge in without awakening the envy of their fellow creatures . . . " (2). The second book tells the story, "edited" by Cooper, of a shipmate's life squandered in the United States merchant marine. Cooper had once saved Ned Myers' life; and in January, 1843, Myers wrote to Cooper to ask if he had sailed aboard the "Stirling" on its voyage to London in 1806. Cooper in replying invited the converted drunkard to Otsego Hall, where the two men spent five months together and wrote Ned's memoirs.

These were the books that prepared for the characterization of Miles Wallingford and the fictional techniques Cooper used in telling his history. The subtitle to *Ned Myers, A Life Before the Mast,* gracefully acknowledges Richard Dana's previous memoirs; "a copy had been timidly presented to Cooper by young Dana's father" in 1840.[4] Also, of course, *Ned Myers* and the rest have a general debt to the biographical and travel narratives of the time. Since the story was Ned's, however, Cooper made a conscious effort "to adhere as closely to the very language of his subject as circumstances will at all allow; and in many places he feels confident that no art of his own could, in any respect, improve it" (vii). Imposing only a historian's order on Ned's experiences, Cooper arrived at a new informality

---

[4] James Grossman, *James Fenimore Cooper,* p. 184. Cooper's borrowings from and relation to various narratives of exploration and seamanship have been admirably collected and recorded in Thomas Philbrick's *James Fenimore Cooper and the Development of American Sea Fiction.*

of tone and clarity of style, and he kept the pose of "editor" through the Littlepage novels.

For Miles Wallingford's history, Cooper expands the "I" until it is, if not Everyman, something like a hypothetical American. It is partly this quality of projection that accounts for Miles's size in the novel. Like the representative man of Emerson's essays or nineteenth-century histories,[5] he means more than he actually is.

We are told that the Wallingfords bought Clawbonny, their country estate, from the Dutch in 1707. Miles's father bore a scar, left by a head-wound received in the Revolution, that was something of a family totem. Having invented a device to arrest their millwheel, the senior Wallingford had clambered onto the wheel to prove his faith in the machinery and had been killed when his invention failed. His seaman's grip would have saved him, had his head not been crushed; "the principal injury had been received on that much-prized scar" (I, 7). Miles, then a thirteen-year-old lad, was present at the time; and while his memory does not return again and again to the scene, its significance is amply insisted on by Cooper. Because of his attempt to thwart a native force (the stream) through his own ingenuity, the senior Wallingford is crushed between the machine and a natural power.[6]

Since Miles was born the day Cornwallis surrendered, he and the United States have literally started life together. He is thus historically a representative man. Yet his personal history is symbolic, and his growth is described as he alternately inhabits two different worlds:

---

[5] See David Levin, *History as Romantic Art,* chap. iii.

[6] This theme, which will sound familiar to Henry Adams' readers, is the same that Leo Marx has designated as "the great issue of our culture."—"Two Kingdoms of Force," *Massachusetts Review,* I (October, 1959), 95.

the social world on shore and the shipboard world at sea. His story is that of a character who voluntarily isolates himself from his original group, tests himself (like a Hemingway hero) in a series of adventures, and finally rejoins a carefully selected segment of society on shore. During the process, Miles learns, as it were, by accretion. In the course of his adventures, he encounters most of the ways by which men have traditionally approached the truth; he chiefly learns the dangers of a priori speculation and the comparative validity of experience. At one time, early in his adventures, a boatload of sailors is saved only because Miles sees with his own eyes an island that, according to the theories of his superior officers, cannot be where it is.[7]

Miles has two companions when he impulsively runs away to sea; one is his boyhood friend, the Episcopalian minister's son, Rupert Hardinge. Rupert soon proves to be incompetent, demanding, lazy, selfish, and dishonest. The third boy, the Negro Neb, quickly becomes valued by Miles (and eventually by others) for his loyalty, unselfishness, and seamanship. Since all three have removed themselves from all of their original influences

---

[7] Cooper could have obtained the background for such scenes from Locke or any of the literature based on his psychology; or it may come also from a source as ancient as Epicurus, who counseled: "We must not conduct the study of nature in accordance with empty assumptions and arbitrary rules but in agreement with the demands of the phenomena; what our life needs is not subjective theories nor superficial opinions but the means of living without disturbances"; and, "If a man enters into a struggle with the self-evident testimony of the senses he will never be able to share in true peace of mind." Peter Green, quoting these passages, says that Epicurus, in "positing Sensations as the only valid criteria from which reason could work . . . showed himself not so much an empiricist as a pioneer in scientific and psychological method."— *Essays in Antiquity* (Cleveland, 1960), pp. 81–82.

Denial of the testimony of the senses accounts for the ridiculous errors of such "scientists" as Dr. Ergot in *The Wept of Wish-Ton-Wish* and Obed Bat in *The Prairie*. Natty Bumppo never argues with this "self-evident testimony" and consequently "sees" more clearly and correctly than those around him.

and are almost without funds, their ensuing adventures are a study in equality of opportunity. Rupert fails to take advantage of his chance and returns to shore to take advantage of other people instead. Miles applies himself industriously and rises in rank; and Neb (who had to stow away to get on board the first ship) also prospers, although Miles warns that it is doubtful that Neb can ever "acquire exactly the same credit as a white man" (I, 63).

Miles's adventures at sea have all the discontinuity of a picaresque novel; and by the second volume he has decided that "there is no question that man, at the bottom, has a good deal of the wild beast in him" (II, 276). His experiences fully justify this conclusion about the nature of man, and yet Miles is no misanthrope. While holding onto his original principles, he has roamed freely across class and racial barriers and has found beyond them his two closest friends. These other men, Neb and Moses Marble (a first mate), function in the novels as antithetical extensions of Miles's own self.

The crucial difference between Neb and Miles is their attitudes toward responsibility. Neb understands and acts on personal loyalty, but he quite naturally has no conception of abstract and impersonal responsibility; as a result, Neb invariably eats and sleeps undisturbed, unconsciously assuming that someone will be responsible for the ship. Miles occasionally envies Neb this ability, particularly during severe storms which Miles considers a threat and Neb welcomes as magnificent entertainment. Neb identifies himself with Miles's honors, but has no notion of his problems or worries. In action, however, which Neb understands, he consistently protects and often saves Miles's life, and he could be

considered a life force. The two have not been long at
sea before Miles concludes: "A sterling fellow was
Neb, and I got in time to love him very much as I
can conceive one would love a brother" (I, 120). At
the end of the first volume, Neb saves Miles from
drowning, and Miles's description of the affair ends in
a peculiar mixture of admiration, prejudice, gratitude,
and brotherly insensitivity.

> I was dragged into the boat, I scarcely know how, and
> lay down completely exhausted. . . . In a moment, Neb,
> dripping like a black river-god, and glistening like a wet
> bottle, placed himself in the bottom of the boat, took my
> head into his lap, and began to squeeze the water from
> my hair, and to dry my face with some one's handker-
> chief—I trust it was not his own.   (I, 536)

Their mutual affection continues, and they retire to
Clawbonny together at the end of the second volume;
as Neb says, "I belong to you, you belong to me, and
we belong to one anodder" (I, 417).

Whereas Neb tries to conserve Miles's life, Moses
Marble acts out a contrary impulse to self-destruction.
Marble is clearly one of the men Tocqueville described
as being "thrown back forever upon himself alone." In
the narrative, Marble outranks Miles through much of
the first two voyages; and on the second voyage, the
death of the captain elevates Marble to command. He
makes mistakes. In an incident indebted both to Washington Irving's Astoria and to the "Somers" mutiny
affair,[8] Marble orders an Indian (named Smudge)

---

[8] Cooper's connection with the "Somers" affair (largely through
his relations with Captain Alexander Slidell MacKenzie) involves
coincidences more numerous and incredible than any of Cooper's
novels can offer. By the time he wrote his "Review" for Proceedings
of the Naval Court Martial in the Case of Alexander Slidell Mac-

hanged, then almost immediately regrets the action. Under the influence, as Miles recognizes, of a "mortified feeling" (I, 281) at the mistakes he has made, Marble tries desperately to recover their losses; he only makes more errors and endangers more people, and finally insists that Miles take over command. By this time, they have all arrived at a Pacific island, and Marble announces his intention to remain there forever. Marble's psychology here seems drawn from *Ned Myers,* for Ned confesses, "Now, nature has so formed me, that any disgust, or disappointment, makes me reckless, and awakens a desire to revenge myself, on myself, as I may say" (165). As Miles tries to dissuade Marble, the dialogue reveals Marble's immediate depression and his long-standing feeling of estrangement.

Marble tells Miles that he was a foundling left in a basket on a tomb-stone in a stone-cutter's yard. " 'They hadn't the decency to pin even a name . . . to my shirt; no—they just set me afloat on that bit of tombstone,' " he complains, " 'and cast off the standing part of what fastened me to anything human' " (I, 304). Marble combines self-hatred and his resentment at the world's neglect in an emotional state for which Ned Myers had furnished the paradigm: "As is common with

---

Kenzie in 1844, Cooper was entangled personally, politically, professionally, and morally with the issues arising from MacKenzie's 1842 hanging of two crewmen and a midshipman for "mutiny." One of Cooper's conclusions was that laws had to be administered justly to be effective. He dramatizes this in *Afloat and Ashore* by having Marble (who is unfit for command) order the pointless execution of an Indian. Melville, also working from the "Somers" case (in which he too had a personal interest), uses a very different kind of commander to dramatize a different conclusion in *Billy Budd.* See James Grossman, *Cooper,* pp. 188–97 for an excellent discussion of Cooper's position and Cooper's relation to Miles Wallingford. Excerpts of writing from and about Cooper can be found in Harrison Hayford's casebook, *The Somers Mutiny Affair* (Englewood Cliffs, N. J., 1959). Also see Beard, *Letters and Journals,* IV.

those who have great reason to find fault with themselves, I was angry with the whole world. I began to think myself a sort of outcast . . . " (173). Marble's mood vacillates between self-pity and irony during the questioning (he assumes he is an American only because it is unlikely " 'any person would import a child a week old, to plant it on a tombstone' "). The more Miles argues, the more Marble insists on his estrangement. He has, he protests, no friends, no relatives, no property, no home, no one waiting for his return, no place to rest, " 'not even a cellar to lay my head in' " (I, 320). He finally echoes the words of Harvey Birch: " 'To me all places are alike, with the exception of this, which, having discovered, I look upon as my own.' " Before hiding away so that Miles will be forced to leave without him, Marble gives Miles a last message for civilization: " 'Tell 'em that the man who was once found is now lost.' "

Months later Miles and Marble meet again in the middle of the Atlantic. Marble has found that his country and friends, Miles in particular, mean something to him after all. Also, being alone was not what he had expected.

"I took it into my head that I should be all alone on the island, but I found, to my cost, that the devil insisted on having his share. I'll tell how it is, Miles, a man must either look ahead or look astarn; there is no such thing as satisfying himself with the present moorings. . . . This generalizing [Marble's term for thinking] night and day, without any port ahead, and little comfort in looking astarn, will soon fit a man for Bedlam. I just weathered Cape Crazy, I can tell you, lads, and that too in the white water!" (I, 444, 445)

Miles himself by now realizes "we had seen so much in company, that I regarded him as a portion of my experience" and that "I loved Marble, uncouth and peculiar as he sometimes was" (I, 439). Marble, as an uncouth and peculiar portion of Miles's experience, has expressed for Miles an impulse to isolation and destruction that drives him repeatedly to sea.

The trio that sails in the "Dawn," then, is one of tried friends; Marble has overcome his initial prejudice against Neb, or rather it no longer matters. The three have formed a voluntary fraternity to which social groupings are irrelevant. Since Miles is a ruined man ashore, the final voyage of the "Dawn" is his last chance; and the ship's wreck is tragic. The three friends are the last men left on board; but Neb, and then Marble, is lost at sea; when Miles, thinking of them, hears their voices sometime later, he believes he is having hallucinations. At daybreak, however, they find that the pieces of wreckage they float on have been providentially brought together and they board one raft. Another storm begins and they cannot see a hundred yards ahead; yet they are in a strange way satisfied.

There we sat, conversing sometimes of the past, sometimes of the future, a bubble in the midst of the raging waters of the Atlantic, filled with the confidence of seamen. (II, 337)

Afloat, these three are Miles's essential community. None is perfect, but their affection overrides their difficulties, and they have earned each other's understanding.

When they return to shore, however, as they eventually must, Neb and Marble become ineffectual. Even Miles considers their efforts to rig a seaman's tackle that will extricate him from debtors' prison as farcical. Ashore, Miles needs someone like Lucy Hardinge, who understands shore institutions and sees through social masks. Intelligent and spirited Lucy is one of Cooper's best heroines, and James Grossman remarks that she reminds Cooper's biographers of Mrs. Cooper. There is nothing of the sentimental heroine about Lucy; and after more than thirty years of marriage, Miles insists on "the immense importance of having a companion, in an intellectual sense, in a wife" (II, 452). What Miles consequently does to reconcile his life is to combine those friends who have survived the trials ashore with those he brings back from sea. He makes Marble the captain of a new ship (which bears the mnemonic name of "Smudge"), marries Lucy, and retires with her and Neb to Clawbonny.

Through his mobility, eclecticism, and compromise, Miles attains a harmonious life. The slightly ironic narrative voice tells a history of illusions lost and knowledge gained through experience. Perhaps the most important discovery he makes about his relation with the world is that he needs human companionship and esteem. He confesses at one time that

> There are men so strong in principle, as well as intellect, I do suppose, that they can be content with the approbation of their own consciences, and who can smile at the praises or censure of the world alike; but I confess to a strong sympathy with the commendation of my fellow-creatures, and as strong a distaste for their disapprobation.

I know this is not the way to make a very great man; for he who cannot judge, feel, and act for himself, will always be in danger of making undue sacrifices to the wishes of others. . . . (I, 361)

Nothing more clearly describes the moral geography of Cooper's world than this. Between the two poles of principle and popularity lies the borderland a free man lives in. The argument for a life of pure principle as the proper goal of a great man is ancient: Epicurus preached that the desire for approval and respect put a man in the power of others and prevent his being truly self-contained and tranquil. Yet the desire for society's approbation is recognized as a part of human nature in Cooper's books, and the struggle of his lone figures with their own social instinct is one of the most telling points of their character.

In an age in which Togetherness is all, it is hard to believe that our forefathers gave this problem as much serious attention as they did; but it was for this very reason that John Adams confessed himself a vain and weak man. He generalized that

the desire of the esteem of others is as real a want of nature as hunger; and the neglect and contempt of the world as severe a pain as the gout or stone. It sooner and oftener produces despair, and a detestation of existence. . . .[9]

Thus far Cooper and Adams agree, and the despair Adams describes is the same as that which occasionally grips Harvey Birch and Miles and which motivates Marble to try his experiment at isolation. Yet an in-

---

[9] *Works*, IV, p. 234.

structive difference of thought exists, for Adams goes on to say that "it is a principal end of government to regulate this passion, which in its turn becomes a principal means of government." In Cooper's novels, "this passion" has nothing at all to do with government as an institution; the problem is personal. Only Natty Bumppo even claims to have overcome it. "'When I first came into the woods to live,'" he says in *The Pioneers*, "'I used to have weak spells when I felt lonesome; and then I would go into the Cattskills, and spend a few days on that hill to look at the ways of man; but it's now many a year since I felt any such longings . . . '" (300).

Miles is not so great a figure as Natty, and one reason he is not is that he compromises between two needs: the need to be detached and self-sufficient in order to lead a thoroughly principled life and the need for human companionship and esteem. Withdrawing to Clawbonny with but few companions, he illustrates a belief Cooper expressed frequently:

> While there is no greater mystery to a selfish manager than a man of disinterested temperament, they who feel and submit to generous impulses understand each other with an instinctive facility. When any particular individual is prone to believe that there is a predominance of good over evil in the world he inhabits, it is a sign of inexperience, or of imbecility; but when one acts and reasons as if all honor and virtue are extinct, he furnishes the best possible argument against his own tendencies and character. . . . In all cases of intimacies, there must be great identity of principles, and even of tastes in matters at all connected with motives, in order to insure respect, among those whose standard of opinion is higher than

common, or sympathy among those with whom it is lower.
(*The Two Admirals,* 104)

Having grown up in two worlds, by the time he reaches
maturity and settles down to the good life of the gentry
Miles has weighed and found wanting most of the
people in both. He is another of Cooper's problems in
perspective, for the mature man may seem larger and
more solid than the adventurous youth mainly because
he has whittled away and discarded so much of both
worlds.

X

THE INDIAN CONFOUNDED
OR CONVERTED

And change with hurried hand has swept these scenes:
The woods have fallen, across the meadow-lot
The hunter's trail and trap-path is forgot
And fire has drunk the swamps of evergreens.
Yet for a moment let my fancy plant
These autumn hills again,—the wild dove's haunt,
The wild deer's walk. In golden umbrage shut,
The Indian river runs, Quonecktacut.
Here but a lifetime back—where falls tonight
Behind the curtained pane a sheltered light
On buds of rose or vase of violet
Aloft upon the marble mantle set—
Here in the forest-heart, hung blackening
The wolf-bait on the bush beside the spring.

—Frederick Goddard Tuckerman*

THIS HAD BEEN a wild and unspoiled continent; and to
writers of the first half of the nineteenth century, the
America that was the land of infinite and unexplored
possibilities was still tantalizingly close. They could not
free themselves, even had they wanted to, from the
dream of a golden age; yet they could not quite locate
that age in time. A few placed it in the past, but even
more of them, encouraged by the opening of the west,

---

* From *The Complete Poems of Frederick Goddard Tuckerman*,
ed. N. Scott Momaday, p. 27. Copyright © 1965 by Oxford University Press, Inc. Used by permission of the publisher.

saw it just ahead. When he used a romanticized past as a metaphor for a hopeful future, Cooper combined both dreams.

He also shared, even while he regretted, the American sense of discontinuity of experience. From the time of William Bradford's *History,* Americans have felt their national experience as a separation from the Old World and a new chance for mankind. Refusing to consider rapid changes as continuous process, we see our history as a series of crises marking the end of one era and the beginning of another. Our response to a Supreme Court decision or the failure of a filibuster is often the feeling that things will never again be as they were. Both Cooper and Dickens, in the nineteenth century, remarked this American tendency to cry havoc at every change,[1] and our historians have supported the novelists. In their autobiographies, Henry Adams set the end of the good old world in 1844, Henry Cabot Lodge located it in the 1830's, and it has been since so frequently relocated within the nineteenth century by the American historian that he sounds like Chicken Little.[2]

Our tendency to read and write history in terms of mutually exclusive polarities probably accounts for

[1] Cooper mentions, for instance, that the ship "Crisis" bore "a very capital name for a craft in a country where crisises [*sic*] of one sort or another occur regularly as often as once in six months. –*Afloat and Ashore,* p. 121. In *Martin Chuzzlewit,* Dickens says, "Martin knew nothing about America, or he would have known perfectly well that if its individual citizens, to a man, are to be believed, it . . . always *is* at an alarming crisis, and never was otherwise . . . " (I, 283).

[2] Avery O. Craven agrees largely with Adams, believing the years 1844–50 to be crucial (*Civil War in the Making*); Marcus Cunliffe, like Lodge, picks the 1830's (*The Nation Takes Shape*); Civil War historians, of course, choose the war years themselves; while still others, such as David Riesman and Henry Steele Commager, locate the end of the old world in the last decade of the nineteenth century.

these interpretations. As Marcus Cunliffe suggests, the organizing principle of many of the older interpretations of American history was antithesis: West versus East, America versus Europe, industrialism versus agrarianism.[3]

Such head-on, no-quarter-given opposition enters many of Cooper's novels; no compromise is possible between the groups of squatters and landowners, Indians and whites, Dutch and Puritans, or even those who cherish privacy and those who snoop. The values of each group are absolutes; and where there is opposition, there must also be extinction. The manner of extinction may vary— the Indians die violently, while the Dutch and gentry are pressed to death like Giles Cory—but the result is the same, the end of something. A true synthesis of societies is impossible in Cooper's world; the best that society as a whole can achieve is the tolerant coexistence that a controlling disinterested gentry or maritime order makes possible.

A lone man in Cooper's novels, however, can make a compromise. Certain individuals, profiting from the freedom of the sea, for instance, can temporarily and in particular circumstances join forces. The smuggler and the revenue officer can reach a limited agreement; Captain Cuffe and the man he is about to hang can

---

[3] "American Watersheds," *American Quarterly*, XIII (1961), 493. A provocative editorial on "that passion for oppositions which is itself one of the deepest German diseases" locates this passion also in America and suggests a connection between the German education of many nineteenth-century American historians (see David Levin, *History as Romantic Art*) and this method of organization (*The Times Literary Supplement*, October 26, 1962, p. 825). To mention only two examples of the same method applied to literature, we find R. W. B. Lewis' *The American Adam* searching for a "dialogue" and Marius Bewley's *The Eccentric Design* investigating the "opposition between tradition and progress, between democratic faith and disillusion, between the past and the present and future; between Europe and America, liberalism and conservatism, aggressive acquisitive economics and benevolent wealth" (p. 18).

admire each other as persons when each is temporarily estranged from his representative group. The man permanently estranged has a permanent freedom of this type. While this does not free him from dilemmas, it does allow him to see experience in a way critics now consider "modern." Such cultural historians as Henry Nash Smith and Leo Marx visualize the polarities, as Cunliffe says, not as

> collisions primarily between opposed groups of men, but rather as contradictory ideals and desires, held simultaneously and uneasily within the mind of a single individual. Very broadly, these opposed aspirations represent the tug between past and future: between primitivism and progress, wilderness and settlement, simplicity and multiplicity, "Arcadia" and "Enterprise." To assume that the polarity is so to speak *internalized*, a dilemma in the individual minds of men as diverse as Andrew Jackson and Henry Adams, is to see American history in a new light.

It is also to describe the mind that produced the characters we have yet to consider: Conanchet, Onoah, and Natty Bumppo.

The two most clearly opposed forces within America were the Indians and the white settlers. This conflict was recognized as a death struggle; it alone produced men who devoted their lives to hunting down and killing members of the other group. Not for bounty, but out of everwhelming hatred for the other race, do Cooper's Michael O'Hearn and Scalping Peter, Bird's Jibbenainosay, and Melville's Indian Hater become hunters of men. Yet Cooper also singled out characters who grope toward reconciliation of the races. In the Leatherstocking Tales, *The Wept of Wish-Ton-Wish* and *The Oak Openings,* Cooper explored the possibility of the co-existence of antithetical cultures. In each of these novels, individuals step forth from their group much as ancient heroes went into single combat, but these are mediators rather than champions and their purpose is conciliation rather than victory. Like Miles Wallingford and Harvey Birch, these men are not representative in any sense of standing for a group. They have presumably inherited the culture of the group they grew up in, but they alienate themselves from it and stand ready to question, even to forfeit, assumptions that hinder a synthesis. They are the scouts of the area of possibility.

Some critics, bothered chiefly it seems by Natty's assertion that scalping is wrong for whites but right for Indians, have described this state of mind as "cultural relativism." It is a label easily come by, and once it is applied to a character it makes understanding that character unimportant and explaining his permanence almost impossible. The charge of relativism (which can be leveled at even Candide's superlative world) keeps us from recognizing as possible a state of mind F. Scott Fitzgerald described as the mark of intelligence: "the ability to hold two opposed ideas in the mind at the same time, and still retain the ability to function." It prevents awareness of the American experience as the internalized dilemma Cunliffe mentions. And finally, it assumes the white man's conscious and unanimous fidelity to ethical absolutes.

As a historian, Cooper was too aware of human fads and follies to censure the Indian. By referring to the scalp-lock as "chivalrous," he placed the custom

among those formally rigid rules as stringent, but as
irrational, as the rules of duelling. As for barbarity,
Cooper denied civilization its clear conscience.

> . . . No empress of Rome could have witnessed the
> dying agonies of the hapless gladiator, no consort of a
> more modern prince could read the bloody list of the
> victims of her husband's triumph, nor any betrothed fair
> listen to the murderous deeds of him her imagination
> had painted as a hero, with less indifference to human
> suffering, than that with which the wife of the Sachem
> of the Narragansetts looked on the mimic representation
> of those exploits which had purchased for her husband
> a renown so highly prized. (*The Wept of Wish-Ton-
> Wish*, p. 353)

Mores have always, as Cooper reminds us, governed
the manner in which men consider the death of another;
and death, whether as spectator sport or the means to
enrich a monarch, has always been accepted for insufficient reasons. The trophies a society honors often
drip with blood.

Although Cooper had (he thought) finished with
Natty Bumppo after the third of the Leatherstocking
Tales (*The Prairie*, 1827), he took up the Indian-white
conflict again in 1831 in *The Wept of Wish-Ton-Wish*.
The novel itself fails, but it is richly suggestive of what
Cooper felt was the might-have-been of the American
past. It also specifies the parts of that past that had
largely been lost to the American present and future.
The characters in the novel, which breaks in half with
roughly a decade dividing the two parts of the action,
fairly represent the peoples living in colonial New
England. In the first half, the important groups are a
border family led by the Puritan patriarch, Mark Heath-

cote; a tribe of Narragansett Indians; and a group of British soldiers intent on hunting down a regicide who has fled to America.

In the second half of the novel, the Heathcote household is but a part of what is by then a Puritan settlement centered, geographically and psychologically, in the church headed by the Reverend Meek Wolfe. The British do not reappear, but they remain as a threat in the background, and the impersonal power of government reinforces the villains. Three groups of Indians are important. The first is the leagued tribes directed by Philip, who has decided the Indian can survive only if the whites are driven out or killed. The second is what remains of the Narragansetts, who have been burned out of their homes by whites the previous winter; they are allied with Philip. The third group is a Pequot and Mohegan coalition led by Uncas; these are the villains who join with the Puritans and colonial government against their own race. This unnatural league is of long standing; and before the novel opens, the Pequots and whites have killed the chief of the Narragansetts, Miantonimoh, on Sachem's plain.

Two important individuals are interrelated throughout the book. The regicide, known only as Submission, is suspected of being present before he is actually seen.[4] The other character, Conanchet, is a Narragansett boy and the only son of Miantonimoh. Neither figure is really explained, in the first half of the novel, either to the characters within the story or to the reader. Through dialogue, hearsay, mysterious actions, and quotations

---

[4] This character is based on William Goffe, one of the judges of Charles I, who hid out in a cave called "The Judge's Cave" near New Haven, according to local legend. Cooper had visited the place while attending Yale.

from Cotton Mather, Cooper builds a network of supernatural suggestion and leaves much unexplained. A
conch shell sounding outside the gates of the stockade
is later explained as an Indian ruse; but a mysterious
stag which leads a hunter astray in the forest, leaves no
tracks, and vanishes at a thunderclap in clear weather
remains unexplained. This tale is reinforced by that of
a traveler who reports, a short time later, that demons
have been hurling lightning bolts at the churches along
the coast and that the devil has aroused his Indian
agents in an unholy war against the settlers.

In the action, the boy Conanchet becomes a mediator
between the Indians and whites; he is aware of obligations to both groups; and his moral dilemma is reflected
in his sorrowful comment that "this world is very wide"
and his perplexed question: "Why have the Yengeese
and the redmen met?" (151) When his tribe attacks
the Heathcote home in order to release him from
captivity, his distress is aggravated by the fact that he
has limited power in either group. Young as he is, he
can only influence the Indians by invoking his father's
name; when he stops a tribesman from killing little Ruth
Heathcote, then a child of eight, the savage releases the
girl reluctantly and whispers "'Miantonimoh,' as softly
as if it recalled a feeling of sorrow." Still, Conanchet has
not won the right to stop the carnage. Belonging to
neither group, but warily trusted by both, he uses his
freedom to effect the safe entry of Ruth and Submission
into the blockhouse, but he cannot keep his tribe from
setting fire to it. After the holocaust, Conanchet stands
among the ruins, feeling triumph and melancholy and
hearing, as if it were hallucination, old Mark Heathcote's voice praying to the dread god of the white man.

Like two Greek gods, the spirits of Mark and Mianton-imoh contend for Conanchet; and Mark's prayer seems a voice from another world just as, in his dreams, the spirit of Conanchet's father asks vengeance on the whites.

Cooper uses the burning of the blockhouse, a later scene in which the Heathcotes are taken prisoner, and a meeting between Submission and Philip to stress the behavior and values admired by both Christians and pagans. As the blockhouse burns and those within remain silent, the Indians are impressed by their fortitude. Afterwards, Indians avoid the spot; those who approach it do so "rather in the reverence with which an Indian visits the graves of the just, than in the fierce rejoicings with which he is known to glut his revenge over a fallen enemy" (189). Both groups also admire self-possession, as Cooper says:

> It would have been a curious study for one interested in the manners of the human species, to note the difference between the calm, physical, and perfect self-possession of the wild tenants of the forest, and the ascetic, spiritually sustained, and yet meek submission to Providence, that was exhibited by most of the prisoners. (317)

A third common ground is indicated by Indian admiration for warriors. Although Philip cannot begin to understand Submission's religious doctrines, the fact that Submission has taken the head of his king elicits Philip's admiration and suggests that understanding between them is possible.

Even more suggestive is what we know of Conanchet's life during the bittersweet years that divide the first half of the novel from the second. He marries

Ruth Heathcote the younger, who was taken captive in the original skirmish, and they survive the midwinter destruction of their Rhode Island village by a group of whites (who include Ruth's father, Content Heathcote). The whites refer to the raid as a "scourge" or "chastisement," but Cooper presents it as a massacre in which Indian women and children were brutally slaughtered. When the government (an impersonal force remote from the evil it causes) places bounties on Indians, Conanchet is driven to league with Philip in a war of extinction. The warfare brings him once again to the valley of the Wish-Ton-Wish, and Conanchet is astounded to find the Heathcotes "reborn" from the ashes of the blockhouse. Conanchet now commands the Narragansetts with an absolute and hard-won authority, but he is ready to believe that the Indians are too weak to combat the mighty God of the Yengeese (313). He takes Philip aside and tells him of the earlier raid.

"My people had lost their sachem, and they came to seek him. Metacom [Philip], the boy had felt the power of the God of the Yengeese! His mind began to grow weak; he thought less of revenge; the spirit of his father came no more at night. There was much talking with the unknown God, and the words of his enemies were kind. He hunted with them. When he met the trail of his warriors in the woods his mind was troubled, for he knew their errand. Still he saw his father's spirit, and waited. [Conanchet describes the burning of the blockhouse, then continues.] The soul of Conanchet was moved at that sight, for there was much honesty in them within. Though their skins were so white, they had not slain his father. But the flames would not be spoken to, and the place became like the coals of a deserted council-fire. All within were turned to ashes. If the spirit of Miantonimoh rejoiced, it was well; but the soul of his son was very heavy. The weakness was on him, and he no longer thought of boasting of his deeds at the war-post." (314)

The thoughts that eventually confound Conanchet are here: he lacks (even more than Hard-Heart, Uncas, Tamenund, or Susquesus) a real tradition of Indian deity to oppose to the Christian's god; his affinity with his own tribe has been interrupted and troubled; finally, tradition would have him revenge his father while his impulse is to discriminate, to acknowledge his personal liking for the Heathcotes and slay only the killers of his father. The categorical imperatives demanded by Mark and Philip (forgiveness for all or revenge on all of white color) prohibit, however, such selective action.

Mark's argument is familiar; Philip's is expressed in Beowulfian terms as he says he "sees" a dark spot on Sachem's plain.

"It is the rich blood of a great warrior. The rains cannot wash it out; it grows darker every sun. The snows do not whiten it; it hath been there many winters. The birds scream as they fly over it; the wolf howls; the lizards creep another way." (320)

He adds to this reminder of filial obligation a taunt: Conanchet's wife who "'speaks with two tongues'" is holding her hands before his eyes until he is blind (321). Conanchet stands firm and dismisses Philip with a haughty, "'My mind is my own'" (324). Yet it is a troubled mind, and he struggles until his death to keep this integrity in spite of repeated assaults on it. The most serious temptations to betray himself reach him through Submission (who personifies discontinuity of experience) and Narra-mattah (Ruth Heathcote the younger, who embodies attachment).

The parallel situation of Conanchet and Submission, hinted at through their mysteriousness in the early part of the book, is made explicit in the latter half. Both men have similar qualities; their naturally stern natures are softened by humane and charitable feelings; both are decisive and accustomed to lead; each one realizes that it is not possible, or even desirable, to deceive the other. What England is to Submission (the homeland from which he has been driven), so the land of the Narragansetts is to Conanchet, and their forlorn fates strengthen the trust they have long felt. Unlike Natty, who is a voluntary exile, these men are proscripts whose banishment augments their homesickness and their friendship (371). Each man suffers from an overwhelming sense of discontinuity with his own past at the same time that he acknowledges his duty to his people. Submission's statement, " 'My mind is ever with my people; yet is there place for other friendships,' " is echoed shortly afterward by Conanchet's " 'My mind is ever with my people' " (346). As these two leaders of warring peoples move toward reconciliation, they draw in a third member, Philip himself; and these three are groping toward peace when the Pequots and colonials attack in an action Meek Wolfe's "inward monitor" has told him is divine judgment (362).

The final scenes have ramifications that spread, sometimes confusingly, beyond the tale itself. Their sequence is based on analysis of who is safe with whom, much like the old problem about the fox, goose, and corn. Had the colonists arrived before or with the Pequots, Conanchet could have escaped with Philip and the colonists would have protected Submission. As it is, the Pequots arrive first; and since they will kill Submission if they find him, Conanchet finds it necessary to declare, "'Our lives are one.'" Conanchet first protects Submission from Philip (who thinks the white man's peace council has been a trap) and then protects Submission from the Pequots by exposing his own person in order to lure them away from the old man's hiding place. The meeting place has been revealed by a renegade Indian who ransoms his own life with his treachery. Before Philip escapes, he brains this Indian in the one satisfactory act of justice in the entire denouement.

Out of the wild scramble of racial and political allegiances at the end of the book, one clear statement emerges: Only by getting a forest creature, or a half-wild one, to act as a mean between civilization and wilderness can the settlement man touch savage life. Only an Indian can locate the place where Philip, Conanchet, and Submission (himself guided there by Conanchet) are conferring. Only Indians can run Conanchet to ground, hunting him in relays as they hunted deer. This situation is common to Cooper and to later American literature. In Faulkner's "The Bear," Sam Fathers and the wild dog, Lion, are needed to conquer the bear; Ahab needs the Parsee and Manilan natives to reach Moby Dick. In Cooper's novels, there must always be a human link between the civilized and the wild for any interaction, affirmative or tragic, to take place. In this novel, in fact, Cooper inverts and parodies the linking savage in a second character, Whittal Ring. Like the Italianate Englishman of the Renaissance, Whittal has become excessively like the Indians who have been his companions since they captured him. Whittal is a half-wit and, like all half-wits, enjoys immunity; only he can freely cross the figurative no man's land that separates the races.

Once Conanchet is their prisoner, his captors conform to Cooper's belief that groups of men escape responsibility by dividing it. The Puritans indicate the necessity for Conanchet's execution, then withdraw, leaving him in the hands of his enemies. When they have gone, Conanchet is offered, and refuses, several chances to live if he will betray his loyalties. The demands of the colonists and those of Philip cannot be reconciled, and Conanchet is now to learn that the man who *must* choose between two groups, both of them wrong, is not free. If life offers only choices that he must reject, he prefers (like Bartleby) to choose extinction.

Relinquishing Narra-mattah and his son is difficult, nevertheless, and Conanchet transfers what feeble hopes are left him to another world.[5] He tries to explain to his wife that "'a just and great chief cannot shut his ear to the Good Spirit of his people. Mine calls his son to hunt among the braves that have gone on the long path. Thine points another way'" (402). He confesses to her that he is a "'child among the cunning'"; the phrase, spreading through memory, touches upon Jesus and the Elders and gives Conanchet some of the aura that belongs to innocence. He hopefully promises her that if there should be, after all, but one heaven, he will look for her and his son there. "'Let Narra-mattah forget her chief till that time, and then, when she calls him by name, let her speak strong; for he will

---

[5] Yvor Winters has pointed out that Parkman's *The Conspiracy of Pontiac* contains essentially the same incidents that make up the story of Narra-mattah. Parkman mentions specifically a Mary Jemison who was captured by the Senecas, married two of them successively, and hid in the forest with her children to keep from being returned to white society as a peace treaty ordered (II, 248–56).

be very glad to hear her voice again'" (403). Then, afraid only for his fortitude, Conanchet speaks his last words triumphantly to his executioner: "'Mohican, I die before my heart is soft!'"[6]

When the Heathcotes arrive, they find Narra-mattah sinking into a willed death at the side of her husband. The pleas of her mother restore the girl mentally to her childhood; she rouses herself to pray a child's prayer; and when she looks at the dead chief beside her, she whispers, "'an evil spirit besets me'" (411). Although the family bury her beside Conanchet, marking his grave "The Narragansett" and hers "The Wept of Wish-Ton-Wish," her death satisfies only her mother, who is delighted that she departs "'in the blessedness of infant innocence'" (410). If Nara-mattah dies, as she apparently does, because she cannot live apart from Conanchet, the last-minute return to her childish fear of Indians as evil spirits seems an obvious failure of nerve on Cooper's part. The baby is simply lost in the final action (except for the adjective "stricken" applied to it), and the whole question of miscegenation is blotted out in a mother's tears.[7]

---

[6] This speech, which threatens to cancel the complexity of Conanchet's character and situation, reveals Cooper's apparent dependence on William Hubbard's *Narrative of the Troubles with the Indians in New England* (Boston, 1677; re-printed, Brattleborough, 1814). Hubbard tells of an Indian, Conanchet, who was captured by Pequods during King Philip's War. Carried to Stonington and sentenced to death, he swore that he would "die before his heart was soft, or had spoken anything unworthy of himself" (162).

[7] The book still disturbed Cooper's contemporaries, one of whom wrote that Conanchet "exhibits rather too much wavering of purpose—but is on the whole a worthy representative of Uncas and Hardheart, and evinces all the fine qualities to reconcile those who can be reconciled to the revolting union of red and white."— *Southern Review*, February, 1830, as quoted by Clavel, *Critics*, p. 223.

Within the novel, two incidents touch on this question. Ruth Heathcote wounds her daughter by obviously finding the baby

Until Cooper takes away from the book his Indian gifts of Narra-mattah's happy marriage and the child, its fictional statement is fairly complicated but clear. Three individuals (Conanchet, Submission, and Narra-mattah) can sustain somewhat uneasily that state of mind in which, as D. H. Lawrence says, the white man's spirit "can cease to be the opposite and the negative of the red man's spirit. It can open out a new great area of consciousness, in which there is room for the red spirit too."[8] Thus Submission at one time remarks that many Christians could learn their own religion from Conanchet and adds, "'I can almost say that my heart is Indian'" (383). Submission survives the action; but once he has lost touch with Conanchet's Indian spirit, he can only return to white society. Conanchet, awed by the power of the white man's God and depressed by the ruin of his tribe, surrenders his own earthly hopes and those of his people. He expresses this metaphorically when he tells Narra-mattah that his son is a child of the clearings and cannot live in the shade. He assumes not only that the white blood is stronger than red, that the child belongs more to the settlements than to the forests, but also that no compromise is possible. He assents intellectually to the idea that the two races are forever opposed. The tragic part of Conanchet's confusion is that the racial polarities

repulsive. In another scene, one of the settlers suggests that since a woman (named Abundance) had given birth to triplets during the Indian attack, Narra-mattah's child could be added as a fourth; considering the circumstances at the time of the multiple births, the colonist suggests that one baby might well look like an Indian. Content Heathcote (the maternal grandfather) admits that he has been ashamed of the child, but that the Lord has given him the strength to resist such vain thoughts (368).

[8] *Studies in Classic American Literature*, p. 61.

he surrenders to are denied by his experience. He knows (as Submission and Narra-mattah know) that individuals can transcend race and combine both spirits; but he also finds that when two rigid and exclusive societies have the power, such individuals are crushed between them. He is intelligent enough to see that one or the other of these social groups will prevail; and yet insofar as he denies the truth of his personal experience, he thinks his way to a lie.

More than any other character in the book, Conanchet embodies the impulse to assimilation. As the action shows, however, the *via media* to which his liberalism guides him is the most dangerous of all possible routes through a world made up of aggressively autonomous communities. He desires reconciliation, but the book's statement is that American history held no blessing for the peacemakers.

Cooper's final attempt to harmonize red and white without mixing them comes in *The Oak Openings* (1848), a novel set in the Michigan forests during the war of 1812. The idea of America as Eden, inherent in Cooper's wilderness stories and often expressed by his Indian orators, is here openly stated as Cooper compares the new lands of the West with mankind's lost Paradise.

There is nothing imaginary in the fertility of the West. . . . Time may lessen that wonderful fertility, and bring the whole country more on a level; but there it now is, a glorious gift from God, which it is devoutly to be wished may be accepted with due gratitude, and with a constant recollection of his unswerving rules of right and wrong, by those who have been selected to enjoy it. (v)

Awareness of the land as a divine gift and of man's obligation to honor it (an attitude characteristic of Cooper's gentry) is related explicitly to Eden within the novel when Ben Boden tells a Chippewa that God put Adam and Eve "to live together in a most beautiful garden, in which all things excellent and pleasant was to be found—some such place as these openings, I reckon" (231).

By relocating Eden in the still unsettled West, Cooper gives Americans a second beginning; and the population of the oak forests hints at what he has in mind. One suspects this book is generally indebted to the story of Pontiac's magnificent attempt, about the middle of the eighteenth century, to unite all the Indians against the whites. Cooper assembles for his tale all the chiefs of the various branches of the Ojebways (as he spells it) who meet to plan a unified resistance to westward moving Americans.

Even more obviously than most of Cooper's novels, this book pairs characters. Gershom Waring, a degenerate Yankee whiskey trader, is paired with a drunken and treacherous Indian, the Weasel. A white bee-hunter, Ben Boden, and an Indian, Pigeonswing, originally occupy the middle ground between the races. Accompanied only by his mastiff, Hive, Boden lives a solitary life, relishing "most of all, the self-reliance that was indispensable equally to his success and his happiness" (26). Like Natty Bumppo, he is given to spiels of philosophizing about the meaning of events, is dedicated to the preservation of trees, and takes only enough from the wilderness to subsist. Yet he is so bleached, leeched, and deodorized that even these obvious attempts to give him Natty's appeal fail. Henry Nash Smith has, in the main, well described the process by which Cooper seems to have arrived at Ben Boden, and correctly remarks the simultaneous destruction of Natty's "subversive overtones."[9] Cooper seems to have changed this book as he wrote. Boden is originally a lone bee-hunter living among the Indians, and Cooper draws attention to his smallpox scars. Like the Indians, he has suffered from the white man's plague.[10] Almost everyone knew, in the first half of the nineteenth century, that small-

---

[9] *Virgin Land*, pp. 75, 76. As Smith points out, Cooper was trying (as early as *The Prairie*) to rid himself of the conventional genteel heroine and hero; he tried to combine (in bee-hunters Paul Hover and Ben Boden) Natty's skills and some of his virtues with a man a proper heroine could marry. The dangerous insufficiency of Smith's explanation that Natty is "too old" for such a role is indicated by Cooper's treatment of Boden; Boden and Pigeonswing are originally the central characters, but as Boden becomes interested in and marries Margery ("Blossom") Waring, he drifts out of the action and ends on its periphery as the conventional heroine's hero.

The character of Boden is a reworking of Paul Hover with additions from Cooper's own experience. Cooper had just returned from a trip to the prairies and Michigan in 1847 when a farmer arrived to "call down" a hive of errant bees which had flown to Cooper's land; Susan writes that her father was fascinated by the process, and the actions are given to Boden in this book (*Pages and Pictures*, 379-82).

The bee has special associations in nineteenth-century literature. Always a link with the Virgilian pastoral tradition, the bee (which had been imported to America from the old world) symbolized colonization (as in Bryant's "The Prairies" of 1832). Other internal evidence in this book suggests that Cooper and his readers were also aware of the Mormon symbolism. Joseph Smith had "discovered" Eden (on the site of Independence, Missouri) in 1831; and in 1847 (the year Cooper went west), the first Mormons reached the permanent "Stake of Zion" in Salt Lake City. Parson Amen's theories sound somewhat like *The Book of Mormon*.

[10] In the Indian thought of the book, smallpox stands for proscription and ugliness. The Indian Onoah compares settlers' cabins to smallpox scars (263) and exiled Jews to men with smallpox (266). William Gilmore Simms had written in *The Yemassee* (1835) that suicide was rare among Indians, but that Cherokees had been known to kill themselves when they saw their ravaged appearance on recovering from smallpox.

pox and whiskey were lethal to the Indian; hence both become for Cooper convenient symbols of civilization's silent and corroding destruction of native beauty.

Cooper's preparation of Boden as a linking character between the two races is largely wasted as a third pair of characters begins to dominate the action. One of these is Parson Amen, a Methodist minister who has come to convert the Indians to Christianity and to persuade them to return to Judea where, according to his theory, they really belong.[11] Amen is originally half a comic team meant to represent possible Indian conquest either through faith or the sword. In the tableau that makes his scheme clear, Cooper describes Amen and Corporal Flint as they stand back to back, surrounded by Indians; the Corporal holds his musket at ready and exhorts the minister, who is praying aloud, to "give 'em another volley; you're doing wonders, and their front has given ground" (373). Soon after this, however, Amen ceases to be a minor comic figure and becomes a Christian hero. Were we to diagram the action, his path would cross with that of Onoah, an Indian chief who is also known as "Tribeless," "Scalping Peter," and simply "Peter." As Parson Amen's dignity increases, Onoah goes from savage strength to a paralyzed condition Cooper presents as true Christianity.

Both men are driven by a ruling passion originally. Onoah's is, says Cooper,

---

[11] According to Roy Harvey Pearce's *The Savages of America*, James Adair's *History of the American Indians* argued, as early as 1775, Hebrew origin as against Tartar origin (the more common theory at the time). "Learned religionists . . . tried with fantastic scholarship from about 1815 on, once more to convince their readers and themselves that Indians were really Hebrews, descended from the Lost Ten Tribes" (61). The partial list of publications supporting this statement suggests that Cooper's novel and *The Book of Mormon* may have a common debt to the religious writings of the time.

A scheme worthy of the loftiest spirit living; the regenera-
tion and union of the people of his race, with a view to
recover the possessions they had yielded to the pale-faces;
but it was a project blended with the ferocity and revenge
of a savage—noble while ferocious. (178)

As originally presented, Onoah is as much the product
of schematics as the Amen-Flint tableau, the bee-colony
associations, and the pock-marked Eden of the setting.
Cooper's control of his material at the beginning of
this book has a kind of mathematical beauty that is
totally lost before the end. Onoah starts as a fine figure
of an Indian; he wears no war paint, but carries a
mixture of symbols of rank and authority: a gorget of
red pipestone (for peace), a rattlesnake totem (snakes
usually mean war), an old Jesuit medal with a cross
on it (which he wears for "political" reasons), and a
hand drawn on his chest in an attitude that clearly
indicates *noli me tangere* (164, 165). He has a "fearful
reputation at all the garrisons, though he never showed
himself in them" (43), and he seems to have no particular tribe, though he is well-known to all the Ojebways,
the Six Nations, and the Cherokees. He passes at ease
and in safety among them, but even to them he is a
mysterious and ubiquitous figure.

With him the past was as much of a mystery as the future. No Indian could say even of what tribe he was born.
The totem that he bore on his person belonged to no
people then existing on the continent, and all connected
with him, his history, nation, and family, was conjecture
and fancy. (183)

Like Moses Marble or Tocqueville's modern man or
the Indian race itself, he seems either lost or partheno-
genetic. His wearing the antithetical symbols of Indian

life is appropriate, for as though all the vanquished and extinguished tribes of America had bequeathed to him their own unused power to repulse the white invaders, Onoah has but one reason for living: to exterminate the white races.

All the white people, however, insist on trusting Onoah; Cooper once more raises questions of appearance and reality and shows how thin a mask can deceive those intent on deceiving themselves. Even Onoah's multiplicity of names (including "Scalping Peter") is ignored by Parson Amen as he falls victim to his own theories: "'names: they hurt no one, and will soon be forgotten. A descendant of Abraham, and of Isaac, and of Jacob, is not placed in this wilderness by the hand of divine power for no purpose; since he is here, rely on it, it is for good'" (169). Amen's obsession, which in turn deludes others of the group, is fully as strong as Onoah's. The parson produces some wonderful parodies of higher criticism as he applies his obsession to scriptural exegesis; for instance, he decides that Onoah is not of the tribe of Benjamin, but of the tribe of Naphthali.

"'Napthali is a hind let loose: he giveth goodly words.' Now, what can be plainer than this? A hind let loose is a deer running at large, and, by a metaphor, that deer includes the man that hunts him. Now, Peter has been— nay, is still—a renowned hunter, and is intended to be enumerated among the hinds let loose; he giveth goodly words, would set that point at rest, if anything were want- ing to put it beyond controversy, for Onoah is the most eloquent speaker ear ever listened to!" (171)

To Parson Amen, the deer and antelope of America are but scapegoats altered (329). He is delighted with his theory, and can hardly wait to publish his findings.

" 'I can scarcely open a chapter in the Old Testament, that some passage does not strike me as going to prove this identity between the redmen and the Hebrews: and, were they all collected together and published in a book, mankind would be astonished at their lucidity and weight' " (197). Deceived by his own thesis, Parson Amen lets himself and the others be lured to the oak openings where an Indian council is to be held.

Once there, Cooper treats the reader to a number of debates. He gives Onoah statements about perceptual ambivalence, Indian unity, and the fragmentation of white culture. Inveighing against tribal wars, Onoah says, " 'To the redmen he [the Great Spirit] gave eyes of the same color, and they always see things of the same color. To a redman there is no change' " (276). By contrast, the pale-faces have eyes of many colors and see things in different ways. Onoah so successfully emphasizes Indian unity, tradition, and immutability that Parson Amen, trying to tell them they were once white, meets hostility. Boden, perceptive for once, has the wit to see Amen's mistake: " ' . . . You went to work to skin them, in a lump, making so many poor, wishy-washy pale-faces of all the redskins in a body' " (277).[12]

The Indians' solemn discussion of Parson Amen's theories is an exquisite example of American humor. Translating Amen's lofty thoughts into literal examples, the chiefs attain the distinctive incongruity of idea and

---

[12] Boden's speech correctly implies that these Indians, although familiar with Catholic priests, have never considered that religion meant becoming un-Indian. Cooper generally insists that the Catholic and Moravian missionary attempts were the most intelligent, since these groups tried to leave Indian identity and traditions intact as much as possible. It is probably Heckewelder's tolerance (as a Moravian) that caused Cooper to use him as a source of information about Indian life. (See Arthur C. Parker, "Sources and Range of Cooper's Indian Lore," p. 451).

tone that characterizes American humorists in the Mark Twain and Will Rogers tradition. One Indian reasons that his tribe, the Pottawattamies, cannot be Jews because:

"It never was *lost*. It *cannot* be lost. No tribe better knows all the paths, and all the best routes to every point where it wishes to go. It is foolish to say you can lose a Pottawattamie. A duck would be as likely to lose itself as a Pottawattamie. I do not speak for the Ottawas: I speak for the Pottawattamies. We are not Jews. We do not wish to be Jews; and what we do not wish to be we will not be. . . . What he [Amen] says may be true of other tribes, but it is not true of the Pottawattamies. We are not lost; we are not Jews. I have done." (336)

Although he carefully stipulates that he is not qualified to speak for all the tribes, Crowsfeather's speech well expresses their common sense of outrage at having their identity threatened. A second Indian, turning his attention to the behavior of the white men, says he is not surprised the Jews are lost. "'It seems to me that all pale-faces get lost. They wander from their own hunting-grounds into those of other people. It is not so with Injins'" (337). Furthermore, he says, the minister's law that one should return good for evil is not a good law. "'I do not wonder that the tribes which follow such a law get lost. They cannot tell their friends from their enemies'" (338).

Suddenly the comedy ends. Peter has led the chiefs to agree with his demand that the whites be killed, but even he cannot control the hatred he has aroused. From this point on, he is consistently referred to as "Peter," and he begins his process of conversion with a double betrayal. Influenced by Margery's kindnesses to him, he warns her and her bridegroom (Boden) that they are in danger; then he leads the unsuspecting Parson back

to the Indians for a second chance to convince them.
Some of these Indians have been exposed to Christian
teaching before, and this time the villainous Weasel
asks Parson Amen about Christ's stay on earth. The
minister knows as well as the Weasel does what the
effect of this story will be, but he answers truthfully
that wicked men put this good man to death. The
Indians are furious at the implications. "'The Jews did
this. My brother wishes us to think that redmen are
Jews! No; redmen never harmed the Son of the Great
Spirit. They would receive him as a friend, and treat
him as a chief'" (379). Now beyond the control of
Peter, the Indians decide to execute the Parson and
the Corporal. Amen, notified that he is to die, prays
for Peter and the rest of the Indians and this act com-
pletes Peter's conversion. He shudders at the sound of
the tomahawk blow that kills Amen. "It was," Cooper
says, "the first time such a weakness had ever come over
him" (382). While the Indians are dispatching Corporal
Flint, Peter leaves the scene and leads the remaining
whites to safety. He breaks completely with his people
and subscribes whole-heartedly to the theory that the
pale-faces "'have been told to come here, and to tell
what they know to the poor ignorant Injins'" (408).
While Peter does not go so far as to agree with Cotton
Mather that the devil inspires the Indians, he does
believe that God loves the Indians less than the whites
or he would not have left them so long in their ignorance. Like Conanchet and others, he surrenders to the
idea that the white men will triumph, but he goes
further than Cooper's other chiefs in feeling that the
victory is also just.

Peter's instant conversion cuts him off effectively
from his ancestors, his race, and even his former self.

Instead of the obstinate confidence in himself and his traditions which had once so much distinguished this chief,
there was substituted an humble distrust of his own judgment that rendered him singularly indisposed to rely on
his personal views in any matter of conscience, and he was
truly become a child in all that pertained to his religious
belief. (438)

What was, on page 178, a "scheme worthy of the loftiest
spirit living" is by page 438 "obstinate confidence in
himself and his traditions," but Cooper tries to fuse
the two by explaining that "the very qualities that would
induce such a being to attempt the wild and visionary
scheme of vengeance and retribution that had now
occupied his sleeping and waking thoughts for years
might, under a better direction, render him eminently
fit to be the subject of divine grace" (400). Cooper's
ability to detect the latent saint in a rogue makes Peter
like those literary figures discussed by R. W. B. Lewis
in his *Picaresque Saint*, and one of Lewis' observations
seems pertinent. Speaking of the portrayal of the "truly
sanctified" in literature, he says that such portraits tend
either to "soft sentimentality" or "stiff abstractions" and
that both are "betrayals of art by their transcendence of
man."[13] The character of Peter notably softens; he
himself reports that when anyone receives the Holy
Spirit, the heart "'is changed to de heart of woman,
and we all be ready to bless our enemy and die'" (476).
The action of the book reinforces this suggestion that
the only good Indian is dead as an Indian. Peter seems
obsessed throughout, but his conversion cancels his
obsession with Indian survival and makes him a child
among the Christians.

The scene in which Parson Amen is killed breaks

---

[13] *The Picaresque Saint* (New York, 1959), p. 215.

the novel into pieces. Parson Amen is changed from a comic figure to a pathetic one, and the changes in his and Peter's characters almost obscure the irony of the actual situation. (It is partly because the Indians are irate at Parson Amen's implication that they were involved in the crucifixion that they kill, rather than honor, the good man.) Yet no one in the novel recognizes the parallel. The Indians, with the single exception of Peter, will go right on being Indians, but Cooper seems to have given the Christians grounds for demanding conversion or death. Any racial reconciliation is, in this book, postponed until the millennium. America is described as a "commingling of believers, which is doubtless to precede the first fusion of sects, and the predicted end" (216). Attributing only to the Indians the opinion that the white men have invaded the continent for selfish reasons, Cooper hopefully and cautiously tries to justify the inroads as Prescott justified the actions of Cortez: the white man is merely "obeying the great law of his destiny" (200) and is a tool in the hands of an inscrutable Providence.

The ways of Divine Providence are past the investigations of human reason. How often, in turning over the pages of history, do we find civilization, the arts, moral improvement, nay, Christianity itself, following the bloody train left by the conqueror's car, and good pouring in upon a nation by avenues that at first were teeming only with the approaches of seeming evils. In this way there is now reason to hope that America is about to pay the debt she owes to Africa; and in this way will the invasion of the forests and prairies and "openings" of the redmen be made to atone for itself by carrying with it the blessings of the gospel, and a juster view of the relations which man bears to his Creator. (468)

The final scenes of the novel hammer at this Crusader's ethic. Cooper himself meets Peter on the Great Lakes, and Peter explains that the Lord sent the Indian to live on the earth originally, but that He has now sent the pale-face. Yet it is a shock to find Peter asserting that whatever is, is right. "Nobody any right to complain. Bad to find fault wid Great Spirit. All He do right; nebber do anyt'in bad'" (468).

The effect of conversion on Peter's fictional character is fatal. He abandons his dreams and his being, throws himself on the mercy of Providence, and trusts that all will be well in a millennial or mystical future. Cooper's final solution looks toward that time Whitman describes in "Passage to India," the time when "the true son of God shall absolutely fuse" man and nature. Yet the annihilation of Peter's character may well be the result less of mysticism than of a movement, on Cooper's part, away from Aquinas' theocentric humanism toward a more Lutheran emphasis on death and annihilation of the self as vital doctrine. Theologically, then, it is appropriate that Peter's extinction as a character seems a loss to Cooper's fictional world. The ending of the book shuts out what Lawrence called "a new great area of consciousness, in which there is room for the red spirit too." It loses that marvelous sense of richness and complexity of human interdependence that Queequeg is aware of when he says, "It's a mutual, joint-stock world, in all meridians. We cannibals must help these Christians!" Consequently, even though *The Oak Openings* is Cooper's last statement on the Indian-white conflict, it is not true to his world as a whole. That world, as he and his readers have always known, is embodied most completely in the figure of Natty Bumppo.

XI

THE MAKING OF NATTY BUMPPO

And they [The Leatherstocking Tales] go backwards, from old age to golden youth. That is the true myth of America. She starts old, old, wrinkled and writhing in an old skin. And there is a gradual sloughing of the old skin, towards a new youth.
You start with actuality.

—D. H. Lawrence*

FEW OF Cooper's characters can shed their race-old skins and become new whole men, and yet his Americans squirm and wriggle in a state between age and youth. More successfully than Ponce de Leon, Cooper located the youth America always promised. In the social novels, he found signs of it in the hope and energy of democracy; and with this much of his thought the age agreed. America's true motto was thundered by Daniel Webster in 1825 when some bleachers collapsed at Bunker Hill and he was told that to restore order among his listeners was impossible. "Nothing," roared Daniel, "is impossible, sir; let it be done." Cooper himself would have qualified Webster's edict with warnings about the nature of man and the designs of Providence, but his books suggest that democracy's mistakes could be the sprawling awkwardness of the newborn, and he died still fighting for the spirit and ideals he thought proper for the early years of a great civilization. These, too, like democracy itself, had to be reborn, for the youthfulness out of

---

* *Studies in Classic American Literature.*

261

which something worth keeping might come was, for Cooper as for Jefferson and Adams, as ancient as Greece.

In the wilderness novels, and particularly in the Leatherstocking tales, youth is in the ancient forests. As Lawrence says, Cooper found it by starting with actuality, and *The Pioneers* is properly the first of the series. To begin with *The Deerslayer* and follow Natty as he ages through *The Last of the Mohicans, The Pathfinder, The Pioneers,* and *The Prairie* is to lose Cooper's shaping of the series and the character. For Natty increasingly embodies the romantic impulse to assimilate and enrich rather than the Puritanic impulse to impoverish and suppress. Cooper indicated this intention in the 1850 Preface to the Leatherstocking Series:

. . . In a moral sense this man of the forest is purely a creation. The idea of delineating a character that possessed little of civilization but its highest principles as they are exhibited in the uneducated, and all of savage life that is not incompatible with these great rules of conduct, is perhaps natural to the situation in which Natty was placed. He is too proud of his origin to sink into the condition of the wild Indian, and too much a man of the woods not to imbibe as much as was at all desirable, from his friends and companions. In a moral point of view it was the intention to illustrate the effect of seed scattered by the wayside . . . removed from nearly all the temptations of civilized life, placed in the best associations of that which is deemed savage, and favorably disposed by nature to improve such advantages, it appeared to the writer that his hero was a fit subject to represent the better qualities of both conditions, without pushing either to extremes. (v)

Nothing could be more democratic than Cooper's seed analogy, and yet he insists on giving Natty the high principles, pride of origin, and tendency to eclecticism that do not notably belong to the common man. This result is, as Balzac said, "un magnifique hermaphrodite moral né de l'état sauvage et de la civilisation, qui vivra autant que les littératures."[1] Such a man is able to examine the life he lives and to make not money but himself.

Probably the most workable approach to Natty is through the fictional process of characterization. Characters come alive for us as we understand how they differ from their group (Cooper would say "class"). The first book written, *The Pioneers,* is the only one that shows Natty in normal settlement society. He can be understood here not only by what he says and does, but by comparison with other frontiersmen and by his difficulties with the normal pattern of living in the community. He will never again suffer urban constraint; for even if one grants that the military garrison of *The Pathfinder* is a community of sorts, Natty relates to it only temporarily and tangentially.

A second consideration is what Elizabeth Bowen refers to as the "expense of potentiality" and a corresponding elimination of a character's alternatives for action. She writes:

> The diminution of a character's alternatives shows (because it is the work of) advance—by the end of a novel the character's alternatives, many at the beginning, have been reduced to almost none. . . . By the end of the novel, the character has, like the silkworm at work on the cocoon, spun itself out. Completed action is marked by the exhaustion (from one point of view) of the character.[2]

---

[1] *Revue Parisienne,* July 15, 1840. Quoted by Marcel Clavel, *Fenimore Cooper,* p. 383.

[2] "Notes on Writing a Novel," *Orion,* II; reprinted in *Collected Impressions* and in *Modern Literary Criticism,* ed. Irving Howe, p. 61.

By the end of *The Pioneers*, Natty Bumppo has only two alternatives. He can stay in the settlement and conform to its rules, which is one kind of death, or he can plunge into the wilderness and await in a more congenial environment the more natural and exalted death that depends on the will of God. His dilemma, then, in the original novel duplicates the central dichotomy of the entire series: what life does a man live before which death? The meaning of the settlements is given in *The Pioneers*, but the meaning of the wilderness is only suggested and the next two books are needed to complete it by filling in Natty's past and future wilderness experience. In each book, Natty finally chooses between the alternatives left him by the action; but while *The Pioneers* exhausts Natty's limited ability to adjust to settlement conditions and *The Last of the Mohicans* elaborates on the potential being expended, *The Prairie* is needed to exhaust the character itself. The three novels could thus stand as Cooper had originally intended. Fortunately, however, Cooper resurrected Natty, guided him safely past the Siren's island in *The Pathfinder*, and unfolded his character most completely in *The Deerslayer*. Here Natty is most "American," his potential richest, and his alternatives most numerous. The Natty Bumppo of *The Deerslayer* can conceivably become or do anything. Everything is possible for him. He has complete freedom and two worlds—one white, one Indian—lie before him.

THE PIONEERS

To begin at the beginning, then, means to start with *The Pioneers*. The action builds from a central misunderstanding that troubles the relations of the chief characters. In addition to his usual device of concealing the identity of one character ("Oliver Edwards" or young Oliver Effingham), Cooper also hides the existence of old Major Effingham, whose welfare underlies many of Natty's actions. Furthermore, he uses a familiar theme—the inability of humans to communicate with each other—to keep even the well-intentioned characters at cross purposes. Because Judge Temple, on one side, and Natty and Oliver Edwards, on the other, do not "know" each other in the sense of Washington's statement to Harvey Birch ("Now indeed I know you."), they judge by appearances and are mistaken. Judge Temple, who appears to have enriched himself opportunely by buying up the lands confiscated from the Effinghams during the Revolution, actually considers himself a steward for his old friends. Natty Bumppo appears to be a surly old hermit, but is actually "a kind of *locum tenens*" (460) with John Mohegan (Chingachgook) on the land the Delawares had given Major Effingham when they adopted him. Natty had once served the Effinghams and is protecting the old Major (now "in his poverty and dotage") from the rest of the world.[3] The basic conflict is between two guardians of the land, and the basic realignment of forces comes when young Oliver Effingham abandons Natty's idea of land use (hunt it as the Indians did) and joins Judge Temple in cultivating it.

At the same time that Natty represents an outmoded

---

[3] This part of Natty's history is usually misinterpreted. His former servitude does not mean that his original rank was even lower than that of the average man and his eventual nobility of character correspondingly more incredible. As we have noted in the chapter on Negroes, Cooper shared the ancient belief that association with educated and moral people is beneficial. Natty's eventual goodness rests firmly on a tripod of reasons: his early service with the Effinghams, his acquaintance with the teachings of Moravian missionaries, and his natural tendency to see clearly and act rightly.

use of the land, he is Cooper's means of analyzing frontier society. When Judge Temple says that Natty has a "temperance unusual in thy class, and a hardihood exceeding thy years" (204), he sets Natty apart from a general group Cooper never shows: the white hunter. Natty Bumppo, the one who wipes his nose on the back of his hand, belongs by occupation to that group of men Irving was to write of thirteen years later in *Astoria*. As the only such character in *The Pioneers*, Natty excels at skills that, because of frontier conditions, all those in the community possess to a lesser extent. Everyone prizes a good shot and no one can resist killing game. When Natty protests that a buck swimming before him in the lake is a "fool to tempt a man in this way," he prepares to yield to a temptation everyone in the community can understand. Yet, as a killer, Natty is both better than and different from everyone else. He kills only what he needs to kill in defense or for food. He kills selectively, choosing his pigeons, his fish, his prime buck. And he kills appropriately when he uses the primitive and silent spear and knife against the buck which has "taken to the water on its own natur', which is the reason God has given to a deer." The difference between the settlers' killing and Natty's is the difference between butchery and art. He judges himself not on the social standard of competition with such men as Billy Kirby but on the artist's standard of perfection. A number of scenes show this, but none more clearly than Natty's comment after he has saved Elizabeth Temple and Louisa Grant from a panther. He dismisses the rescue itself lightly but empathetically ("it was a skeary thing to the young creater"), and immediately turns his thoughts toward judgment of his own performance. "I wonder if I had aimed at the varmint's eye, if I shouldn't have touched the life sooner than in the forehead; but they are hard-lived animals, and it was a good shot, consid'ring that I could see nothing but the head and the peak of its tail" (319). Natty thus forms his opinion of himself by juxtaposing performance, possibility, and perfection. Such scenes establish Natty's independence of mind and place him among those who (like Hemingway's heroes) use their ability to kill as a test of themselves and as a manifestation of man's quest of excellence.

In hunting and woodcraft, Natty is compared with Billy Kirby, the most proficient of the settlers; they relate to each other roughly as do the social and isolate Daniel Boones of American history and legend described by Henry Nash Smith in *Virgin Land*. Within the settlement itself, however, the character most like Natty is not Billy or Chingachgook but Ben Penguillian, an old sailor who lives with Judge Temple. Here, before he had written any of his sea tales, Cooper gave Ben Pump (as he is most often called) the blunt honesty and independence from social norms that characterizes his seamen. Both Ben and Natty have a truly Epicurean gratitude for the past, which they enjoy remembering and talking about, in contrast with Chingachgook, for whom memories are unbearably depressing. Both share a sense of personal obligation that has nothing to do with law; just as Natty feels obligated to care for Old Mohegan and old Major Effingham, Ben Pump (whom Natty has saved from drowning) pays Natty's fine and shares with him what Natty gratefully considers "half the disgrace" of being placed in the stocks.

Ben has, however, two advantages over Natty, who

finds it difficult "to know men's ways . . . since the settlers have brought in their new fashions" (309). Ben knows how to manipulate cash; he has hoarded his savings, knowing that money is power. Furthermore, when he offers to pay Natty's fine, he stipulates that his tavern bill must be settled first; and when he finds himself in jail with Natty, he rapidly increases that tavern bill in order to make confinement tolerable. Secondly, Ben has been trained to accept discipline by rule; whereas Natty, locked in the stocks, feels disgraced and helpless, Ben Pump climbs alongside, grabs Hiram Doolittle by the neck, and hammers Hiram's face out of shape (393). This difference is important. Natty's silent laugh reveals, of course, a deliberate frustration of a natural impulse that might otherwise betray him. For Natty, society's requirements are something heaped atop his own self-imposed restraints. Modern socioligists would consider Ben Pump better adjusted; he cheerfully volunteers for society's restraint (symbolized by the stocks), but then feels free to batter the magistrate when Doolittle wanders within reach. Similarly, he acquiesces to the popular code of behavior, which disapproves hitting a man who is down, but turns it against Doolittle, whom he carefully supports with one hand while pounding him with the other.

Finally, both Ben and Natty search their own experience for indications of truth and error in the present situation. Just as Ben excuses his attack on Hiram by likening it to a naval battle fought at anchor (395), Natty distrusts "'smooth speakers; for I've known the whites talk fair when they wanted the Indian lands most'" (208). Often, Natty's previous experience is only implied; he trusts his dog, for instance, "'more than many a Christian man; for he never forgets a friend, and loves the hand that gives him bread'" (9). Sometimes the inductive leap plunges Natty into depression: "'just as the game grows scarce, and a body wants the best ammunition to get a livelihood, everything that's bad falls on him, like a judgment'" (198). This manner of thinking is characteristic of Natty throughout the series, and the criticism Peter Green makes of Epicurus is no less true of Natty: "His aims were wholly admirable; his axioms often invalid. No one could argue with this protopsychologist when he preached friendship, tolerance, and the whole life. . . ."[4] Whenever he cannot apply the Christian principles taught him by the Moravians, Natty falls back on the humanistic design one can find in Epicurean thought. Both the mode of thought and the goal mentioned by Epicurus are also Natty's: "If a man enters into a struggle with the self-evident testimony of the senses he will never be able to share in true peace of mind."

Such a man should be able to live, if anyone can, peacefully within the settlement; the community, in fact, is still so new and unformed that it excludes no one. Yet Natty cannot remain in Templeton because of reasons attached to a third comparison—of Natty Bumppo and Judge Temple. This particular study in comparison and contrast is inescapable, and we may refer to it summarily. The two characters are alike in being able to remember the virgin beauty of the site of Templeton, in decrying the settlers' prodigality, and in wishing to conserve the land's natural resources. The

---

[4] *Essays in Antiquity,* p. 82.

pressure of urbanization reveals their differences. Judge Temple wants to hoard resources and ration them to future generations; Natty's creed for the present is "'Use, but don't waste'" (253), but he trusts to Providence to provide for the future. Partly because he feels responsible for the welfare of the community, Judge Temple has a "sensitive spot" or an "infirmity" where cash is concerned; Natty never accumulates anything not immediately useful and needs little that can be purchased. The Judge is dedicated to communal interdependence and Natty to individual self-reliance.

Their quarrel ultimately is carried on in terms of government and anarchy, of artificial law and natural justice.[5] Natty's most important action in *The Pioneers* is to burn his hut. It is the only property he ever owns that he cannot take with him, and its burning is as meaningful as Hawthorne's later holocaust. The fire marks an end of an era in which a man could peacefully enjoy his own property; it signals the failure of government. For the law, strong enough to punish Natty for killing a deer out of season, is inadequate to justice or to the essential function of government. Two of Cooper's cardinal beliefs about government were that it should insure a man's right to the peaceful possession

---

[5] Others have indicated this before. Richard Chase says, "In short, Cooper found it necessary in America to be both a conservative and an anarchist." It was, he adds, a dilemma "at the heart of American culture."—*The American Novel and Its Tradition*, p. 52. Henry Nash Smith uses more Oedipal terms to discuss essentially the same conflict between a paternal rule which orders to conserve and a son's desire to grow unhampered. Actually, the Judge's remark that Natty is an exception (because of his temperance and hardihood) is less connected with social status than with anarchy. Anarchists (Kropotkin, for instance) posit or hope for a world in which everyone is as self-controlled and undemanding as Natty Bumppo. Cooper believed men were partly evil; and if Natty is something of an untutored saint, Cooper supplies along with his character a running reminder that such men were rare.

of property and should guard him against "unseasonable invasions" by the "coarse-minded and ignorant." The government of Templeton has failed Natty on both scores and he has been forced to move both Old Mohegan and Major Effingham into a cave—significantly —hidden in the forest.[6]

---

[6] On the purpose of government, Cooper wrote: "It ought to be written in letters of brass in all of the highways and places of resort in the country, that A STATE OF SOCIETY WHICH PRETENDS TO THE PROTECTION THAT BELONGS TO CIVILIZATION, AND FAILS TO GIVE IT, ONLY MAKES THE CONDITION OF THE HONEST PORTION OF THE COMMUNITY SO MUCH THE WORSE, BY DEPRIVING IT OF THE PROTECTION CONFERRED BY NATURE, WITHOUT SUPPLYING THE SUBSTITUTE."—*The Redskins*, p. 367. This is exactly the situation in *The Pioneers*, for the charge on which Natty is finally convicted is of physically attacking Hiram Doolittle when Hiram insists on entering Natty's cabin even after Natty has confessed to killing the deer and has turned over the evidence to Hiram. Hiram successfully abuses the power of a search warrant, and Natty has no protection against him.

The reference to "coarse-minded and ignorant," which suits Hiram precisely, comes from Cooper's definition in *The American Democrat*: "He is the purest democrat who best maintains his rights, and no rights can be dearer to a man of cultivation, than exemptions from unseasonable invasions on his time, by the coarse-minded and ignorant." In everything except education, as we shall see, Natty is a "man of cultivation."

Still another quotation from *The American Democrat* relates to the conflict of *The Pioneers*. "There is getting to be so much publick right, that private right is over-shadowed and lost. A danger exists that the ends of liberty will be forgotten altogether in the means." Again, Natty's liberty (or the right to privacy) is denied him in the name of public right to invade his hut.

An important chain of causality leads up to this burning, but it is difficult to detect because it is set in motion by a sneaking Yankee. Hiram Doolittle's curiosity is frustrated and his acquisitiveness whetted by Natty's locked door. Hiram (whose only value is cash) assumes Natty has silver in there; and when Natty is absent, Hiram puts a knife on the end of a long stick, cuts the leashes of Natty's hounds, and tries to break into the cabin. The hounds, following their instinct, run into the forest and start the deer that swims in front of Natty and causes him to violate the game laws. Hiram, unsuccessful in his attempt at burglary, gets a search warrant from Judge Temple. ("Men, as individuals, may be, and sometimes are, reasonably upright—but bodies of men, I much fear, never. The latter escape responsibility by dividing it.."—*Wyandotté*, p. 23.) Judge Temple gives Hiram the warrant, though he knows Hiram is a scoundrel; had he accompanied the warrant, the chain would

With the burning of the hut, Natty severs his connection with part of his personal history, with settled society, and with fixed property; property is the means through which government and its agents can make his personal life miserable. As he stands there, watching the flames, he appraises himself and the settlers; and when a group comes to arrest him for assaulting Doolittle, he blurts out his bitterness:

"You have driven me, that have lived forty long years of my appointed time in this very spot, from my home and the shelter of my head, lest you should put your wicked feet and wasty ways in my cabin. You've driven me to burn these logs, under which I've eaten and drunk—the first of Heaven's gifts, and the other of the pure springs —for the half of a hundred years; and to mourn the ashes under my feet as a man would weep and mourn for the children of his body. You've rankled the heart of an old man, that has never harmed you or your'n, with bitter feelings toward his kind, at a time when his thoughts should be on a better world; and you've driven him to wish that the beasts of the forest, who never feast on the blood of their own families, was his kindred and race; and now, when he has come to see the last brand of his hut, before it is melted into ashes, you follow him up, at midnight, like hungry hounds on the track of a worn-out and dying deer. What more would ye have? for I am here—one to many. I come to mourn, not to fight; and, if it is God's pleasure, work your will on me." (369-70)

---

have been broken, but he does not. Natty admits killing the deer (thus making the warrant unnecessary), but points out that the panther bounty (from the beast which almost killed Elizabeth Temple) more than pays for the deer fine. Hiram now has no possible reason to enter the hut, but insists on entering anyway; and it is then that Natty shoves him over a bank, thus committing the act of aggression for which he is punished by society. Hiram is the true aggressor and the law his most effective tool.

Natty is seeing society in a new way. It is true that he is used to being alone; he lived by himself at the lake for many years, "'and a cheerful time I had of it'" (298), he remembers. He has never been gregarious, and he considers the need for human society a "weakness."

"When I first came into the woods to live, I used to have weak spells when I felt lonesome; and then I would go into the Cattskills, and spend a few days on that hill to look at the ways of man; but it's now many a year since I felt any such longings. . . ." (300)

Yet, until Hiram Doolittle took advantage of the "'twisty ways of the law,'" Natty never thought of men as animals that hunted in packs or himself as their helpless quarry. His acknowledgement that he is "'old and helpless'" and "'one to many'" disagrees with his life-long feeling of self-sufficiency. Alone in the forest, he is strong; alone in society, he is weak. Natty's recognition of the difference is supported by the Judge's surprise that an "'old, a friendless man, like him, would dare to oppose the officers of justice'" (355).

In the novel, the law works to the advantage of such cowards as Hiram Doolittle, whose "jesuitical, cold, unfeeling, and selfish manner . . . seemed to say, 'I have kept within the law,' to the man he had so cruelly injured" (391). The law allows Hiram, as it later allows the Newcomes in the same region, to triumph over a morally better man. Natty has his own sense of justice—one he extends even to animals: "'the flesh is sweeter, where the creatur' has some chance for its life . . . ' " (272). Natty's idea of justice has a catholic complexity that admits gradations and mitigation; Natty is hurt when Judge Temple, sentencing him, seems to have forgotten the family's huge indebtedness to him. Another child among the cunning, Natty cannot grasp the study of power embodied in the judge. The man who owes him so much is powerless when in robes; yet only when he wears robes has he more power than anyone else in the community. All this denies the testimony of Natty's senses and is simply too much for him to fathom. When the Judge upholds the abstract power of the law and says " 'the dignity of the law requires an open exhibition of the consequences of your crime' " (383), Natty translates the punishment into human terms as showing " 'off a man in his seventy-first year, like a tame bear, for the settlers to look on!' " The Judge worries about the dignity of the law; Natty about the dignity of the man. He finally protests, " 'Is it no harm to bring down the pride of an honest man to be the equal of the beasts of the forests!' "

The threat of the settlements is most dangerous, then, to Natty's idea of himself as a human being and to his opinion of mankind. Once he has done his duty (*not* his legal duty) to Chingachgook and Major Effingham, Natty turns to the woods. He must. As he explains to Oliver and Elizabeth, " 'I lose myself every day of my life in the clearings' " (475). Natty's self, the one he has painfully formed from the experiences of a lifetime, is threatened, and the values he needs to exist cannot be found within settlements. To justify what remains of his life, to bolster his shaken sense of human worth, he falls back on his doctrine ("Use, don't waste") and applies it to himself. As he tells the Effinghams,

" 'The meanest of God's creatur's be made for some use, and I'm formed for the wilderness; if ye love me, let me go where my soul craves to be ag'in!' " To civilization, which hoards its cash, squanders its natural resources, and places law as the unanswerable weapon in the hands of the greedy and cowardly, Natty is himself so much waste. His survival involves more than the clearing of the forests that threatens his profession; to survive as Natty Bumppo, he must leave the settlements and go where his integrity can be preserved.

Natty's sense of the settlement as a threat to character has been prepared for by the decline of Chingachgook. As loyal to him as Natty is, Chingachgook is a burden to Natty, just as Chingachgook's life is itself a burden to the Indian. Like the madman Ralph in *Lionel Lincoln* and Tamenund of *The Last of the Mohicans*, Chingachgook suffers the curse of Tithonus. Like Conanchet, he suffers also from a radical sense of discontinuity with his own past. Both he and Natty have aged, but the drunken John Mohegan is further from the Chingachgook of the later books than Natty is from his younger self. Only when preparing to die does Chingachgook comb his hair back from his face; otherwise it hangs as a veil for his shame. Conversion to Christianity has not saved John from drunkenness but has taught him to feel guilty about it. Consequently, he goes to church but (remembering the debauch of the previous night) refuses communion. Natty, who does not intend to let " 'churchings and merry-makings' " interfere with his hunting, complains that he " 'never knowed preaching come into a settlement but it made game scarce' " (130, 131). Religion does not, in this book, pass Natty's pragmatic test; it ruins the game and the Indians, and he complains that the Moravians "'were always over intimate with the Delawares'" (153). Yet Natty acts like a gentleman; when Mohegan and the minister lose rapport as the Indian is dying Natty concentrates on protecting the feelings of both. In a scene which verges on comedy because of misunderstandings on both sides, Natty explains to the minister that Chingachgook has not "'seen a Moravian priest sin' the war; and it's hard to keep them [Indians] from going back to their native ways. I should think it would be as well to let the old man pass in peace'" (439). Natty is no meddler; but when it becomes necessary, he can stand between two other men and, while agreeing with neither, protect the self-respect of both.

According to Natty, the Indian had actually shrunk at least three inches since middle-age; and "'Old John and Chingachgook were very different men to look on . . .'" (152). More eloquent even than Natty's testimony are two scenes which hint at the Indian's former grandeur and the pleasant life the two men lived. In the first, the famous fishing scene, their quiet canoe contrasts with the boatload of quarreling settlers who are seining the lake. The second begins when Natty finds Chingachgook, dressed again as a chief, sitting on Mount Vision. Affection, admiration, and long experience with Indians combine with Natty's usual forbearance in the explanation that "'when an Indian fixes his eye, he means to go but to one place; and what the wilful creatur's put their minds on, they're sure to do'" (436). Natty realizes that it is Chingachgook's tragedy to outlive his race, and considers his death as "'natur' giving out in a chase that's run too long'" (437). With the death of Chingachgook, Natty himself gives way to depression.

> "Red skin or white, it's all over now! He's to be judged by a righteous Judge, and by no laws that's made to suit times, and new ways. Well, there's only one more death [Major Effingham's] and the world will be left to me and the hounds. Ah's me! a man must wait the time of God's pleasure, but I begin to weary of life." (441)

Weary or not, there is no rest for Natty in the settlements, and he turns to the forest.[7]

THE LAST OF THE MOHICANS

The true death of the real Chingachgook occurred earlier, in *The Last of the Mohicans,* as he sat before the body of his son Uncas and appeared to be "some creature that had been turned from the Almighty hand with the form but without the spirit of a man" (418). This book, the second of the series, justifies Natty's affection for Chingachgook. It also expands Natty's character and shows how far he has moved from the

---

[7] When organized civic constraint and discipline force Natty to seek serenity in the forest, Cooper has established generally the preconditions for a pastoral. From *The Pioneers* on, Natty inhabits a buffer state between raw primitivism and encroaching civilization. As Bruno Snell says of Virgil's Arcadia, it is a "half-way land" where "currents of myth and empirical reality flow into one another." —"Arcadia: The Discovery of a Spiritual Landscape," *The Discovery of the Mind; The Greek Origins of European Thought* (Oxford, 1953), p. 283. *The Pioneers* establishes as a menace the world of hostile urban forces and collective power; consequently, when we next find Natty, Uncas, and Chingachgook quietly talking in the forest, "We are made to feel that the immediate setting, a place of tender feeling and contentment, is an oasis in a land of tragic disorder." The quotation is Leo Marx's description of the setting of Virgil's *Eclogues* ("Two Kingdoms of Force," *Massachusetts Review,* I [October, 1959], 92). Cooper, we remember, had memorized the *Eclogues* twenty-five years earlier.

rationale of civilization, as represented by Major Duncan Heyward and psalm-singer David Gamut. Finally, it portrays Natty as an independent thinker in the process of shaping his own life and character.

The principal characters meet when Heyward, accompanied by Gamut and guided by a treacherous Indian (Magua or "Le Renard Subtil"), escorts Alice and Cora Munro toward Fort William Henry (which is commanded by their father) during the French and Indian war. Heyward is beginning to distrust Magua; and since he himself is lost in the forest (in spite of all the natural signs Natty mentions as showing directions), he requests, for the sake of the women, the aid of Natty, Uncas, and Chingachgook. Except for Natty's white skin, the three would scarcely inspire confidence, for Chingachgook is in black and white war-paint as an "emblem of death," and they are simply sitting, for no reason at all, in the middle of the forest discussing the history of the Delawares.

Tracing the decline of his people, Chingachgook sounds the familiar lament of the dispossessed: "'I, that am a chief, and a sagamore, have never seen the sun shine but through trees, and have never visited the graves of my fathers'" (29). Chingachgook establishes an *ubi-sunt* tone and identifies his son Uncas (whose name is a generic term for chief) as a symbol of the race.

"Where are the blossoms of those summers!—fallen, one by one; so all of my family departed, each in his turn, to the land of spirits. I am on a hilltop, and must go down into the valley; and when Uncas follows in my footsteps, there will no longer be any of the blood of the Saga-mores, for my boy is the last of the Mohicans." (29)

The sequence Chingachgook anticipates will be aborted because the three friends elect to aid Heyward's group; the extinction he keens is closer than any of them can realize.

It is significant that under the circumstances Heyward still has to request, rather formally, the aid of Natty and his friends. Heyward's military rank is meaningless in the forest where Natty and the Indians are an aristocracy of talent. Each has, as Natty explains, some special excellence for which he is famous and which is reflected in his Indian name. By contrast with Christian "fashion," the Indian system of naming is honorable self-assessment.

> "The biggest coward I ever knew was called Lyon; and his wife, Patience, would scold you out of hearing in less time than a hunted deer would run a rod. With an Indian, 'tis a matter of conscience; what he calls himself, he generally is—not that Chingachgook, which signifies Big Sarpent, is really a snake, big or little; but that he understands the windings and turnings of human natur', and is silent, and strikes his enemies when they least expect him." (60)

The practice acknowledges the wisdom of "Know Thyself," and allows each man to be an avatar of some excellence. Uncas is also known as "Le Cerf Agile" and Natty is called "La Longue Carabine" by the Mingos and "Hawkeye" by his friends. Natty takes classical pride in his ability to see and to shoot and predicates a whole family tree full of riflemen: "'I conclude the Bumppos could shoot, for I have a natural turn with a rifle, which must have been handed down from generation to generation . . .'" (27). Uncas is the best tracker; and while each is called upon to use his own particular talent, the three experts confer, according to Indian custom, on all important decisions, and the action thus records the working of a small but perfect government.

As the youngest member, Uncas is as deferential as he should be in a world where wisdom depends on experience. Natty explains:

> "Your young white who gathers his learning from books and can measure what he knows by the page, may conceit that his knowledge, like his legs, outruns that of his father; but where experience is the master, the scholar is made to know the value of years, and respects them accordingly." (256)

A second custom which makes Indians superior to whites is indicated when the Indians, convinced at one time that Natty's argument is sound, abandon "their own previously expressed opinions with a liberality and candor that, had they been representatives of some great and civilized people, would have infallibly worked their political ruin, by destroying forever their reputation for consistency" (238). This little government, where wisdom is weighted and error can be abandoned instantly, works so well that Heyward suspects "the foresters had some secret means of intelligence, which had escaped the vigilance of his own faculties" (233).

In addition to showing this government in action, the initial encounter of the two groups begins to establish Natty Bumppo as a gentleman. Cooper's gentleman must have taste, manners, and opinions based on intelligence and cultivation; Natty's early service (we know from *The Pioneers*) has aided him, but "cultivation" is, and always will be, his weakest quality. The most severe criticism of Natty ever recorded in the tales comes when Duncan Heyward of this book is quoted (in *The Prairie*) by his grandson: "'In short, he [Natty] was a noble shoot from the stock of human nature, which never could attain its proper elevation and importance, for no other reason, than because it grew in the forest'" (130). Natty's deficiencies are due to his lack of education; he has all the other qualities Cooper lists: liberality, refusal to stoop to meanness, truthfulness, superiority to scandal or meddling, pride of character. These last traits, plus intelligence, he shares with the Indians and has to a certain extent learned from the Indians. Cooper does not openly insist on this identification but makes it through the discrepancy between the behavior we would expect of Natty and his actions. Natty and his friends are, first of all, disinterested; when found, they are sitting in the forest, discussing history and seeming as little interested as Jane Austen in any contemporary wars. Although all three will act heroically in the adventures to follow, they do not volunteer; they wait until their help is asked, discuss the request, then make their commitment and stand by it. They do not meddle or pry into the affairs of the people they aid; the Indians ask no questions at all, and Natty only enough to satisfy himself that he is not aiding a traitor. They behave, in short, according to the Senecan precepts that governed the gentry; they are useful, when properly asked, to as many people as they can help. A little later, when (because they have no ammunition) they are no longer useful, they feel no qualms about leaving the original party, replenishing their gunpowder, and then returning to rescue their four charges who are, by then, Indian captives. Such behavior is often difficult for Duncan Heyward, governed by his artificial code of honor, to understand immediately.

Duncan Heyward's ignorance of Indians and the forest is, so far as Cooper is concerned, his most valuable asset. Writing before the stream-of-consciousness technique had been developed (a fact for which we, considering Alice Munro, can be grateful), Cooper had difficulty handling point of view in books about an illiterate hero. Natty could be given a limited amount of soliloquy, but most of the exposition had to be carried by dialogue. If any were needed, the excuse for Natty's talk was to be found in an authentic Indian oral tradition and in the simple truth that one learns, on the frontier, by talking. Still, the plausibility of Natty's analyzing aloud was reinforced by the presence of an intelligent young man (as the heroine's hero always is) who needs to learn what Natty and the Indians know.

As a result, Duncan is confused about those happenings and errs in those ways that will underscore the differences between the values and habits of civilization and those of Natty's group. Duncan, asking help, offers money; Natty reminds him that money is useless in the forest and suggests he offer prayers instead. Duncan dislikes taking cover when others are exposed, dissembling when dealing with a traitor, or departing from orthodox ways of fighting; Cooper recasts the old saying about Rome into Natty's statement: " 'Whoever comes into the woods to deal with the natives, must use Indian fashions, if he would wish to prosper in his undertakings' " (39). Duncan's "white reason" that considers a certain number of troops expendable in battle can be suicidal, as Natty reminds him: "'a man must ask himself, in this wilderness, how many lives he can spare'" (399). A long and precarious wilderness experience is implicit in Natty's casual remark that "'life is an obligation which friends often owe each other in the wilderness'" (80) and in his matter-of-fact statement that "'when men struggle for the single life God gave them, even their own kind seem no more than the beasts of the woods'" (47). Duncan has accepted society's standards of honorable conduct and is consequently concerned about how his actions appear to others; for Natty, the importance of honor is psychological and personal rather than social: "'. . . it is better for a man to die at peace with himself than to live haunted by an evil conscience'" (86).

In *The Pioneers*, Natty talked mostly of the past; here he is given to epigrammatic statements that sum, rather than recount, his experiences. He says the things a man would say who has examined his own life for what it tells about human nature. "'An Indian is a mortal to be felt afore he is seen'" (51). "'. . . A friend whose face is turned from you often bears a bloodier mind than the enemy who seeks your scalp'" (272). "'When a man consorts much with a people, if they are honest and he no knave, love will grow up atwixt them'" (234). "'Why, I believe it is natur' to give a preference to one's own quarrels before those of strangers'" (235). Such are Natty's explanations to Heyward for the shifting alliances, splitting tribes, and inscrutable (to Heyward) behavior of the Indians.

Such opinions are to be trusted. Having named his hero Natty (for Nathanael, the "given of God" or the prophet in whom, Jesus said, there "is no deceit"),

Cooper endowed him, as Hawkeye, with extraordinary
sight that begins to acquire some of the metaphysical
extension of Conrad's famous statement about making
the reader "see." In this book, Cooper adds a natural
temperament that is a "singular compound of quick,
vigilant sagacity, and of exquisite simplicity" (54). He
also elaborates on Natty's sense of an ordered universe;
Natty's devotion to order and his horror of anything
chaotic as "unnatural" amount to a rude ethic. One of
his bitterest complaints against the French and English
is based on this; he blames " 'white cunning' " for the
" 'confusion' " of tribes that sets people who speak the
same tongue to fighting each other. Such tactics throw
" 'everything into disorder' " and destroy " 'all the harmony of warfare' " (234). Like Sergeant M'Fuse of
Lionel Lincoln, Natty sometimes speaks of warfare as
though he were an eighteenth-century rules critic judg-
ing a new drama. Rules as such are not important, but
confusion and disharmony are signs of man's willful
disordering of a Providentially ordered theocentric universe. In this, too, he stands with the gentry against
the audacity that arose from nominalism.

The order that nature symbolizes for Natty is described by him at some length when he speaks of a
"rebellious" stream that left the course Providence first
gave it.

"If you had daylight, it would be worth the trouble to
step up on the height of this rock, and look at the perversity of the water. It falls by no rule at all; sometimes
it leaps, sometimes it tumbles; there, it skips; here, it
shoots; in one place 'tis white as snow, and in another 'tis
green as grass; hereabouts it pitches into deep hollows,
that rumble and quake the 'arth; and hereaway, it ripples
and sings like a brook, fashioning whirlpools and gul-

leys in the old stone, as if 'twas no harder than trodden clay. The whole design of the river seems disconcerted. First it runs smoothly, as if meaning to go down the descent as things were ordered; then it angles about and faces the shores; nor are there places wanting where it looks backward, as if unwilling to leave the wilderness to mingle with the salt. Ay, lady, the fine cobweb-looking cloth you wear at your throat, is coarse and like a fish-net, to little spots I can show you, where the river fabricates all sorts of images, as if, having broken loose from order, it would try its hand at everything. And yet what does it amount to! After the water has been suffered to have its will, for a time, like a headstrong man, it is gathered together by the hand that made it, and a few rods below you may see it all, flowing on steadily towards the sea, as was foreordained from the first foundation of the 'arth." (57)

This, to Natty, is the ""religion of the matter, in believing what is to happen is to happen'" (52). Rebellion, perversity, willfulness, all such attempts to destroy predetermined order are to Natty irreligious. Furthermore, to struggle against such an order is futile, and Natty consistently (like the seamen) finds his freedom within the governance of Providence and his own self-control.

When Cooper also gives Natty the belief that Providence is (while inscrutable) benevolent and that the soul is immortal, he has prepared for Natty's peculiar psychological resilience. He creates a character who can sit in the ruins of Fort William Henry, surrounded by corpses and alert to the noises made by human and bestial scavengers prowling the battlefield the first night after the massacre, and calmly say to Heyward:

"I believe that paradise is ordained for happiness; and that men will be indulged in it according to their dispositions and gifts. I therefore judge that a red-skin is not far from truth when he believes he is to find them glorious hunting grounds of which his traditions tell. . . . it is comfort to know we serve a merciful Master, though we do it each after his fashion, and with great tracts of wilderness atween us—what goes there?" (228, 229)

"What" is an Oneida whom Uncas scalps; moments later, Natty goes to sleep and Chingachgook and Uncas chat and laugh for a time in "soft and playful tones of affection." The incongruity of activities inside and outside the fort reveals that Natty, like the Indians, possesses a mind at peace with itself. He is not insensitive, but his beliefs control the perspective of present happenings and allow him to accept calmly, even comfortably, his separation from other men.

Natty is, all things considered, pre-Christian rather than Christian. It is true that in *The Pioneers* he is brought to trial with two counterfeiters (the thieves of a society devoted to cash), but in *The Last of the Mohicans* Cooper explicitly denies Natty's Christianity. David Gamut, the psalmist, instructs Natty, "' . . . seek no victims to my *manes*, but rather forgive my destroyers; and if you remember them at all, let it be in prayers for the enlightening of their minds, and for their eternal welfare'" (330). Natty thinks this over, then, mindful of his own experiences as usual, says,

"There is a principle in that . . . different from the law of the woods; and yet it is fair and noble to reflect upon." Then, heaving a heavy sigh, probably among the last he ever drew in pining for a condition he had so long abandoned, he added, "It is what I would wish to practise myself, as one without a cross of blood, though it is not always easy to deal with an Indian as you would with a fellow Christain [sic]. God bless you, friend, I do believe your scent is not greatly wrong, when the matter is duly considered, and keeping eternity before the eyes, though much depends on the natural gifts, and the force of temptation." (330)

Natty makes the same allowance for the natural man that brought Epicureanism into disrepute once the Romans took it over. Like Plotinus Plinlimmon of Melville's *Pierre*, he questions whether rules suited to heaven can ever be satisfactory for earth.

We shall probably never know how Cooper came to make Epicureans of Natty and his Indian friends; he toyed with the idea of history as something of a spiral moving slowly and with apparent reverses toward perfection; and the wilderness may have struck him as a removal in time as well as space into ancient ways of living. Or Cooper may have been in revolt (subconsciously?) away from civic virtues and toward social or personal dedication. Again we must remember that the nation's hopes were, for such men as Webster, founded on the total strength of a great number of strong individuals rather than on sheer numbers of men willing to place their undistinguished selves at the service of the republic. Whatever the reason, Natty and the Indians, with their devotion to *ataraxia* and their dedication to personal standards of honesty and friendship, gain in credibility through their Epicureanism, which strikes us as both strange and hauntingly familiar. Furthermore, it is a system of thought well suited to the uneducated minds of Natty and the Indians. Epicurus' basic attitude was a deep moral reverence, and his approach to the gods was literal, rather than abstract. (He disliked Plato's astral theory because it was undignified for gods to roll around the

sky as balls of fire, and he was a regular prude about
their fabulous love affairs.) Natty worries, in this book,
about being cooped up in the heavenly mansions the
white ministers speak of; later the Indian's idea of
heaven as the happy hunting-ground will bother him
because heaven means to be free from necessity and
consequently hunters there torment the dumb animals
for sport.

Such concerns make Natty seem childish, but Cooper
reminds us of the ancient equation of childlikeness and
innocence. The two terms not only form an equation
with the women and Conanchet ("a child among the
cunning") but underlie a statement he gives to Herr
Müller of *The Headsman:* " 'This is a glorious world
for the happy, and most might be so, could they
summon courage to be innocent' " (71). Since innocence
leads inevitably to a certain boyishness in the character,[8]
we must be careful not to assume that Cooper was
writing against reason, learning, maturity. Innocence
is properly opposed to the rote learning in schools of
the mistaken notions in a narrow education, to the
institutionalized religion that puts cant between man
and God, to speculation and a priori decisions that
deny experiential truths, to anything—in short—that
keeps a man from examining, with every means he
has, life itself. The antithesis of Natty Bumppo is not
Edward Effingham but Obed Battius *(The Prairie)*,
who identifies his own jackass as a *Vespertilio horribilis
Americanus* because the "image of the Vespertilio was

---

[8] Leslie Fiedler has written at length about the immaturity of
heroes in Cooper and American fiction generally; see, for instance,
An End to Innocence (Boston, 1955), particularly "Come Back to
the Raft Ag'in, Huck Honey!", pp. 142–51. Fiedler finds in American literature an "implacable nostalgia for the infantile, at once
wrong-headed and somehow admirable" (144).

on the retina" of his eye. By contrast, Natty, if a child, is the child who saw and said that the Emperor wore no clothes.

For Natty, not even the ideal should obscure the real and the possible; he tells David Gamut that if any man

> "will follow me from sun to sun, through the windings of the forest, he shall see enough to teach him that he is a fool, and that the greatest of his folly lies in striving to rise to the level of One he can never equal, be it in goodness, or be it in power." (135)

We have seen (with such characters as Red Rover) how Cooper believed the romantic agony of young Werther or Byron's heroes identified the hero *manqué*. By accepting the limitations of his own humanity (and that of others), Natty spares (or denies) himself any brooding anguish. When he impulsively shoots his rifle at a Mingo although they are trying to keep the party hidden, Natty says only, " 'It was an unthoughtful act. . . . But then it was a natural temptation! 'twas very natural' " (44). On another occasion, he uses the last of their desperately needed powder to end the misery of a wounded Mingo (and he hates Mingos) who is slowly losing his grip on a tree limb high overhead. Again, he is momentarily ashamed:

> " 'Twas the last charge in my horn, and the last bullet in my pouch, and 'twas the act of a boy!" he said; "what mattered it whether he struck the rock living or dead! feeling would soon be over." (83)

Yet, forty years later he remembers this scene and that he killed because he pitied and admired the Mingo.

". . . Never, before nor since, have I seen human man
in such a state of mortal despair as that very savage; and
yet he scorned to speak, or to cry out, or to own his forlorn condition! It is their gift, and nobly did he maintain
it!" (*The Prairie*, p. 274)

Natty's youthful impulsiveness has here caused him to
act out of admiration for a stoicism that boys traditionally
are supposed to admire. Such errors are, however, quite
consistent with his idea of himself as a man and not
a god; he is humanly wrong, and then only often enough
to keep him from becoming the "monster of goodness"
that Cooper feared he might be.

More serious charges of juvenility have been leveled
at Natty by those critics who, like Fiedler, seem chiefly
worried by Natty's relations with other men and the
lack of relations with women. Again, the truest reading
of *The Last of the Mohicans* is probably the most
classical; marriage was not in those days considered a
test of heroism. Women have little value for Natty, as
he indicates when he says, sounding a bit like Huck
Finn, that anyone "'who thinks that even a Mingo
would ill-treat a woman, unless it be to tomahawk her,
knows nothing of Indian Natur' . . . '" (258). In
his world, women are more a nuisance than an asset
(as Cora and Alice Munro have proved abundantly)
and Natty is scandalized by Magua's suggestion that
Natty exchange his life for Cora's. "'It would be an
unequal exchange, to give a warrior, in the prime of
his age and usefulness, for the best woman on the
frontiers,'" he says. Then he states his idea of a fair
exchange; "'I might consent to go into winter-quarters,
now—at least six weeks afore the leaves will turn—on

condition you will release the maiden'" (379). Like
Achilles, he is well aware of how much his withdrawal
from the warring forces is worth.

The life Natty elects is devoted to masculine pursuits.
He confesses that he first joined the Delawares because
they were a "scandalized and wronged race," and the
implication is that he saw in them a chance to be of
use; Cooper adds the further explanation that he continues with the Indians partly out of a "secret love
of desperate adventure which had increased with his
experience, until hazard and danger had become, in
some measure, necessary to the enjoyment of his
existence" (274). By this time, he has also formed close
friendships with Chingachgook and Uncas, and Cooper
tests the strength of Natty's ties through a study of
revenge and death. Indians, we remember, traditionally
revenge the deaths of members of their tribe; and the
closer the relation to the dead man, the more imperative
are the demands for vengeance; Conanchet, like Hamlet,
was haunted by his father's ghost. Natty transfers this
same obligation to the white "tribe" and assures Duncan
that should he be killed his death will be avenged.

Should Uncas be killed, however, revenge is not
enough; Natty himself will die, if he can arrange it,
in the place of the son of Chingachgook. He honestly,
but bluntly, tries to explain to Heyward why he will
not do for him what he proposes to do for Uncas:

"You have risked life, and all that is dear to you, to bring
off this gentle one [Alice Munro], and I suppose that
some such disposition is at the bottom of it all. As for me,
I taught the lad the real character of a rifle; and well has
he paid me for it. I have fou't at his side in many a

bloody skrimmage; and so long as I could hear the crack of his piece in one ear, and that of the Sagamore in the other, I knew no enemy was on my back. Winters and summers, nights and days, have we roved the wilderness in company, eating of the same dish, one sleeping while the other watched; and afore it shall be said that Uncas was taken to the torment, and I at hand—There is but a single ruler of us all, whatever may be the color of the skin; and Him I call to witness, that before the Mohican boy shall perish for want of a friend, good faith shall depart the 'arth, and 'Kildeer' become as harmless as the tooting we'pon of the singer!" (320)

The proper tradition behind this speech, heroic boasting and all, is the kind of feeling our literature associates with David and Jonathan, Damon and Pythias, or Achilles' doing for the sake of a friend what he will not do for the state. (Any homosexual implications are also a Greek gift.) Natty has no words for this feeling, born of admiration and compassion (in the root sense of the word), and the best he can do toward expression is to draw an analogy with what Heyward's feeling for Alice seems to be. When Uncas is finally killed in battle, the same sympathies draw him to the grieving Chingachgook with, Cooper says, "a force that no ideal bond of union could bestow" (422).

As Chingachgook ends his threnody, saying "'I am alone—,'" Natty interrupts, "'no, Sagamore, not alone. The gifts of our colors may be different, but God has so placed us as to journey in the same path. I have no kin, and I may also say, like you, no people. . . . The boy has left us for a time; but, Sagamore, you are not alone'" (423). In leaving those of his own race and staying with Chingachgook, Natty acts from his affections and his sense of true kinship. Some time in his

own hidden past (or, in the series, in *The Pioneers*),
Natty has been thrown back on "himself alone" as
Tocqueville predicted, but his alliance with Chingachgook keeps him from the companion fate of being
confined in "the solitude of his own heart." To be free
so to act, he has had to discard, as he says, his "people,"
as well as their pretension to racial and religious superiority over the Indians. He has had to go beyond society
and look, clear-eyed, for the honesty, faith, and friendship he sought. And having found these he suffers, with
Chingachgook, the frustration of his future hopes. Natty
often speaks of Uncas as a son in *The Last of the
Mohicans,* and Cooper finally allows him, in *The
Prairie's* Hard-Heart, the adopted son Uncas might have
been. In this third book, meant to be the last of the
series, Cooper combines the echoed experience of Uncas
with a sense of the pressures the solitary old hunter
fled at the end of *The Pioneers.* With these converging
backgrounds, the myth begins.

THE PRAIRIE

Many critics have written well about Cooper's use
of set scenes in the book that was supposed to end
Natty Bumppo's fictional career.[9] Charles Brady is

---

[9] Among these are Henry Nash Smith (*Virgin Land* and the
Introduction to the Rinehart edition of *The Prairie*), Marius Bewley
(*Eccentric Design*), and Donald A. Ringe (*James Fenimore Cooper*);
the article by Charles A. Brady, "Myth-Maker and Christian
Romancer" is also good, as are the articles by Howard Mumford
Jones and James F. Beard, Jr., which relate Cooper's literary tech-
niques to the work of contemporary artists. Cooper finished *The
Pioneers* in Europe, where, according to James Beard ("Cooper and
His Artistic Contemporaries"), he "sat long afternoons in the
Louvre while [Samuel F. B.] Morse copied paintings and Cooper
exclaimed, 'Lay it on here Samuel—more yellow—the nose is too
short—the eye too small—damn it if I had been a painter what a
picture I should have painted.' " While the Leatherstocking Tales

probably correct in suggesting that these betray Cooper's
conscious recognition of his hero's mythopoetic function;
and nowhere is this awareness more apparent than in
the widely-admired opening scene in which the members
of Ishmael Bush's caravan first catch sight of the old
trapper.

> The sun had fallen below the crest of the nearest wave
> of the prairie. . . . In the centre of this flood of fiery
> light a human form appeared, drawn against the gilded
> background as distinctly, and seeming as palpable, as
> though it would come within the grasp of any extended
> hand. The figure was colossal; the attitude musing and
> melancholy; and the situation directly in the route of the
> travellers. But imbedded, as it was, in its setting of
> garish light, it was impossible to distinguish its just pro-
> portions or true character.
>
> The effect of such a spectacle was instantaneous and
> powerful. The man in front of the emigrants came to a
> stand, and remained gazing at the mysterious object with
> a dull interest, that soon quickened into superstitious awe.
> His sons, so soon as the first emotions of surprise had a
> little abated, drew slowly around him, and as they who
> governed the teams gradually followed their example, the
> whole party was soon condensed in one silent and won-
> dering group. Notwithstanding the impression of a super-
> natural agency was very general among the travellers, the
> ticking of gunlocks was heard, and one or two of the
> bolder youths cast their rifles forward, in readiness for
> service. (8)

Natty does not approach or retreat but stands "within
the grasp of any extended hand," ready to serve those

---

furnished subjects for many paintings here and abroad, the picture
Cooper commissioned Cole to paint showed the Natty Bumppo of
The Prairie climbing a hill and beckoning to his companion to
follow (Beard, p. 486). The description of the painting suggests
Cole thought of Natty more as a guide than as an exile, or lonely
wanderer.

to whom he can be of use if they ask it. The image suggests what we can expect of a man and predicts Natty's function in the book. His "musing and melancholy" attitude is that of a contemplator. Not Natty but his "situation" (place in time and space) is directly ahead of the Bushes, but the "garish light" (crude and glaring frontier setting) obscures "just proportions and true character" (classical virtues, both). Furthermore, the Bushes, unable to comprehend such a figure, react as animals would, standing at gaze like dumb brutes and then (since they are bold rather than timid animals) preparing to attack.

Brady mentions that the scene in which Natty dies brings together "all of the underlying greater themes of the Tales—paternity, the mystery of race, the god in his aloneness,"[10] but the opening scene is a careful overture to them. It properly shows Natty alone and prepares for the integrity that will resist equally the threats of the Bushes and the personal appeal of Hard-Heart. He has by this time formed himself and is qualified to be the mediator that he is in the action; for this book contains, as Natty remarks, " 'four parties within sound of a cannon, not one of whom can trust the other' " (240). He is the only person who can communicate with all four groups, slipping easily from one tongue to another and varying his language to suit his hearers or match his own thoughts. He transcends the particular interests of any group, but has something in common with all of them and judges infallibly; as he explains, " 'it is needful to be honest in one's self, to be a fitting judge of honesty in others' " (441). He has, in short, achieved the godlike status of a contemplator:

---

10 Charles A. Brady, "Myth-Maker and Christian Romancer," p. 88. See also Bewley, *Eccentric Design*, p. 110.

The contemplator looks upon the world and man with the calm eye of one who has no design on them. In one sense he feels himself to be close to all nature. He has not the aggressive detachment or unfeeling isolation that comes from scrutinizing men and objects with a will to exploiting them. In another sense he is truly detached because he looks on none of them with intent to manipulate or control or change, on neither man nor beast nor nature.[11]

De Grazia's description of the Aristotelian ideal man not only fits Natty but explicitly denies Ishmael Bush, for Ishmael is the negation through which Natty is ultimately defined.

Henry Nash Smith has rightly observed that "the conceptual pattern of *The Prairie* develops from the juxtaposition of Ishmael with Leatherstocking."[12] They are yet another of those pairs (like the Effingham

---

[11] Sebastian de Grazia, *Of Time, Work and Leisure*, p. 20.

[12] Smith, however, goes on to say that the characters form a spectrum in which "Hard Heart expresses a cult of nature. Inez expresses a cult of civilization or, to use a term that for Cooper was synonymous, of refinement. The cult of nature places the locus of value at the bottom of the series of social stages. The cult of civilization places it at the top. In bringing these two characters together Cooper is affirming contradictory judgments concerning the course of social evolution in the New World."—Introduction to *The Prairie* (New York, 1950), p. xv. This schema, by assuming that Cooper's analysis was completely social and superficial, forces a contradiction on Cooper; Hard-Heart (who is no simple savage) and Inez (who is insignificant in the action) are not truly antithetical characters. Cooper later said the introduction of Inez and Middleton was "a great blemish" in the novel (Susan Fenimore Cooper, *Pages and Pictures*, p. 157.)
Professor Smith's refusal to take into consideration thought prior to the eighteenth century (where this contradiction does exist) leads to further trouble. Summarizing Cooper's fictional representation of the progress of civilization, he writes, "The Western frontiersman is thus the American analogue of 'those who have paved the way for the intellectual progress of nations in the old world.' Cooper's grasp of European history is far from secure; he seems to be trying to equate the American backwoodsman with Scott's lawless Highland chieftains" (xiii). The rest of Cooper's description of "those who have paved the way for the intellectual progress of nations" (70) is: "Both might be called without restraint, the one [the European]

cousins) Cooper likes to use to achieve niceties of analysis. Natty and Ishmael dress somewhat alike—they wear furs, carry rifles, pouches, horns—but Ishmael's fur is "of a fineness and shadowing that a queen might covet" (5) while Natty's is merely "worn with the hair to the weather" (10). Natty's rifle is worn from "long and hard service" while Ishmael's has a stock "of beautiful mahogany, riveted and banded with . . . precious metal."[13] Ishmael's other "prodigal and ill-judged ornaments" make him as conspicuous an acquirer as Mary McCarthy's character who always "looked as though she were going through customs"; Ishmael wears a gaudy silken sash, silver buttons on a dirty coat, and three Faulknerian worthless watches dangle "from different parts of his person" (5). He is the acquisitive Yankee in apotheosis, laden with possessions he neither takes care of nor knows how to use.

With the arrival of the Bush caravan, the hostile forces of society again impinge on Natty's consciousness. Both men hate the settlements, Natty detesting them for their "waste and wickedness" (442) and Ishmael feeling about them as a man would who, with his family, has been "published on the logs and stubs of the settlements, with dollars enough for reward to have made an honest

---

being above, the other [the borderer in America] beyond the reach of the law—brave, because they were inured to danger—proud, because they were independent—and vindictive, because each was the avenger of his own wrongs." Cooper lists as differences the facts that the European was a knight and religious while the American borderer is not. The prototype Cooper had in mind would seem to be Catholic and medieval.

13 This is the gun Ishmael will fire (unsuccessfully) at Ellen Wade and successfully at the cord by which he hanged Abiram White. Anyone who has read Albert Guerard's and Thomas Moser's comments on the Freudian symbolism of ineffective weapons in the writings of Conrad cannot escape similar implications in Cooper, whom Conrad described as his "constant companion." See Natty's dream on page 312.

man rich . . . " (103).[14] Although Ishmael and Natty share bitter memories about laws, they disagree about the nature of justice. Natty's idea of justice is indicated by his statement to Hard-Heart, who cannot believe his land was sold without the chiefs being present and asks where they were.

> "Right enough—right enough, and where were truth and honesty also? But might is right, according to the fashions of the 'arth; and what the strong choose to do, the weak must call justice. If the law of the Wahcon-dah was as much hearkened to, Pawnee, as the laws of the Long-knives, your right to the prairies would be as good as that of the greatest chief in the settlements to the house which covers his head." (220)

With Ishmael, justice is a relative thing, depending on whether or not his mind is in, as his wife says, " 'its honest corner' " (410) and upon what his impulses are at the moment. The power that Ishmael grabs when he "contrived to shift the responsibility of all that had passed from his own shoulders to those of his prisoners" (412) is frightening enough to anyone who knows psychopaths, but Ishmael's additional notion of himself as one " 'called upon' " (like Meek Wolfe) to become judge, jury, and executioner for his fellow men is horrifying (409). Understanding only one rule from the Bible ("an eye for an eye"), Ishmael embodies the great American nightmare of the early nineteenth century.

---

[14] Lillian Fischer (in "Social Criticism in Cooper's Leather-stocking Tales: The Meaning of the Forest," an unpublished Ph.D. dissertation, Yale University, 1957) points out that tree stumps are not accidentally mentioned as the posting places of "wanted" notices for Ishmael (p. 158).

Figures like Ishmael Bush, Cooper's brutal soulless squatter in *The Prairie,* underlined one of the threats which
these men saw in the process of westward settlement. If
men were naturally self-centered and rapacious, bent on
pursuing their own private ends, and nature was an
amoral or a neutral force [both conditions are true in
Cooper], then what was there in the classless and open
society of America to prevent its becoming a social jungle
the equal of which the civilized world had never seen?
What was to preserve the sanctity of the home and family, upon which it was felt depended the stability of
society, from the forces which were daily tearing it apart?
What, finally, was to provide the nation at large with a
coherent set of common aims which would prevent its
breaking up into a number of armed bands and hostile
factions each bent upon satisfying its wants at the expense
of society as a whole? [15]

Only getting on, Cooper would answer, with that
"pursuit of our total perfection" that Matthew Arnold
was later to call culture. To this end, Ishmael and Natty
are comparative studies in detachment. Ishmael's is the
aggressive detachment of the manipulator who toys
with other people's lives until his actions come full
circle and Esther wails, "'O! Ishmael, we pushed the
matter far" (426). He is probably the character Cooper
had in mind when Natty speaks of presumptuous man
who "'would mount into the heavens, with all his
deformities about him, if he only knew the road . . . '"
(283). In the same passage Natty says that if man's
"power is not equal to his will, it is because the wisdom
of the Lord hath set bounds to his evil workings." Natty
accepts human limitation and becomes, consequently,
more godlike than Ishmael, who tries to become like

---

[15] William R. Taylor, *Cavalier and Yankee,* p. 98.

God. Natty's detachment (shown usually by his refusal to meddle and his self-containment) allows him to witness the murder of Asa and say nothing of it until accused of being the murderer himself. Then he says calmly that he learned discretion from the redmen (420).

At the same time that Cooper is portraying a wasted Natty who feels keenly his own degradation as a trapper, he makes of him (as the Bushes first suspected) a supernatural being who lives, as Natty says, "in the air." He is even freer of time and space than old Tamenund, who has some of the same qualities. His reiteration of the classical refrains (Much have I seen, traveled, suffered, and long have I lived) build eventually an ubiquitous figure. He has earned authority, not just for his woodcraft, but for having seen the waters of both seas that bound America and for holding in his mind a country grown "'larger than I once had thought the world itself to be'" (82). His outlook has grown proportionately; and when Ishmael accuses him of having a "'redskin heart,'" Natty replies calmly, "'To me there is little difference in nations'" (84). Even his garrulity (realistically justified as a sign of loneliness and old age) adds to this sense of ubiquity as his conversation ranges through theory and memory while he ignores, to the exasperation of his companions, such immediate and pressing facts as prairie fires raging about them, Indians creeping up in the dark, and imminent torture at the hands of the Sioux. Through Natty's memories and his role as a disinterested mediator among four warring factions. Cooper pulls into notice the several strands from previous books and achieves an illusion of immortality.

True to the pastoral tradition, encounters in *The Prairie* are as improbable as those in a Shakespearean forest, but the accompanying revelations of true identity come early rather than late in the action. This strategy keeps identification of a minor character from vitiating the death scene toward which Cooper is building, and it also augments, throughout the intervening action, the figure of Natty. Thus Duncan Uncas Middleton, who arrives to retrieve his kidnapped bride from the Bushes, proves to be named for his grandfather (the Duncan Heyward of *The Last of the Mohicans*) and the dead Uncas of the same book. He has been brought up on stories about Natty Bumppo, whom he describes as "a man endowed with the choicest and perhaps the rarest gift of nature: that of distinguishing good from evil" (130). Having attested to the singularity and endurance of Natty in the oral tradition of his family, Duncan shows Natty a pup descended from Natty's old dog, Hector (who begins to show similarities with Ulysses' Argos). A second connection, through Duncan's middle name, is carried over and expanded with Natty's hope that Hard-Heart, the Pawnee, will prove to be related to his beloved Delawares. Natty tells Hard-Heart,

"Young warrior . . . I have never been father or brother. The Wahcondah made me to live alone. He never tied my heart to house or field, by the cords with which the men of my race are bound to their lodges; if he had, I should not have journeyed so far, and seen so much. But I have tarried long among a people who lived in those woods you mention, and much reason did I find to imitate their courage and love their honesty. The Master of Life has made us all, Pawnee, with a feeling for our kind. I never was a father, but well do I know what is the love of one. You are like a lad I valued, and I had even begun to fancy that some of his blood might be in your veins. But what matters that? You are a true man, as I know by the way in which you keep your faith; and honesty is a gift too rare to be forgotten. My heart yearns to you, boy, and gladly would I do you good." (330)

Since they find in each other the same Epicurean values (respect for truth and honesty and desire for peaceful companionship) that Natty revered in the Delawares, Hard-Heart rejects the famous Sioux chief's offer to adopt him and joins " 'that just warrior' " as a son.

As a result, when Natty dies in a Pawnee village, he is attended by representatives of both the white and the Indian worlds. Throughout *The Prairie*, Natty has been preparing to answer the roll call for the Last Judgment, although he speaks of it in military terms, reporting himself ready " 'to answer to my name as a soldier at evening roll-call' " (363). He pulls together references to his military service, death, and the capsule biography furnished by his successive names when he says,

". . . various have been the names by which I have gone through life; but little will it matter when the time shall come, and all are to be muster'd, face to face, by what titles a mortal has played his part! I humbly trust I shall be able to answer to any of mine in a loud and manly voice." (199)

Seeing himself many men become one, but responsible for all, Natty stands firmly by the convictions of his final self. He rejects Hard-Heart's offer of horses and arms at his funeral, and specifies that there be no boasting service for him; he does this out of respect for his own integrity and in the face of his personal attachment to the Indians. He makes, then, two bequests. His rifle (symbol of his success and excellence) he sends by Middleton back east (to Oliver Effingham, presumably); his traps (symbols of exile and decline) he gives to Hard-Heart. Choosing carefully from white and Indian customs, he further requests that his dead dog be buried with him and that he be buried in the Pawnee camp ("'beyond the din of the settlements'"), but that a white man's tombstone be erected on the grave. Just at sunset, the old man stands upright, supported on one side by Duncan Uncas Middleton and on the other by Hard-Heart.

> For a single moment he looked about him, as if to invite all in presence to listen (the lingering remnant of human frailty), and then with a fine military elevation of his head, and with a voice that might be heard in every part of that numerous assembly, he pronounced the word—
> "Here!"

The scene duplicates, of course, that other occasion of judgment in which Natty, pronounced guilty by the settlement's jury, has been called to the bar of the law by Judge Temple.

> "Nathaniel Bumppo," commenced the Judge, making the customary pause.
> The old hunter, who had been musing again, with his head on the bar, raised himself and cried, with a prompt military tone—
> "Here." (*The Pioneers*, 383) [16]

---

[16] Professor Levin has pointed out the similarity to the "Here am I" of Samuel 1:3. Lillian Fischer (in "Social Criticism in Cooper's Leatherstocking Tales") says this scene is "full of private meaning" since Natty, "standing upright at the last . . . is a monu-

This duplication of the judgment scene rounds off the action of *The Pioneers,* and, as many people have noticed, the beginning and ending of *The Prairie* are a balance of tableaux. Large as Natty is in this book, the entire novel has an air of resolution as it shows simultaneously the fruition and the slow but inevitable waste of the potential that has been Natty Bumppo. Similarly, he is without contradiction both a man who " 'always found that intercourse with my kind was pleasant and painful to break off, provided that the companion was but brave and honest' " (296) and one who, undismayed, sees himself as a solitary figure " 'if he can be called solitary who has lived for seventy years in the very bosom of natur' where he could at any instant open his heart to God without having to strip it of the cares and wickedness of the settlements . . . ' " (296). Natty's death is unlike that of two other solitary men, for Conanchet's uncertainty and confusion called for stoicism while Harvey Birch's was a release from ignominy; Natty, by contrast, has a faith that makes

---

ment to all he had lived for" (p. 170). She explains that the "private meaning" is due to Horatio Greenough's having likened the obelisk to the word: "If I understand its voice, it says, Here! It says no more." (See F. O. Matthiessen, *American Renaissance,* p. 143.) That Cooper meant Natty for a human monument is undoubtedly correct. (It reminds us of Willa Cather's comment, in her *O Pioneers!,* "Of all the bewildering things about a new country, the absence of human landmarks is one of the most depressing and disheartening.") The direction of the influence, however, is highly uncertain; Cooper recorded his first "Here" in 1822; Greenough designed an obelisk for a Bunker Hill monument in 1825; Natty's death scene was published in 1827 (the year Cooper became "like a father" to Greenough and started getting commissions for him), and Greenough's comment about the obelisk was not published until Emerson recorded it in his journal in 1852.

While we are tidying up remarks about this death scene, it should be said that D. H. Lawrence's lengthy and admiring comment on it unaccountably has Natty facing east (toward his native forests) rather than west as he dies. Lawrence missed the American equation of death, future, and the West.

stoicism unnecessary, and he has been understood by the good people he has met.

The Prairie shows that Cooper still believed people would revere and willingly follow a model character; he had tried to humanize Natty and the gentry both, but Natty emerges as more "real" because more vulnerable. At the same time, by yielding to a contrary impulse to deify Natty (a luxury he had never allowed himself with the gentry), Cooper achieved an odd sense of a life already lived in the past. He documented this at one step removed from the action by having Natty explain:

> "If I could choose a change in the orderings of Providence—which I cannot, and which it would be blasphemy to attempt, seeing that all things are governed by a wiser mind than belongs to mortal weakness—but if I were to choose a change, it would be to say, that such as they who have lived long together in friendship and kindness, and who have proved their fitness to go in company, by many acts of suffering and daring in each other's behalf, should be permitted to give up life at such times, as when the death of one leaves the other but little reason to live." (295)

This allusion to his former happiness with the Mohicans reminds us that Natty is just living out his allotted time, but Cooper's simultaneous humanizing and deifying extends beyond Natty's lifetime and into mythology. If Natty consequently moves among the four inimical groups on the prairie with the free ease of a spectre gliding through the insubstantial shades of another world, it is largely because he is already a member of the living dead.

THE PATHFINDER

After rounding off Natty's life, Cooper turned to sea romances, three novels set in Europe, *The Wept of Wish-Ton-Wish*, political satire *(The Monikins)*, his sketches of Europe, the history of the Navy, three expository works, and one novel of social criticism. These last cost him his popularity in America; and when he needed money and his publishers pleaded once more for another Leatherstocking Tale, he resuscitated Natty. In the final preface for *The Pathfinder* (1840), he admits that the book did not regain his public.

> It was, perhaps, a too hazardous experiment to recall to life, in this manner, and after so long an interval [seventeen years] a character that was somewhat a favorite with the reading world, and which had been regularly consigned to his grave, like any living man. It is probably owing to this severe ordeal that the work, like its successor, *The Deerslayer*, has been so little noticed. . . . (iii)

This is not the whole truth; Cooper's unpopularity with the newspapers had some effect. More importantly, Cooper here threatens to "civilize" Arcadia and domesticate Natty. He is revived at an age later than the time of *The Last of the Mohicans* and before the time of *The Pioneers*. Natty is a scout working for the British out of a fort on Lake Ontario in the middle of the eighteenth century.[17] His special friend within the fort

---

[17] This vocation in itself is exceptional, as it shows Natty being superintended, regulated, and observed as an employee. He has, it is true, wide discretion (he admits once to sending Chingachgook to do something he should have done himself), but this employment is the nearest Natty ever comes to being a common worker. His position also affects Chingachgook, who becomes more of a servant than ever before.

is a Sergeant Dunham, a man some thirty years older than Natty. Outside the fort, he travels with Chingachgook and a young white man, Jasper Western. The Scots in charge of the fort distrust Jasper because he (having been reared in Canada) speaks French, the language of the enemy. Consequently, Jasper is much like Oliver Effingham, the young man accepted by Natty and Chingachgook but distrusted by the white group in power. The opening of the novel is also familiar; the sergeant's daughter Mabel and her uncle Cap (a salt-water sailor) are being escorted through the enemy-infested forest by a treacherous Indian guide when they come upon Natty, Chingachgook, and Jasper.

As this opening, pieced together from *The Last of the Mohicans* and *The Pioneers* suggests, *The Pathfinder* is a pastiche and one of the most labored of Cooper's novels. Even the character of Natty seems derivative, and Charles Brady comes close to the right analogy for the Natty of this book when he says Hawkeye "stands somewhere between the picaro of the eighteenth-century narrative and the possessed, irrational hero of Gothic romance. . . . "[18] The great prototype who is both picaro and possessed is, of course, Don Quijote de la Mancha. The important thing about this parallel, for our present purposes, is that Natty possessed and in the hire of some calculating Scots is not at all

---

One interesting textual change in Cooper is related to Natty's not working for wages. In the first edition of *The Pioneers*, Natty says some settlers "bought" him to get them a stuffed panther. Cooper later changed the term to "hired" (or someone else did; Cooper's revisions are always uncertain for he gave his publishers great powers). The change could have been made because (according to *Webster's Dictionary* then in use) "to buy" meant "bribe" or "pay dearly for" in colloquial American. (See *The Pioneers* [New York, 1823], II, 107.)

[18] "Myth-Maker and Christian Romancer," p. 86.

like the freely ranging demigod Cooper buried at the end of *The Prairie*.

In Cooper's novels as in classical thought, an obsessed man (John Paul Jones was one mentioned earlier) is not free, and Natty is obsessed with (or possessed by, as you will) the ideal of the sergeant's daughter Mabel long before he meets her. In their talks together, the sergeant (who never acquires any physical presence) has talked at length about his happy life with Mabel's mother (now dead) and about Mabel herself. By the time Mabel approaches the fort to visit her father, Natty's feeling for her rivals that of Don Quijote for the unseen Dulcinea; she is perfection, the unattainable, and he is eager to devote his life to serving her. Cooper catches Natty's infatuation nicely; as the parties, once joined, run the usual gantlet toward the fort, Natty's recurring exhortation, "The sergeant's daughter must be saved," is as predictable (and as clearly obsessive) as Cato's "Carthage delenda est."

Exposing Natty to the threat of domesticity and saving him from his own obsession is the central problem of the book, and one not easily solved. Mabel is a douce heroine, and so like Alice Munro that Cooper referred to her as "Alice" part of the time and "Mabel" the rest in the first edition. To justify Natty's continued interest in her, Cooper endeavored to convince the reader of Mabel's superiority through acclamation. All the single men want to marry her (or pretend to—Cooper's analysis of Scotch canniness is devastating); even the commander of the fort has to remind himself that he is engaged. The traitorous Indian, Arrowhead, is enamored, of course; and even his wife (Dew-in-June) "had got to entertain an admiration and love for her [Mabel] which, though certainly very different, was scarcely less strong than that of her husband" (372). Even this is not enough, however; for the whole book depends on Mabel and she is weak; she cannot be artful and be a Cooper heroine. Cooper's remedy was to weaken Natty, also; the initial obsession is part of this vulnerability, innocence another. Natty is, Cooper writes, "a sort of type of what Adam might have been supposed to be before the fall . . . " (139). Elaborating on the prelapsarian theme, Cooper says,

> . . . The most striking feature about the moral organization of Pathfinder, was his beautiful and unerring sense of justice. This noble trait (and without it no man can be truly great; with it, no man other than respectable) probably had its unseen influence on all who associated with him; for the common and unprincipled brawler of the camp had been known to return from an expedition made in his company, rebuked by his sentiments, softened by his language, and improved by his example. . . . He was a fair example of what a just-minded and pure man might be, while untempted by unruly or ambitious desires, and let to follow the bias of his feelings, amid the solitary grandeur and ennobling influences of a sublime nature; neither led aside by the inducements which influence all to do evil amid the incentives of civilization, nor forgetful of the Almighty Being, whose spirit pervades the wilderness as well as the towns. (139, 140)

As Cooper tries to explain Natty as a strange combination of Adamic innocence, respectability, child of nature, and model influence, the character of Natty (as we know him) fades. A little later, still insisting on Natty's innocence, Cooper makes him seem six feet of idiot:

. . . The Pathfinder was a mere child: unpractised in
the ways of the world, he had no idea of concealing a
thought of any kind, and his mind received and reflected
each emotion with the pliability and readiness of that
period of life; the infant scarcely yielding its wayward
imagination to the passing impression with greater facility
than this man, so simple in all his personal feelings, so
stern, stoical, masculine, and severe, in all that touched
his ordinary pursuits. (294)

This kind of exposition goes on for pages; Cooper does
more writing *about* Natty in this book than in any of
the other tales. Why he feels called upon to do this is
a matter of conjecture, but the best guess is probably
that he is trying to force Natty into a role that both
the character and part of Cooper's own temperament
resist.

When Natty talks about himself, his obvious gauche-
rie as a lover is still obvious, but it is bearable because
filtered through and qualified by his own thoughts.
Before he has seen Mabel, he confesses, he has promised
the sergeant that he would consider marrying her; this
means, to him, that he must "'quit some of my wander-
ing ways, and try to humanize my mind down to a wife
and children'" (134). This sacrifice would apparently
be offset, for him, by erasing one danger that he sees
in living alone: "'the man that lives altogether in the
woods, and in company with his enemies, or his prey,
gets to lose some of the feelin' of kind, in the end'"
(92). Natty does not here consider the possibility of
male friends, and it is significant that Chingachgook's
role is very minor in this book; he is altogether missing
from most of the action.

When Mabel actually appears, Natty approaches her

as though she were a new species, saying of such "'gentle and pure-hearted creatur's,'" "'I have seen some of you before, and have heard of others'" (92). At the same time, he considers himself and confesses to the sergeant that "'it is not Mabel that I distrust, but myself. I am but a poor ignorant woodsman, after all, and perhaps I'm not, in truth, as good as even you and I may think me'" (134). The plot forces Natty to re-evaluate himself and judge by domestic rather than masculine standards. He begins to dislike the Natty that is "'too rude, and too old, and too wild like, to suit the fancy of such a young and delicate girl'" (135), and he tells the sergeant that he never knew his own "'worthlessness'" before. Such self-deprecation not only makes him vulnerable where Mabel is concerned but gives the villain (David Muir) a chance to take advantage of him. Natty is a pathetic figure as he confesses to David that "'one may be rude, and coarse, and ignorant, and yet happy, if he does not know it . . .'" (318). Gentle Mabel, in short, is the most destructive force Natty ever meets.

Were this all, once Natty is convinced of his own worthlessness he could shoulder his rifle and retire to the forest. But the sergeant keeps him around, encouraging false hopes, and actually bequeathing her to Natty as he is dying. During this time, Natty finds that his former joys have vanished. When Mabel suggests Natty may be happier alone than "'when mingling with your fellow-creatures,'" Natty replies that he used to think so, but that "'other feelin's have got uppermost . . .'" (282). He admits that he formerly thought himself happy "'when ranging the woods, on a successful hunt, breathing the pure air of the hills, and filled with vigor and health, but I now feel that it has all been idleness and vanity . . . '" (285). Even his shooting becomes domesticated, and he fires at potatoes or drives nails into trees with his bullets to win a calabash for Mabel. (He finally lets Jasper win the shooting contest, at Jasper's request, but tells Mabel about it later—which is not like Natty.) Eventually, even his pleasure in memories of "'scoutin's, and of my marches, and out-lyings, and fights, and other adventures'" pales before "'feelings in which there are no wranglings and blood-shed, and of young women, and of their laughs, and their cheerful soft voices. . . . I sometimes tell the sergeant that he and his daughter will be the spoiling of one of the best and most experienced scouts on the lines'" (199). Because of Mabel, he neglects his work, sending Chingachgook on a trail "'where I ought to have been too, but for a great human infirmity'" (281). Mabel disrupts his nights as well as his days, for he dreams that she is at the root of every tree. Then, in his dream, he tries to shoot a fawn, but Killdeer misses fire and the fawn "'laughed in my face, as pleasantly as a young girl laughs in her merriment, and then it bounded away, looking back as if expecting me to follow'" (292).

Only at the end of the book does Natty start to act like himself again. Too honest to take advantage of the sergeant's bequest, and learning that Jasper loves Mabel, too, Natty calls the three principals to a meeting, tells Mabel they both love her, meticulously inventories the strengths of Jasper and himself and ends with a blunt: "'Now stand up, and choose atween us'" (486). The more Mabel protests that such procedures are "improper," the more firmly Natty seems determined to get the whole thing decided. As James Grossman says, "he has a Noble Savage's faith, as naive and strong as a Shavian hero's, in reasonable discussion. Civilized sentimentality cannot hold out against him." [19] Mabel chooses Jasper, of course, and Natty interprets his bequest from the sergeant as a power of attorney to release her. They leave Natty alone on the island, "almost overcome with a sense of his loneliness. Never before had he been conscious of his isolated condition in the world. . . . Now all had vanished . . . and he was left equally without companions and without hope. Even Chingachgook had left him, though it was but temporarily; still his presence was missed at the precise instant which might be termed the most critical in our hero's life" (494).

The only conclusion one can draw from all this is that Mabel's effect is disastrous. She undermines Natty's self-respect, destroys his pleasures, ruins his professional ability, makes him dream of his own impotence, and leaves him crushed by his isolation. The terms Cooper uses are revealing; he opposes the real condition of "vigor and health" to a "feeling" of "idleness and vanity," and Natty refers to his feeling for Mabel as a "human infirmity." Again we have illusion and reality; the difference is that with the Natty of *The Pathfinder* (as with Don Quijote), the illusion is for a time more real than reality. Only by losing Mabel does Natty regain himself. According to the action (not Cooper's exposition), a streak of misogyny very like that found in Conrad and Faulkner was also latent in Cooper. It is not noticeable in most of the novels because the heroine's hero is already fabricated by the time she meets him; the threat is to the man who is trying to

---

[19] *James Fenimore Cooper*, p. 143.

fashion himself into the greatest man he could possibly become.

Since so much of Natty's life is devoted to producing himself, it is a relief that, late in the novel, he shows signs of putting Mabel in her properly parenthetical place among his interests:

"I've often thought . . . that he is happiest who has the least to leave when the summons comes. Now here am I, a hunter and a scout, and a guide, although I do not own a foot of land on 'arth, yet do I enjoy and possess more than the great Albany Patroon. With the heavens over my head to keep me in mind of the last great hunt, and the dried leaves beneath my feet, I tramp over the ground as freely as if I was its lord and owner; and what more need heart desire? I do not say that I love nothing that belongs to 'arth; for I do, although not much, unless it might be Mabel Dunham, that I can't carry with me. I have some pups at the higher fort, that I valy considerable, though they are too noisy for warfare, and so we are compelled to live separate for a while; and then, I think, it would grieve me to part with Killdeer; but I see no reason why we should not be buried in the same grave, for we are, as near as can be, of the same length—six feet, to a hair's breadth; but, bating these, and a pipe that the Sarpent gave me, and a few tokens received from travellers, all of which might be put in a pouch, and laid under my head, when the order comes to march, I shall be ready at a minute's warning. . . . " (460, 461)

This is the old Natty, not tied to property, proud of his talents, relishing his freedom, confident and content. As he himself says without realizing how true it is, " 'Ah's me! Mabel, I have indeed been on a false trail since we met!' " The a priori infatuation that put Mabel on Natty's retina (to use the figure Cooper developed with Dr. Obed Bat) blinded Natty to his true path.

One last observation about *The Pathfinder* and *Don Quijote de la Mancha*. Both books contain a tension between the contrary impulses to comedy and pathos, and Natty's gauche attempts to persuade Mabel to marry him are as close to comedy as to the obvious failure they portend. The final statements of the two books are completely unlike, however. The Spanish Don lives in a dream and only when dying returns to sanity; his illusions have a reality and truth that make their loss tragic. Natty's illusions, by contrast, give him a distorted view of the world that we cannot accept as either true or desirable; and in relinquishing them he escapes death and impotence and begins to live again.

THE DEERSLAYER

Just one year after *The Pathfinder*, Cooper wrote on back to Natty's first hunt. Eschewing the sentimentality, moralizing, and infantilism that accompanied Natty's rebirth or resurrection in the previous book, Cooper approached the neophyte Natty with a grandfather's tolerance. *The Deerslayer* has for its setting that same Otsego lake from which Natty was driven in *The Pioneers*, but the setting this time is suited to an idyl and its unspoiled hero; and its beauty (as usual in Cooper) becomes a way of testing character. The good people (particularly Natty) respond to the aesthetic appeal of the lake while the crude and insensitive (such as Harry March and Thomas Hutter) cannot.

In addition, so close is man to nature in *The Deerslayer* that they interact to produce something like a naturally justified pathetic fallacy. The setting becomes a part of the process Marius Bewley describes:

> . . . The most flagrant adventures are intrinsic parts of a developing moral theme, the whole of which becomes the form of the completed tale. Neither the characters nor their acts are extraneous to this theme, nor is the theme independent of the physical components of the story. For Cooper at his best, an action is the intensified motion of life in which the spiritual and moral faculties of men are no less engaged than their physical selves.[20]

This interweaving of "spiritual and moral faculties" with physical action and the setting begins when Natty and an acquaintance, Harry March, first reach the lake, and Harry impulsively shoots at a buck. Not only does the noise of the gun endanger them and their friends, but they do not need the meat. The sound of Harry's rifle, after a short silence, "reached the rocks of the opposite mountain, where the vibrations accumulated, and were rolled from cavity to cavity for miles along the hills, seeming to awaken the sleeping thunders of the woods" (43). The buck, unhurt and never having seen a man or heard a bullet before, only shakes his head at the initial report, but the echoes from the forest "awakened his distrust" (44). To Natty, they sound "'like the voice of natur' calling out ag'in a wasteful and onthinking action." Even Harry reacts with uncharacteristic whimsy, saying:

---

[20] *The Eccentric Design*, p. 73. Bewley later offers a perceptive comparison of Harry March, "the artistic progenitor of Senator McCarran's racial ideal," with Natty; "if there is a poetry of tolerance, Deerslayer is its expression." Equally valuable is the analysis Yvor Winters offers, in "Fenimore Cooper, or the Ruins of Time," to support his contention that the opening of the seventh chapter of *The Deerslayer* "is probably as great an achievement of its length as one will find in American fiction outside of Melville."

"You'll hear plenty of such calls, if you tarry long in this quarter of the world, lad. . . . The echoes repeat pretty much all that is said or done on the Glimmerglass [the local name for the lake], in this calm summer weather. If a paddle falls, you hear of it sometimes ag'in and ag'in, as if the hills were mocking your clumsiness; and a laugh or a whistle comes out of them pines, when they're in the humor to speak, in a way to make you believe they can r'ally converse." (44)

When Natty kills his first Indian, nature testifies to the fairness of his shot; his and his enemy's rifles are discharged so nearly together that "the mountains, indeed, gave back but a single echo" (113). Afterward, unusually "full and long" echoes reverberate around the lake (127). While echoes, a part of the pastoral formula, let Cooper suggest a relatedness of man and nature (as in *Home as Found*), they here bear an additional meaning by indicating the portent of the shot.

In this responsive setting, Natty first begins to discover himself as an adult. The Indian custom of naming men for their achievements is nowhere more significant for him than in this book; and when he recounts his former names, shed successively like so many outgrown snakeskins, he summarizes his life to the present. He has been, first of all, Nathaniel Bumppo. When his parents died, he went to live with the Delawares and became Straight-tongue, the Pigeon, Lap-ear (for his ability to find game), and then Deerslayer. As Deerslayer, Natty realizes that he is considered inferior by those "'who set more valie on the scalp of a fellow-mortal than on the horns of a buck'" (57). For Natty, this occasion of his first warpath should mean still another change of name.

The nature and meaning of Natty's approaching

ordeal is given a second dimension by the scoffing of
"Hurry Harry" March, a veteran scalp-taker, brawler,
and Natty's chance companion. Harry tries to nettle
the younger man, asking, " ' . . . did you ever pull a
trigger on an inimy that was capable of pulling one on
you?' " (7). When Natty admits he has not, Harry
asserts his own "manhood"; " ' . . . the sooner you
wipe the disgrace off your character, the sounder will
be your sleep; if it only comes from knowing there is
one inimy the less prowling in the woods. I shall not
frequent your society long, friend Natty, unless you
look higher than four-footed beasts to practise your rifle
on' " (7). Indifferent to this threat (and hence superior
to those Cooper heroes like Miles Wallingford who
confess themselves sensitive to the approbation of their
fellows), Natty replies that he awaits a friend (Chingachgook) " 'who will think it no disgrace to consort
with a fellow creatur' that has never yet slain his kind.' "

Throughout the book, Cooper maintains a counter-
point of uncertainty and self-assurance. Natty frankly
confesses his probationary state (30, 64, 92), his doubts
welling up from his knowledge of human fallibility.
As he learns through experience about himself, he finds
that he will not shoot an unarmed man even when
threatened, that he can kill fairly when he must, that
he can refrain from boasting, that he can withstand
psychological torture, and that he remains firm when
the Indians " 'hold up avarice afore me on one side,
and fear on t'other, and think honesty will give way
atween 'em both' " (312). Furthermore, he is uninflu-
enced by the fact that the honesty of the two men he
is protecting has long since given way under these
identical pressures. Yet Natty never presumes to extend

his confidence in himself; each test brings its own doubts that can be canceled only by knowledge. Cooper illustrates this in the scene in which the Indians first throw tomahawks at Natty, then shoot at him in what they consider the more harrowing trial. Natty, to whom the tomahawk is as foreign as guns are to Indians, is relieved when he confronts the weapon he has mastered (525).

At the same time that he shows lack of self-knowledge as debilitating, Cooper grants Natty the confidence of the just. Natty refuses to be badgered by Harry March into agreeing that killing is proof of manhood; that man is, says Natty, "'the most of a man who acts nearest the right'" (30). Neither his personal hatred for Mingos nor the laws that promise bounty for their scalps affect Natty's view of what is right: "'When the colony's laws, or even the King's laws, run ag'in the laws of God, they get to be onlawful, and ought not to be obeyed'" (37). The action supports Natty's anarchism by having Hurry Harry and Thomas Hutter, raiding the Indian camp, seize not a Mingo but the Mingo's own prisoner, Hist. Acting out of hatred and greed and with the blessing of the law, Harry March and Hutter attack the one person Chingachgook and Natty have come to rescue.

In spite of the violence in it, the term "idyl," often applied to *The Deerslayer,* is correct. It is justified by the setting and by the hero's youth, multiple adventures, and chivalric purpose. Like the heroes of older romances, Natty never questions that it is "'the duty of the strong to take care of the weak, especially when the last belong to them [women] that natur' intended man to protect and console by his gentleness and strength'" (75). He accepts, as a law of nature, the ancient code that governed chivalry: "'to defend our lives, and the lives of others, too, when there's occasion and opportunity'" (91). It is beyond these certainties, which he never questions, that Natty finds moral doubts. In the old romances, when an arm thrusts a sword above the water of a lake, the hero knows it is meant for him. Furthermore, he always knows where to take it and what to do with it when he gets there. For Natty, the rules of chivalry are not so simple. Three distinct codes present themselves to him in *The Deerslayer;* and though he finds his weapon (the rifle), the use he is to make of it is not completely clear.

To follow Christianity in its purest form (as advocated by Hetty Hutter) would require him to give up the rifle entirely. To obey the Indian system of honor requires revenging every wrong and bringing back the trophies that "rightfully" belong to the honor of the Delawares. (When Chingachgook learns Natty has killed a man, he wants to go get the scalp, saying "'The honor belongs to the tribe; it must not be lost!'", 154.) To follow the values of the borderers means to "unhumanize" his nature, to kill women and children for cash, and to accept the right of might and the values of a materialistic society.

Cooper helps Natty narrow the choices by giving him a temperament too realistic to accept any course that obviously will not succeed. Hetty Hutter's simple Christianity does not work. Her confidence in her own ability to make the Indians obey the very commandments her father and Harry March ignore is as unwarranted as David Gamut's assertion, just before the massacre at Fort William Henry, that he has "'words'" that "'shall quiet the most unruly temper.'" She can only burst into tears when Rivenoak asks the inevitable Indian question: " 'He [the white man] comes from beyond the rising sun, with his book in his hand, and he teaches the redman to read it; but why does he forget himself all it says?' " (194). Both James Grossman and Charles Brady have pointed out Hetty's resemblance (and to a lesser extent Natty's) to the Dostoevskian thoroughly good mental defective. The truth is probably that both writers were drawing from the tradition of the "pure fool" in folk literature; Dostoevski's Myshkin has been related to Ivanushka, the simpleton of folktales, and thence to the *yurodivyi*, the saintly imbecile. Hetty Hutter matches such characters, except that Cooper insists perhaps too strongly on her innocence as invulnerability.[21]

As compared with Hetty, Natty is a blessed relief when he declares that his own spiritual state is " 'not good enough for the Moravians,' " yet " 'too good for most of the other vagabonds that preach about in the woods' " (110). When he discusses with Hurry Harry the injunction of turning the other cheek rather than seeking revenge, Natty's own interpretation adjusts the doctrine according to the real nature of man. " 'I don't understand by this any more than that it's *best* to do

---

[21] Hetty, followed docilely by a mother bear and her cubs, antedates Hawthorne's own romanticism which lets the very innocent communicate with wild animals (as in *The Marble Faun*). Further complicating Hetty's invulnerability is the Indian custom of respecting the mental defective, plus the notion that there is an "awe which nature has instilled into all of the inferior for the highest animals of the creation."—*Jack Tier*, p. 257. In this book, the awe keeps sharks from eating a sailor; in *The Prairie* it keeps the carrion birds from devouring a "victim which, frightful and disgusting as it was, still bore too much of the impression of humanity to become the prey of their obscene appetites" (158). The Miltonic influence seems strong; writing of Adam and Eve's "shadie bower" in book IV of *Paradise Lost*, Milton said, . . . Other creature here/Beast, Bird, Insect, or Worm durst enter none;/Such was their awe of man."

this, if *possible*. Revenge is an Injin gift, and forgiveness a white man's. That's all. Overlook all you *can* is
what's meant; and not *revenge* all you can.'" And to
Hetty's suggestion that he should have returned good
for evil done him by an Indian instead of braining
him with his own tomahawk, Natty says,

> " . . . That may do among the missionaries, but 'twould
> make an onsartain life in the woods. The Panther craved
> my blood, and he was foolish enough to throw arms into
> my hands at the very moment he was striving a'ter it.
> 'Twould have been ag'in natur' not to raise a hand in
> such a trial, and 'twould have done discredit to my train-
> ing and gifts." (507)

Natty's insistence that the present life has value and
that a man's training and talents deserve respect saves
him from puerility. Yet he and Hetty have (as Cooper
notes) similarities; both approach religious questions
simply and literally, have an instinctive sense of right
and wrong, believe the settlements are full of wickedness, and expect to meet again in heaven. The affinity
between the two is explained most quickly by comparing
Cooper's description of Hetty with the words that end
the novel. Hetty is

> one of those mysterious links between the material and
> the immaterial world, which, while they appear to be
> deprived of so much that is esteemed and necessary for
> this state of being, draw so near to, and offer so beautiful
> an illustration of the truth, purity, and simplicity of an-
> other. (559)

The conclusion to *The Deerslayer* returns to much the
same idea.

We live in a world of transgressions and selfishness, and no pictures that represent us otherwise can be true; though happily for human nature, gleamings of that pure spirit in whose likeness man has been fashioned, are to be seen, relieving its deformities, and mitigating, if not excusing its crimes. (573)

The important similarity is in their common saintliness; the one character in the novel, however, who can see the world as it is and at the same time prevent this knowledge from quenching the "gleamings of that pure spirit" he embodies is Natty Bumppo.

The second code to which Natty is exposed is that of worldly values represented by Thomas Hutter, Harry March, the settlements, and Judith Hutter. Of this group, only Judith is really a temptation, for Natty's lack of respect for the other men is constant throughout the novel. In the Preface, Cooper announces his intention of contrasting the two women, but describes Judith as one "full of art, vanity, and weakness" and calls attention to the preference Natty gives to Hetty over "beauty, delirious passion, and sin." We can grant beauty to Judith, for everyone considers her beautiful, but what delirious passion and sin have to do with Natty is a mystery to this day.

The fictional Judith that emerges is more complex and ambiguous than this. Harry March intimates that she is not all she should be, but then he is trying (through fair means or foul) to get her to marry him. It is true that Judith wishes to have nothing to do with a certain Captain Warley, the senior officer of a nearby fort, who is said to be "the very individual with whom the scandal of the garrisons had most freely connected

323

the name of this beautiful but indiscreet girl" (547).
But Natty does not know any of this. All he knows is
that she is forward (she proposes to him) and that,
according to Harry, she has managed to get herself
talked about. It seems a strange point for Cooper to be
unsympathetic on, and one always wonders how much
Spartan history (where the achievements of disciplined
men were destroyed by wanton women) lies behind
Cooper's treatment.

Judith looks better in action than under analysis.
She proves herself quick, skillful, resourceful, and
courageous. She tries to improve her character, giving
up her beloved finery when she finds Natty disapproves;
and yet she risks his good opinion and dresses herself
in brocades in an attempt to awe the Indians into
releasing him. It looks as though she might succeed
when little Hetty informs the chief that Judith is really
no emissary from the Queen but is Muskrat Hutter's
daughter from the middle of the lake. The authorial
statements about Judith sometimes relent, compounding
the ambiguity. She is described as being "goaded by a
sense of wrongs not altogether merited, incited by the
helplessness of a future that seemed to contain no resting
place . . . " (433). Even Natty seems occasionally
aware of complexities in her nature and the circumstances that trap her; he warns her, " ' . . . never do
anything in bitterness, or because you feel as if you'd
like to take revenge on yourself for other people's back-
slidings'" (440). The truth of the matter is that in
spite of the moral advice Cooper decided to work into
the novel, Natty is simply not interested in getting
married. He tells Chingachgook that he never felt about
any girl as Chingachgook feels toward Hist "'though

the Lord knows my feelin's kind enough towards 'em all" (450). He thinks of women as a group, hypothetically, or not at all.

With the "civilized" values represented by Harry March and Thomas Hutter, Natty has even less difficulty. They deal in cash rather than honor; they cannot be trusted not to shoot down an emissary of peace; and they lack even the most primitive forms of loyalty. Natty engineers their release from the Indians; but when he is captured, they abandon him. Worse, while Natty is a captive, Harry fires at an Indian on shore in the dark and succeeds in killing a young girl who has gone down to meet her lover. As Natty says, "'that shot might just as well have been fired into my breast'" (398). Finally, Harry March refuses to stay and help the Hutter girls defend themselves and their home unless Judith will marry him. In short, white civilization's representatives will do nothing for its own sake; everything they do must be paid for in commercial coin, and their way of life is, of the three presented, the least temptation to Natty.

The third system is, of course, the Indians'. Most of their values are familiar by now, and Cooper sides with them. Even when they are about to put Natty to the torture, the author's mention of the problem Rivenoak must solve in disposing of Sumach (the middle-aged widow of the slain warrior and the mother of a sizable brood) puts the reader "in the midst of a truly Homeric age, where grand heroic warfare goes hand in hand with opportune domestic arrangements between victor and vanquished." [22] Such scenes keep even the enemy Indians from appearing fiendish. Fur-

[22] James Grossman, *Fenimore Cooper*, p. 148.

thermore, the whole matter of Natty's furlough and voluntary return for torture relates honor to life. As Marius Bewley says,

. . . . This episode is the key to the significance of Deerslayer's life, which is moulded in the imagination with the firm spiritual contours of the saint. It reveals Natty's vision of life to us as a passionate dedication to truth—and truth, not as the pragmatical nothingness it was to become in American life, but as a religious conception.[23]

Only Chingachgook and Hist can understand Natty's devotion to truth as something good of itself, and only with them will he have the freedom to form himself fully. Of the three routes opened to Natty at the end of *The Deerslayer*, the way of the Indian is the only clear path for him.

Compounded of ancient and American legends of the past and of a dream for the future, Natty Bumppo most completely synthesizes Cooper's thought about the human condition in America. Natty, like Falstaff, is a great synthetic character, an embodied truce of conflicting impulses. The adventures Cooper invented for him reveal the conviction that a man's primary function is to form a self consistent with the ideals of absolute truth. To do this, Natty must be free; and since he will not deny another what he himself needs, his respect for the integrity of others emerges as an expansive tolerance. He is a plea that diversity be allowed to survive.

As an uncommon common man trying to live as a man should, Natty is most threatened by the popular

---

[23] *The Eccentric Design*, p. 99.

opinion that judges worth by wealth, by insufficient justice that puts him at the mercy of his neighbors so long as he owns property, and by women. All come together in his explanation, in *The Prairie,* that the Wahcondah "made me to live alone. He never tied my heart to house or field . . . ; if he had, I should not have journeyed so far, and seen so much" (330). Were Natty a modern hero, this would be a disguised plea for compassion, but he is only counting the cost of his freedom. Journeying far and seeing much are good in Cooper's world; and if, as Richard Chase says of him, Natty "seems ultimately to deny the whole idea of society," we see why he must. Natty's business is to form himself, to find his place in the universe; and this is essentially a religious (rather than political) activity. It is also by its nature a solitary one, which leads us into the territory of antithesis, for a solitary quest for perfection of individual character was at the very heart of democratic hope. Yet all Cooper's loyalty to republicanism and all his fictional inventiveness could not show him how to expand Natty's figure within society.

Cooper kept him outside it, in an aloneness that is neither tragic nor aggressive—just necessary. The other isolated Americans he wrote of became society's victims (like Harvey Birch and Conanchet), or were lessened by their compromises with it (like Miles Wallingford). The one (Onoah) who became convincingly Christian ceased to be a man. These are the characters that attest the impossibility of a Natty Bumppo in society; they all represent some form of loss and they support D. H. Lawrence's complaint that the Leatherstocking Tales are a "wish-fulfillment vision, a kind of yearning myth." Yet Natty is impossible much as some of the modern

327

heroes discussed by R. W. B. Lewis are impossible; these are dedicated "not so much to a supernatural god as to what yet remains of the sacred in the ravaged human community," and their characters are revealed through a series of "encounters between the hero and beings and customs it is his purpose to outwit; and between the hero and those rare beings with whom communion may be fleetingly possible." [24]

Hope died hard in Cooper, and he furnished Natty's world with a number of these "rare beings." Yet Cooper never again risked Natty, after *The Pioneers,* within democratic society. At the end of his life, Cooper had not been able to reconcile the classical values Natty represents with the democracy that was taking shape. Still, William Cullen Bryant, who was Cooper's friend, said that Cooper died while planning another Leatherstocking Tale in the belief "that he had not yet exhausted the character." [25]

---

[24] *The Picaresque Saint,* pp. 32, 34.

[25] "Discourse on the Life and Genius of Cooper," in *Memorial of James Fenimore Cooper,* p. 68.

BIBLIOGRAPHY

BIBLIOGRAPHY

ADAMS, BROOKS. *The Law of Civilization and Decay.* New York: Macmillan Co., 1897.

ADAMS, JOHN. *The Works of John Adams,* ed. CHARLES FRANCIS ADAMS. Boston: Little & Brown, 1850–56.

AUDEN, W. H. *The Enchafed Flood.* London: Faber & Faber, n.d.

BEARD, JAMES F. "Cooper and His Artistic Contemporaries," *James Fenimore Cooper: A Re-appraisal.* Special issue of *New York History,* ed. MARY E. CUNNINGHAM, Cooperstown: New York State Historical Association, LII (1954), 480–95.

———. "The First History of Greater New York: Unknown Portions of Fenimore Cooper's Last Works," *NYHSQB,* XXXVII (1953), 109–45.

BEWLEY, MARIUS. "Problems of the Literary Biographer," *Hudson Review,* XV (Spring, 1962), 143–48.

———. *The Eccentric Design: Form in the Classic American Novel.* London: Chatto & Windus, 1959.

BOWEN, ELIZABETH. "Notes on Writing a Novel," *Modern Literary Criticism,* ed. IRVING HOWE. New York: Grove Press, 1958. (First published in *Orion,* II.)

BRADY, CHARLES A. "Myth-Maker and Christian Romancer," *American Classics Reconsidered: A Christian Appraisal*, ed. HAROLD C. GARDINER, S. J. New York: Charles Scribner's Sons, 1958.

BROOKS, VAN WYCK. *The World of Washington Irving*. New York: Dutton & Co., 1944.

BROWN, HERBERT ROSS. *The Sentimental Novel in America: 1789–1860*. New York: Pageant Books, 1959.

BRYANT, W. C. "Discourse on the Life and Genius of Cooper," *Memorial of James Fenimore Cooper*. New York: Putnam, 1852.

CADY, EDWIN HARRISON. *The Gentleman in America*. Ithaca, N. Y.: Syracuse University Press, 1949.

CHARVAT, WILLIAM. "Cooper as Professional Author," *James Fenimore Cooper: A Re-appraisal*. Special issue of *New York History*, ed. MARY E. CUNNINGHAM. Cooperstown: New York State Historical Association, LII (1954), 496–511.

————. Introduction to *The Last of the Mohicans*. Cambridge, Mass.: Riverside Press, 1958.

————. *The Origins of American Critical Thought*. New York: A. S. Barnes & Co., 1961.

CHASE, RICHARD. *The American Novel and Its Tradition*. New York: Doubleday & Co., 1957.

CLAVEL, MARCEL. *Fenimore Cooper and His Critics*. Aix-en-Provence: Imprimerie Universitaire de Provence, 1938.

————. *Fenimore Cooper: Sa vie et son ouevre: La jeunesse (1789–1826)*. Aix-en-Provence: Imprimerie Universitaire de Provence, 1938.

CONRAD, JOSEPH. "Tales of the Sea," *Notes on Life and Letters*. New York: Doubleday, Page & Co., 1925.

COOPER, JAMES FENIMORE. *Afloat and Ashore: A Sea Tale*. (Pathfinder edition.) New York: G. P. Putnam's Sons, n. d.

————. *America and the Americans: Notions Picked up by a Traveling Bachelor*. 2 vols. 2nd ed.; London: Henry Colburn, 1836.

————. *The American Democrat: Or Hints on the Social and Civic Relations of the United States of America.* Cooperstown: H. & E. Phinney, 1838.

————. *Autobiography of a Pocket-Handkerchief.* Chapel Hill: Private printing, 1949.

————. *The Bravo.* (Pathfinder edition.) New York: G. P. Putnam's Sons, n. d.

————. *The Chainbearer: Or The Littlepage Manuscripts.* (Pathfinder edition.) New York: G. P. Putnam's Sons, n. d.

————. *The Crater: Or Vulcan's Peak.* (Pathfinder edition.) New York: G. P. Putnam's Sons, n. d.

————. *The Deerslayer: Or The First War-Path.* (Pathfinder edition.) New York: G. P. Putnam's Sons, n. d.

————. *Early Critical Essays,* edited, with an Introduction, by JAMES FRANKLIN BEARD. Gainesville, Fla.: Scholars' Facsimiles and Reprints, 1955.

————. *The Headsman: Or The Abbaye des Vignerons.* (Pathfinder edition.) New York: G. P. Putnam's Sons, n. d.

————. *The Heidenmauer: Or The Benedictines.* (Pathfinder edition.) New York: G. P. Putnam's Sons, n. d.

————. *Home as Found: Sequel to Homeward Bound.* (Pathfinder edition.) New York: G. P. Putnam's Sons, n. d.

————. *Homeward Bound: Or The Chase.* (Pathfinder edition.) New York: G. P. Putnam's Sons, n. d.

————. *Jack Tier: Or The Florida Reef.* (Pathfinder edition.) New York: G. P. Putnam's Sons, n. d.

————. *The Last of the Mohicans: Or A Narrative of 1757.* (Pathfinder edition.) New York: G. P. Putnam's Sons, n. d.

————. *A Letter to His Countrymen.* New York: John Wiley, 1834.

————. *The Letters and Journals of James Fenimore Cooper,* edited, with introductions to each section, by JAMES

FRANKLIN BEARD. Cambridge, Mass.: Belknap Press, 1960 and 1964. (The four volumes in print span the years 1800–1844.)

————. *Lionel Lincoln: Or The Leaguer of Boston.* (Pathfinder edition.) New York: G. P. Putnam's Sons, n. d.

————. *Mercedes of Castile: Or The Voyage to Cathay.* (Pathfinder edition.) New York: G. P. Putnam's Sons, n. d.

————. *Miles Wallingford: Sequel to Afloat and Ashore.* (Pathfinder edition.) New York: G. P. Putnam's Sons, n. d.

————. *The Monikins.* (Pathfinder edition.) New York: G. P. Putnam's Sons, n. d.

————. *Ned Myers: Or, A Life Before the Mast.* London: George Routledge & Sons, n. d.

————. *The Oak Openings: Or The Bee-Hunter.* (Pathfinder edition.) New York: G. P. Putnam's Sons, n. d.

————. *The Pathfinder: Or The Inland Sea.* (Pathfinder edition.) New York: G. P. Putnam's Sons, n. d.

————. *The Pilot: A Tale of the Sea.* (Pathfinder edition.) New York: G. P. Putnam's Sons, n. d.

————. *The Pioneers: Or The Sources of the Susquehanna.* (Pathfinder edition.) New York: G. P. Putnam's Sons, n. d.

————. *The Pioneers: Or The Sources of the Susquehanna* New York: Charles Wiley, 1823.

————. *The Prairie.* (Pathfinder edition.) New York: G. P. Putnam's Sons, n. d.

————. *Precaution.* (Pathfinder edition.) New York: G. P. Putnam's Sons, n. d.

————. *The Red Rover.* (Pathfinder edition.) New York: G. P. Putnam's Sons, n. d.

————. *The Redskins: Or Indian and Injin.* (Pathfinder edition.) New York: G. P. Putnam's Sons, n. d.

————. *Satanstoe: Or The Littlepage Manuscript, A Tale of the Colony.* (Pathfinder edition.) New York: G. P. Putnam's Sons, n. d.

———. *The Sea Lions, Or The Lost Sealers*. (Pathfinder edition.) New York: G. P. Putnam's Sons, n. d.

———. *The Spy: A Tale of the Neutral Ground*. (Pathfinder edition.) New York: G. P. Putnam's Sons, n. d.

———. *The Two Admirals*. (Pathfinder edition.) New York: G. P. Putnam's Sons, n. d.

———. *The Water-Witch: Or The Skimmer of the Seas*. (Pathfinder edition.) New York: G. P. Putnam's Sons, n. d.

———. *The Ways of the Hour*. (Pathfinder edition.) New York: G. P. Putnam's Sons, n. d.

———. *The Wept of Wish-Ton-Wish*. (Pathfinder edition.) New York: G. P. Putnam's Sons, n. d.

———. *The Wing-and-Wing: Or Le Feu-Follet*. (Pathfinder edition.) New York: G. P. Putnam's Sons, n. d.

———. *Wyandotté: Or The Hutted Knoll*. (Pathfinder edition.) New York: G. P. Putnam's Sons, n. d.

COOPER, SUSAN FENIMORE. "A Glance Backward," *Atlantic Monthly*, LIX (February, 1887), 199–206.

———. *Pages and Pictures from the Writings of James Fenimore Cooper*. New York: W. A. Townsend & Co., 1861.

CUNLIFFE, MARCUS. "American Watersheds," *American Quarterly*, XIII (Winter, 1961), 480–94.

DAY, A. GROVE. *The Sky Clears*. New York: Macmillan Co., 1951.

DE GRAZIA, SEBASTIAN. *Of Time, Work and Leisure*. New York: Twentieth Century Fund, 1962.

DONDORE, DOROTHY. "The Debt of Two Dyed-in-the-Wool Americans to Mrs. Grant's *Memoirs*: Cooper's *Satanstoe* and Paulding's *The Dutchman's Fireside*," *American Literature*, XII (1940), 52–58.

FIEDLER, LESLIE. *An End to Innocence*. Boston: Beacon Press, 1955.

FISCHER, LILLIAN. "Social Criticism in Cooper's Leatherstocking Tales: The Meaning of the Forest." Unpublished Ph.D. dissertation, Yale University, 1957.

FREDERICK, JOHN T. "Cooper's Eloquent Indians," *Publications of the Modern Language Association*, LXXI (1956), 1004–17.

GATES, W. B. "Cooper's Indebtedness to Shakespeare," *Publications of the Modern Language Association*, LXVII (1952), 716–31.

GLICKSBURG, CHARLES I. "Cooper and Bryant: A Literary Friendship," *Colophon*, Part 20. New York, 1935, no pagination.

GREEN, PETER. *Essays in Antiquity*. Cleveland: World Publishing Co., 1960.

GRIFFIN, MAX L. "Cooper's Attitude toward the South," *Studies in Philology*, XLVIII (1951), 67–76.

GROSSMAN, JAMES. *James Fenimore Cooper*. New York: William Sloane Associates, 1949.

HASTINGS, GEORGE E. "How Cooper Became a Novelist," *American Literature*, XII (1940), 20–51.

HAWTHORNE, NATHANIEL. *The Scarlet Letter* (Centenary Edition of the Works of Nathaniel Hawthorne, ed. WILLIAM CHARVAT, ROY HARVEY PEARCE, and CLAUDE M. SIMPSON; FREDSON BOWERS, textual editor; MATTHEW J. BRUCCOLI, associate textual editor, Vol. I.) Columbus, O.: Ohio State University Press, 1962.

HAYFORD, HARRISON. *The Somers Mutiny Affair*. Englewood Cliffs, N. J.: Prentice-Hall, Inc., 1959.

HOWARD, LEON. *Herman Melville*. Berkeley: University of California Press, 1951.

———. *The Connecticut Wits*. Chicago: University of Chicago Press, 1943.

HOWE, IRVING. *Politics and the Novel*. New York: Meridian Books, Inc., 1958.

HUBBARD, WILLIAM. *Narrative of the Troubles with the Indians in New England*. Brattleborough: William Fessenden, 1814.

IRVING, WASHINGTON. *The Works of Washington Irving*. 27 vols. New York: Putnam & Son, 1864-69.

JAMES, HENRY. Review of Constance Fenimore Woolson's novels for *Harper's Weekly*, Feb. 12, 1887, in *The American Essays of Henry James*, ed. LEON EDEL. New York: Vintage Books, 1956.

JEAN-AUBRY, G. *Joseph Conrad: Life and Letters*. 2 vols. New York: Doubleday, Page & Co., 1927.

JONES, HOWARD MUMFORD. "James Fenimore Cooper and the Hudson River School," *Magazine of Art*, XLV (1952), 243–51.

LAWRENCE. D. H. *Studies in Classic American Literature*. Garden City: Doubleday & Co., 1953.

LEVIN, DAVID. *History as Romantic Art: Bancroft, Prescott, Motley, and Parkman*. Stanford, Calif.: Stanford University Press, 1959.

LEWIS, R. W. B. *The American Adam: Innocence, Tragedy, and Tradition in the Nineteenth Century*. Chicago: University of Chicago Press, 1955.

————. *The Picaresque Saint*. New York: J. B. Lippincott, 1959.

LOWES-DICKINSON, G. *The Greek View of Life*. Ann Arbor, Mich.: University of Michigan Press, 1958.

MARX, LEO. "Two Kingdoms of Force," *Massachusetts Review*, I (October, 1959), 62–95.

MATTHIESSEN, F. O. *American Renaissance: Art and Expression in the Age of Emerson and Whitman*. New York: Oxford University Press, 1941.

————. *Henry James, The Major Phase*. New York: Oxford University Press, 1944.

MELVILLE, HERMAN. *Moby Dick*. New York: Hendricks House, 1962.

————. *The Confidence Man*. New York: Hendricks House, 1954.

————. Review of Cooper's *Red Rover*, *Literary World*, VI (March 16, 1850), 266–67.

————. Review of Cooper's *The Sea Lions*, *Literary World*, IV (April 28, 1849), 370.

Memorial of James Fenimore Cooper. New York: G. P. Putnam, 1852.

MENCKEN, H. L. *The American Language.* 4th ed.; New York: Alfred A. Knopf, 1936.

————. *Supplement I* (1945) and *Supplement II* (1948) to *The American Language.* New York: Alfred A. Knopf.

NELSON, JOHN HERBERT. *The Negro Character in American Literature.* ("Bulletin of the University of Kansas Humanistic Studies," Vol. IV, No. 1, 8-137.) Lawrence, Kansas: University of Kansas Press, 1926.

OUTLAND, ETHEL R. *The "Effingham" Libels on Cooper.* ("University of Wisconsin Studies in Language and Literature," No. 28.) Madison, Wis.: Wisconsin State Press, 1929.

PARKER, ARTHUR C. "Sources and Range of Cooper's Indian Lore," *James Fenimore Cooper: A Re-appraisal.* Special issue of *New York History.* Cooperstown: New York State Historical Association, LII (1954), 447–56.

PARKMAN, FRANCIS. *The Conspiracy of Pontiac.* 2 vols. Boston: Little, Brown & Co., 1899.

PAULDING, JAMES K. *The Dutchman's Fireside: A Tale.* New York: Charles Scribner & Co., 1868.

PEARCE, ROY HARVEY. *The Savages of America: A Study of the Indian and the Idea of Civilization.* Baltimore: Johns Hopkins Press, 1953.

PHILBRICK, THOMAS. *James Fenimore Cooper and the Development of American Sea Fiction.* Cambridge: Harvard University Press, 1961.

POIRIER, RICHARD. *The Comic Sense of Henry James.* London and New York: Oxford University Press, 1960.

PRITCHETT, V. S. *The Living Novel.* London: Chatto & Windus, 1954.

Review of *Lionel Lincoln, North American Review,* XXII (1826), 400.

Review of *The Pioneers, Port Folio,* XV (March, 1823), 236.

Review of *The Wept of Wish-Ton-Wish, Southern Review* (February, 1830).

RIEFF, PHILIP. "The Analytic Attitude," *Encounter,* XVIII (June, 1962), 22–28.

RINGE, DONALD A. *James Fenimore Cooper.* New York: Twayne Publishers, Inc., 1962.

ROURKE, CONSTANCE. *American Humor: A Study of the National Character.* Garden City: Doubleday & Co., 1931.

SCHOOLCRAFT, HENRY R. *Personal Memoirs of a Residence of Thirty Years with the Indian Tribes on the American Frontiers: with brief Notices of Passing Events, Facts, and Opinions, A. D. 1812 to A. D. 1842.* Philadelphia: Lippincott, Grambo & Co., 1851.

SMITH, HENRY NASH. Introduction to *The Prairie.* New York: Rinehart & Co., 1950.

———. *Virgin Land: The American West as Symbol and Myth.* New York: Vintage Books, Inc., 1957.

SNELL, BRUNO. "Arcadia: The Discovery of A Spiritual Landscape," *The Discovery of the Mind, The Greek Origins of European Thought,* trans. T. G. ROSENMEYER. Oxford: Oxford University Press, 1953.

SPILLER, ROBERT E. *Fenimore Cooper: Critic of His Times.* New York: Minton, Balch & Co., 1931.

———. "Fenimore Cooper's Defense of Slave-Owning America," *American Historical Review,* XXXV (1930), 575–82.

———. "Second Thoughts on Cooper as a Social Critic," *James Fenimore Cooper: A Re-appraisal.* Special issue of *New York History,* ed. MARY E. CUNNINGHAM. Cooperstown: New York State Historical Association, LII (1954), 540–57.

SPILLER, ROBERT E. *et al. Literary History of the United States.* New York: Macmillan Co., 1953.

TAYLOR, WILLIAM R. *Cavalier and Yankee.* New York: George Braziller, Inc., 1961.

Times Literary Supplement. October 26, 1962, p. 825.

TOCQUEVILLE, ALEXIS DE. *Democracy in America*. 2 vols. New York: D. Appleton & Co., 1899.

VANDIVER, EDWARD P. "James Fenimore Cooper and Shakespeare," *Shakespeare Association Bulletin*, XV (1940), 110–17.

VAN DOREN, CARL. *The American Novel*. Rev. ed.; New York: Macmillan Co., 1940.

WALKER, WARREN S. *James Fenimore Cooper: An Introduction and Interpretation*. New York: Barnes & Noble, 1962.

WALLACE, PAUL A. "Cooper's Indians," *James Fenimore Cooper: A Re-appraisal*. Special issue of *New York History*, ed. MARY E. CUNNINGHAM. Cooperstown: New York State Historical Association, LII (1954), 423–46.

WAPLES, DOROTHY. *The Whig Myth of James Fenimore Cooper*. New Haven, Conn.: Yale University Press, 1938.

WASSERSTROM, WILLIAM. "Cooper, Freud, and the Origins of Culture," *American Imago*, XVII (Winter, 1960), 423–37.

WATT, IAN. *The Rise of the Novel*. London: Chatto & Windus, 1957.

WINTERS, YVOR. *In Defense of Reason*. Denver: University of Denver Press, 1947.

WOODWARD, C. VANN. "The Antislavery Myth," *The American Scholar*, XXXI (Spring, 1962), 312–28.

ZOELLNER, R. H. "Conceptual Ambivalence in Cooper's Leatherstocking," *American Literature*, XXXI (January, 1960), 397–420.

INDEX

INDEX

Adams, John, 93, 104 n., 127, 148, 149, 150, 151 n., 161-62, 230-31, 262
Afloat and Ashore, 28, 81, 85, 87-88, 152, 185, 219-32
American Democrat, The, 74, 75 n., 169, 173, 177, 271 n.
Anglicans, as group, 108, 151-54; *see also* Gentry
Anna (Updyke), 37-38
Apollo, 57, 63, 66
Aquinas, St. Thomas, 73, 149 n., 260
Arcadia, 65, 277 n., 306
Arcadia (Sidney), 13
Aristotle, 73, 74, 149, 160, 161 n., 169, 177 n., 296
Arrowhead, 308
Auden, W. H., 170
Austen, Jane, 19, 281

Balzac, Honoré de, 263
Bancroft, George, 4

Barbérie, Alida de, 44-46, 97, 100-103
Bat (or "Battius"), Dr. Obed, 132, 223 n., 288, 315
Beard, James Franklin, 9, 148 n., 293 n.
Bewley, Marius, 93 n., 117 n., 140 n., 151 n., 157 n., 175 n. 13, 235 n., 316 n., 326
Bible, The, 105-6, 127, 129, 133-34, 298
Birch, Harvey, 15, 24, 31, 118, 119, 205-17, 227, 230, 237, 304, 327
Boden, Ben, 22 n. 4, 250-52, 255, 256
Bolt, Deacon Ithuel, 141-42, 185, 201
Bonnie, 83-84
Bowen, Elizabeth, 208-9, 263
Brackenridge, Hugh, 172, 173, 175
Bradford, William, 234
Brady, Charles A., 148 n., 154, 215-16, 295, 307, 321

343

345

347

235

Miles and years away from William Faulkner's Yoknapatawpha County, James Fenimore Cooper created a coherent fictional world containing hundreds of characters that represented the possibilities of American life.

Cooper was, by virtue of his analytic intelligence and unsentimental sympathy with America's history, peoples, and land, well suited to the task of explaining America to Americans and to Europeans. He quoted from Fielding, "I am a true historian, a describer of society as it exists, and of men as they are"; and he went back into the past to uncover and describe the peoples and cultures that represented the "given" of American life.

While his concern for character is typical of his time, Cooper's discoveries are not, for he discerned dour facts and stubborn dilemmas that are missing from the hopeful prophecies exuded by such writers as Crèvecoeur, Emerson, and Whitman. He found American life, in fact, so buffeted by rapid and apparently discontinuous changes that he warned: "To see America with the eyes of truth, it is necessary to look often."

His historical novels did just that, revisiting scenes and linking characters until American history becomes a human continuum. His romances were never intended to conjure a